Enigma Books

Also published by Enigma Books

Hitler's Table Talk: 1941–1944
In Stalin's Secret Service
Hitler and Mussolini: The Secret Meetings
The Jews in Fascist Italy: A History
The Man Behind the Rosenbergs
Roosevelt and Hopkins: An Intimate History
Diary 1937–1943 (Galeazzo Ciano)
Secret Affairs: FDR, Cordell Hull, and Sumner Welles
Hitler and His Generals: Military Conferences 1942–1945
Stalin and the Jews: The Red Book
The Secret Front: Nazi Political Espionage
Fighting the Nazis: French Intelligence and Counterintelligence
A Death in Washington: Walter G. Krivitsky and the Stalin Terror
The Battle of the Casbah: Terrorism and Counterterrorism in Algeria 1955–1957
Hitler's Second Book: The Unpublished Sequel to *Mein Kampf*
At Napoleon's Side in Russia: The Classic Eyewitness Account
The Atlantic Wall: Hitler's Defenses for D-Day
Double Lives: Stalin, Willi Münzenberg and the Seduction of the Intellectuals
France and the Nazi Threat: The Collapse of French Diplomacy 1932–1939
Mussolini: The Secrets of His Death
Top Nazi: Karl Wolff—The Man Between Hitler and Himmler
Empire on the Adriatic: Mussolini's Conquest of Yugoslavia
The Origins of the War of 1914 (3-volume set)
Hitler's Foreign Policy: 1933–1939—The Road to World War II
The Origins of Fascist Ideology 1918–1925
Max Corvo: OSS Italy 1942–1945
Hitler's Contract: The Secret History of the Italian Edition of *Mein Kampf*
Secret Intelligence and the Holocaust
Israel at High Noon
Balkan Inferno: Betrayal, War, and Intervention, 1990–2005
Hollywood's Celebrity Gangster
Calculated Risk
The Murder of Maxim Gorky
The Kravchenko Case: One Man's War On Stalin
The Mafia and the Allies
Hitler's Gift to France
The Nazi Party, 1919–1945: A Complete History
Closing the Books: Jewish Insurance Claims from the Holocaust
Encyclopedia of Cold War Espionage, Spies, and Secret Operations
The Cicero Spy Affair

Michael McMenamin
and
Curt J. Zoller

Becoming
Winston Churchill

The Untold Story of Young Winston
and
His American Mentor

Enigma Books

Published by
Enigma Books
New York

Becoming Winston Churchill. The Untold Story of Young Winston and His
American Mentor by Michael McMenamin and Curt J. Zoller was originally
published in hard cover by Greenwood World Publishing. http//
www.greenwood.com/ gwp an imprint of Greenwood Publishing Group, Inc.,
Westport, CT. Copyright © 2007 by Michael McMenamin and Curt J. Zoller. This
paperback edition by arrangement with Greenwood Publishing Group, Inc. All
rights reserved.

First Paperback Edition 2009

ISBN 978-1-929631-87-2

Printed in the United States of America

Library of Congress Cataloguing-in-Publication Available.

To my wife, Carol, whose own study of Churchill's youth inspired and influenced mine. And to my parents, Jack and Maxine, who were children when Bourke Cockran died and who were young and in love when Winston saved the world, something they helped do as well. Their children, grandchildren and great-grandchildren are all very grateful.

M. M.

To my wife, Gert, whose steadfast support made it possible for me to assemble an extensive Winston Churchill collection. And also to all the students and young adults who were told by their parents or teachers 'You'll never amount to anything'. Don't you believe it!

C. J. Z.

Contents

Foreword
to the Paperback Edition

I am pleased that a new edition of *Becoming Winston Churchill* is being made available to a wider American audience. When I read the book, essentially a dual biography of my grandfather as a young man and his mentor Bourke Cockran, I realized at once it was breaking new ground in covering my grandfather's life. As such, while I thoroughly enjoyed it myself, I did not know how the book would be received by Churchill scholars.

There are no more respected Churchill scholars than Sir Martin Gilbert, Churchill's Official Biographer and Allen Packwood, Director of the Churchill Archives Centre at Cambridge University. So, when Sir Martin says the book is "fascinating: a tour de force that brings light and life to one of the great early influences on Winston Churchill" and Allen Packwood calls it "A magnificent and an illuminating study of a largely forgotten relationship", you can be certain you will be reading an original and highly entertaining account of Churchill's life as a young man.

And once you read it, you'll understand why The Churchill Book Club called it "The most important new book about Churchill...one you'll come back to again and again for its extraordinary insights into Churchill's genius". You'll also appreciate why Anne Sebba, the most recent biographer of Winston's mother, Lady Randolph Churchill, wrote in a review that *Becoming Winston Churchill* is 'a hugely readable study [which] brings back into the foreground with power and imagination a spell-binding rabble-rouser, a man who deserves to be remembered as one whose principles, faith in democracy and oratorical skills were passed on to a young man at a critical point in his life, helping to create Winston Churchill, the leader who in turn inspired millions at a critical point in world history."

The authors' use of brief fictional passages to introduce each of the fourteen chapters is unusual but it works. It is especially useful in bringing to life details about the relatively unknown Cockran's remarkable life and career. He was not only hailed as America's greatest orator during his lifetime but he was also a good friend and economic adviser to two presidents, the Democrat Grover Cleveland and the Republican Theodore Roosevelt who was also Cockran's neighbour, each having large estates on Long Island's Gold Coast. Seven passages are written from Winston's point of view and suggest what he was thinking at a particular point in his life later covered in the chapter. The same is done for Cockran in six of the chapters and for Churchill's mother Jennie in one chapter where she is preparing for the dinner party in 1895 where she initially met Bourke Cockran, the first step in a chain of events which was to change her son's life forever.

I know from my own experience that most biographers are so well versed in their subjects' lives that they could do the same, i.e., tell you what their subject *must* have been thinking at a given point in time, even if they don't have a direct source. In this respect, all of the fictional narratives in *Becoming Winston Churchill* are well-sourced and these are disclosed in the chapter notes.

I also have written (*Churchill: Wanted Dead or Alive* and *Chasing Churchill: The Travels of Winston Churchill*) about one of the periods in Winston's life covered in *Becoming Winston Churchill* – the adventure-filled years from 1895 to 1900 where he fought bravely in India, the Sudan and South Africa. The authors mention these well-known adventures only in passing and usually in the context of Churchill's intimate correspondence with his mother where the son vividly describes his battle experiences in language which must have made her cringe. They focus instead on all the time and effort Winston spent during this same period educating himself for the career he planned in politics and as a writer determined to make a name for himself in print as well as combat.

Cockran became a good friend of Jennie's sister, Leonie Leslie and her son Shane, Winston's first cousin, who later married Cockran's sister-in-law. He also stayed on good terms with Jennie who, when Winston was captured by the Boers in 1899, turned to Cockran to help ascertain her son's safety and how he was faring as a prisoner. Cockran, a Democrat who was held in high regard by his political opponents, in turn used his influence with the Republican administration of President McKinley to have the U.S. Consul in Pretoria personally visit Churchill and report back to him on the young man's condition which he in turn telegraphed to Jennie.

The entire Churchill-Cockran correspondence is reproduced in the book and particularly poignant is a long letter from Churchill to Cockran on 30 November, 1899, written while Winston was a prisoner of the Boers and which he concludes with "I am 25 today—it is terrible to think how little time remains!" How little indeed, as my grandfather lived until he was 90!

Finally, the book also covers in more detail than other biographies Winston's romances as a young man and the three beautiful young women he courted and to whom he reputedly proposed marriage prior to meeting the fourth and most beautiful one of all, Clementine Hozier, the one who said "yes". I was particularly struck, however, by Winston's first love Pamela Plowden about whom he once wrote his mother that he didn't think he could be happy with any other woman. They were unofficially engaged but, under parental pressure, she married another.

Pamela and Winston nevertheless remained close friends throughout their lives ("Your Pamela" is how Clemmie referred to her). Early in their romance in 1897, he wrote to her that he destroyed all her letters, presumably in an effort to encourage her to be open about her feelings for him. After each of their marriages, the two continued to correspond episodically over the years including a letter she wrote to Winston in October, 1950, reminding him that he had proposed to her 50 years ago to the day. We know this only because Winston wrote a sweet letter back telling her "how much I cherish yr signal across the years, from the days when I was a freak...but there was one who saw some qualities, & it is to you that I am most deeply grateful...Fifty years!" Fortunately for history, Pamela saved her letters from Winston. My grandfather, who otherwise saved nearly *everything* he received or wrote, was true to his youthful promise and no letters from his Pamela to him survive.

I hope you enjoy reading *Becoming Winston Churchill*. I did. After all, it's difficult to resist a book whose first line is "It began with a love story."

Celia Sandys, 2009
Winston S. Churchill's granddaughter

Foreword

Thousands of books and millions of words have been written about the life of Winston Churchill. Many go over the same ground trying to find a different way to praise, criticise or revise what others have written but in *Becoming Winston Churchill*, Michael McMenamin and Curt Zoller have found a completely new area of my grandfather's life and brought it to life with an imaginative treatment. Although already steeped in the subject it took no more than a few pages before I was caught up in this fascinating story so cleverly told.

Bourke Cockran was the first person to welcome the twenty year old Winston to the United States. The young cavalry officer was not expecting to like America but those few days were the beginning of a lifelong love affair with the land of his mother's birth. The world assumes that the special relationship between Britain and America began with Churchill and Roosevelt. I believe it was conceived when Cockran introduced the young Winston to New York in 1895.

"He was my model, it was he who taught me how to hold thousands in thrall." What a tribute to Cockran by the man who nearly half a century after their first meeting would, through his oratory, give hope and inspiration to millions throughout the world.

The well researched story of Bourke Cockran is interwoven with fictional passages which are clearly very close to the facts. By using this device to describe the relationships between Winston and Cockran, Winston and Jennie, and Jennie and Cockran, the authors bring to life events of a bygone era which eventually determined the course of the twentieth century.

Celia Sandys, 2007

Prologue

It began with a love story.

Born on different sides of the Atlantic, two Americans – a man and a woman – met in Paris in the spring of 1895, each grieving a lost love. They had led political lives at the highest level in their chosen lands. Both were intelligent, attractive and strong-willed. They were immediately, magnetically drawn to one another. They rode horses and bicycles. They went to plays, restaurants, museums and glittering dinner parties. They talked and they fought, in English and in French. They became lovers.

Their affair was intense, but they exhausted themselves, each too strong for the other and they reluctantly parted that summer, friends still. That fall, she asked a favour. Would he take her twenty-year-old son under his wing on his first journey to the land of her birth and provide a strong man's influence, something needed but never received from the boy's late father? The man would and did because he had no child of his own. And because she asked.

He immediately recognized the young man's courage, strength and brilliance, truly his mother's son. He was the first man, but not the last, to see this. For the next ten years, when no one else could or would, he taught the young man all that he knew through word and deed, showing him how to place principle over party, helping him to use the English language as a painter would a palette, offering himself as a role model as if the young man were his own son, stepping silently back once he was done and the young man's public career was well begun.

The two lovers, in turn, remarried but not to one another. Still, along with her son, he was at her side the day she died, twenty-six years after they met, the friend he had promised always to be. Two years later, he was gone as well.

Less than two decades after their deaths, her son's courage saved his country. And the world.

The man was Bourke Cockran. The woman was Lady Randolph Churchill, the American-born heiress Jennie Jerome. Everyone knows her remarkable son.

Becoming Winston Churchill is the story of the legacy left by Jennie's lover to her son and the role it played in Churchill's life during the sixty years after that Paris spring.

Chapter 1
'He Was My Model'

Chartwell, Kent
Winter, 1954

Winston Churchill stepped away from the stand-up writing desk in the study at his country home, Chartwell, and walked over to the window. Cigar in one hand, a weak whisky and water in the other, the eighty-year-old prime minister looked out over the snow-covered weald of Kent. To him, it was the most beautiful view in the world whatever the season, and he turned to it often for inspiration, or to gather his thoughts. He had been revising a speech he was never going to give. At least not in person.

The State University of New York had awarded him an honorary Doctorate of Law and Churchill was to accept in absentia. After all, the only degree he had was from Sandhurst, which had not given him the liberal education he would have received at university. Besides, it was an honour from America and he rarely declined any recognition from the land of his mother's birth, the country which helped him save the world from that mad Austrian corporal. It had been nearly sixty years ago when he first stepped on its shores.

Churchill could see it still in his mind's eye. The incomparable New York City skyline. The Statue of Liberty. The incredible energy which seemed to rise out of the Manhattan bedrock. And then he had seen the tall, sturdy figure of Bourke Cockran on the quay, the great friend of his mother and his two aunts, easily recognized from their description. No other man looked like Bourke Cockran, Aunt Leonie had told him, and she had been right. What his mother and aunts had not prepared him for, however, was the man's magnetic countenance, the breadth of his knowledge, the originality of expression, the brilliance of his mind. And, of course, the voice. Difficult to describe even now, but Churchill had always wished he had a voice like Cockran's. Alas, it was not to be no matter how hard or long he practiced.

Churchill smiled. Whatever did Cockran see in that young cavalry lieutenant in 1895? More than anything his own father had seen, that much was certain. If Churchill had strived throughout his long life to accomplish things to prove his father wrong and to make him proud – and he certainly had – that wasn't the case with Cockran. No, with Cockran, Churchill thought, he had to prove Cockran right. He always was conscious as a young man that he had to live up to the older man's

1

high opinion – oft expressed – of what a glittering career he believed Churchill would have.

Churchill rarely reflected on America without thinking of Bourke Cockran. Churchill had known the last three American presidents rather well and none compared to Cockran. What Churchill could not erase from his mind, however, was a conversation he recently had with the Democratic Party's presidential nominee in the last American election. Decent fellow. A governor from one of those states in the middle of the country. He had asked a common question. Many people Churchill met for the first time asked the same thing. 'Upon whom did you base your oratorical style?'

Churchill had promptly answered as he always did. The governor was surprised. Most people were. They expected to hear him say that his father, Lord Randolph, had inspired him. His father had inspired him to be sure, but not as an orator. 'That great American statesman Bourke Cockran', Churchill told the governor, and because the governor was an American, Churchill had thought to give him a treat. He began quoting at length from Cockran's speeches, which he had memorised nearly sixty years ago. Two of Cockran's best. The 1896 speech in Madison Square Garden where he opposed his own party on the issue of free silver and drew a larger crowd than his party's presidential nominee, William Jennings Bryan. Churchill next had quoted from Cockran's 1903 speech on free trade to the Liberal Club in London after which the Liberal Party leader had attempted, unsuccessfully, to persuade Cockran to leave America and stand for Parliament in Great Britain.

Churchill shook his great head at the memory of the governor's reaction. A blank stare. The man said nothing, but Churchill could tell that he simply didn' t know who Bourke Cockran was. America's greatest orator, they had called him from the mid-1880s until his premature death at age sixty-nine in 1923. A man who had been a close friend and adviser to President Grover Cleveland and later to Theodore Roosevelt. Yet the Democratic presidential candidate in 1952 didn't know who Bourke Cockran was. It was sad, he thought, that even educated Americans had such short memories.

Looking out at the snow, Churchill decided it was time to remind his American cousins once more of Bourke Cockran. He had done so in his last address in America in 1946. His 'Sinews of Peace' speech that everyone else knew as the 'Iron Curtain' speech. If nothing else, Churchill thought, he would have expected the governor to have remembered his quoting Cockran on that occasion.

Churchill had never had much regard for the Republican Party in America. For most of the twentieth century, it had been protectionist to its core, something the free-trader Churchill could not countenance. But if the most recent Democratic presidential candidate did not even know the name of his party's most eloquent champion of free trade and individual liberty, perhaps it was not so bad that his old wartime comrade had defeated him in the last election. If only Ike had chosen a more qualified secretary of state. Churchill smiled. 'Dull, duller, Dulles.' One of his better lines. The cabinet certainly thought it funny. A pity he could never use it in public.

Yes, Churchill thought it was time again to publicly honour his mentor, the biggest and most original mind he had ever met. The man to whom, he once told his cousin, he owed the best things in his career.

Churchill took another sip of his whisky, placed the crystal tumbler down on the stand-up desk, switched on the intercom and called for one of his two secretaries who were constantly on duty. When she arrived, he handed her a marked up copy of the speech.

'There and there', he said pointing to red marks he had made on the draft. 'I want you to insert what I am about to dictate.'

The secretary sat on the edge of her chair, her pad and pencil poised as Churchill began to speak.

I remember when I first came over here in 1895 I was a guest of your great lawyer and orator, Mr. Bourke Cockran. I was only a young Cavalry subaltern but he poured out all his wealth of mind and eloquence to me. Some of his sentences are deeply rooted in my mind. 'The earth,' he said, 'is a generous mother. She will produce in plentiful abundance food for all her children if they will but cultivate her soil in justice and in peace.' I used to repeat it so frequently on British platforms that I had to give it a holiday. But now to-day it seems to come back with new pregnancy and force, for never was the choice between blessing and cursing more vehemently presented to the human race.[1]

Churchill paused. 'That's the first part. Did you get that all?' Seeing her nod yes, Churchill began to speak again.

There was another thing Bourke Cockran used to say to me. I cannot remember his actual words but they amounted to this: 'In a society where there is democratic tolerance and freedom under the

3

*law, many kinds of evils will crop up, but give them a little time and
they usually breed their own cure.' I do not see any reason to doubt
the truth of that . . . You must not – you must not indeed – think
I am talking politics. I make it a rule never to meddle in internal
or party politics of any friendly country. It's hard enough to understand the party politics of your own! Still, I remain, as I have said,
a strong supporter of the principles which Mr. Bourke Cockran
inculcated into me on my youthful visit before most of you were
born.*[2]

'Pray read that back to me', Churchill said.
    *The young woman did and Churchill nodded. It sounded right. He
dismissed her and walked back to the window. Sixty years was a long
time, he thought, and the world had been turned upside down twice in
that time. Still, he could see it all as if it were yesterday.*

'. . . I owe the best things in my career to him . . .'

Even giants can have mentors. So can self-made men. Any young person
can benefit from the attention of someone older who recognizes, nurtures
and helps develop as yet unrealized potential.

    Winston Churchill. May 1940. A giant and a self-made man.
Empowered by his principles, his will and his words, he forever changed
the future of the twentieth century and helped preserve all that people
who love liberty hold dear. He did so by resolutely refusing the entreaties
of his own Foreign Secretary – his most serious political opponent – to
at least enquire of Hitler what his terms for peace would be, the first step
on a slippery slope Churchill defiantly declined to take. With Germany
in complete control of the European continent, it was an act of unques-
tionable, albeit seemingly unrealistic, political courage. In the event, it
made all the difference.

    How did Churchill find the courage to do it? How did he become the
man he was? Maybe, in the end, an individual deserves to be remembered more for the single act of saving Western Civilization than for how
he developed both the oratorical skills that helped him do so and the
political principles which characterized his public career for sixty years.
But the role those principles and skills played and those who helped
nurture and encourage him in the process deserve consideration as well.

This book intends to explore Winston Churchill's coming of age in the years 1895–1908 through the prism of the role played in that process by Churchill's only true mentor.

As a young man, Winston Churchill had one – and only one – mentor who helped shape at an early age his political thought and his speaking style. Churchill acknowledged throughout his long life, privately and publicly, at home and abroad, by the spoken and the written word, how important this man was to his career.

Churchill's mentor was an American, an Irish-born, French-educated lawyer and Democratic Congressman from New York City, a close friend of Churchill's American-born mother, Jennie Jerome – Lady Randolph Churchill. The man's name was William Bourke (pronounced 'Burke') Cockran, a near-forgotten figure in American political history who served as the young Winston Churchill's mentor, unselfishly helping his protégé formulate his political thought and develop his speaking style.

Prior to Randolph Churchill's first volume of his father's official biography, no Churchill biographer had recognized or acknowledged the key role Cockran played in Churchill's life. Thereafter, some biographers did mention Cockran in passing, but most didn't, the notable exceptions being William Manchester, Roy Jenkins and, most significantly, Martin Gilbert, Randolph Churchill's successor as his father's official biographer. Indeed, Gilbert's 2006 book *Churchill and America* contains the most extensive treatment to date of Churchill and Cockran. This book seeks to expand upon Gilbert's foundation and explore in detail who Bourke Cockran was as well as how and why he came to have such an influence on the young Churchill, an influence which was to last throughout his long life.

Bourke Cockran was a fierce defender of individual liberty, a hard-money classical liberal, an ardent advocate of free trade and trade unions alike, an opponent of the death penalty and the income tax and an anti-imperialist. During his lifetime, both Democrats and Republicans, from House Speaker Champ Clark to Cockran's good friend, President Theodore Roosevelt, hailed him as America's greatest orator.

As we shall see, however, Cockran was much more than a politician and orator. While he lived during the height of public oratory as entertainment, in the late nineteenth and early twentieth centuries, it was only a hobby to him. He accepted no payment for his speeches, not even travel expenses. Yet he was the unquestioned king of orators, a man who both inspired and intimidated his friend and contemporary William Jennings Bryan, who would not appear on the same platform with Cockran.

Cockran was a seven-term Democratic member of the US House of Representatives in a public career spanning forty years. He was what today would be called in America a 'citizen politician' because he spent the larger part of his public career – twenty-six years – outside of Congress. He never served more than two consecutive terms in Congress – four years – because he continually placed principle above party and patronage, something which did not endear him to the various political bosses he served under at Tammany Hall. Cockran was, in fact, one of the greatest – and most well-paid – trial and appellate lawyers of his era, deemed so by such pillars of the New York bar as Elihu Root, later to become Secretary of War and Secretary of State under Theodore Roosevelt,[3] and Paul Cravath, founding partner of the iconic Wall Street corporate law firm Cravath, Swaine & Moore.[4]

More importantly, to Cockran at least, he had the ear and confidence as well as the personal friendship of two American presidents, the Democrat Grover Cleveland and the Republican Theodore Roosevelt, serving as a close economic adviser to both. A third president, William McKinley, also a Republican, asked Cockran to become his Attorney General, which Cockran declined because, as a free trader, he would not serve in a protectionist government.

Winston Churchill first met Cockran when he was twenty years old, his father, Lord Randolph, dead less than a year. Churchill's mother introduced them. Their introduction was fortuitous. An historical quirk of fate. And romantic attraction. The forty-one-year-old Cockran was then a wealthy former member of the US Congress, with an annual income in 1895 of over $100,000 from his law practice ($2.3 million in current value) and a national reputation as a captivating speaker. Cockran met Jennie Churchill, then age forty, in Paris in the spring of 1895 following the deaths earlier that year of their respective spouses. They were instantly attracted to one another and they had an affair. The affair was brief, intense and, by some accounts, flamed out by the fall. Yet their friendship endured and they remained close, Cockran by her side along with Churchill when Lady Randolph died prematurely at age sixty-seven in June 1921. Cockran himself passed away less than two years later at the age of 69.

In 1906, the thirty-one-year-old Churchill privately told his first cousin Shane Leslie (who became Cockran's brother-in-law when he married the sister of Cockran's wife, Anne Ide) that Cockran had 'the biggest and most original mind I have ever met. When I was a young man he instantly gained my confidence and I feel that I owe the best things in my

career to him'.⁵ Forty years later in his famous 'Iron Curtain' speech in
Fulton, Missouri, Churchill still quoted the words of his mentor Cockran
and credited the life-long influence he had on him.

'He was my model'

Adlai Stevenson, only hours from his death in 1965, may have forgotten
who Bourke Cockran had been. Winston Churchill never did.

Stevenson, one-time governor of Illinois and two-time unsuccessful
Democratic candidate for president, asked Churchill in the early 1950s
upon whom he had based his speaking style. Bourke Cockran, Churchill
said at once and began to elaborate in great detail. Stevenson had been
dining out on the story ever since. The day before he died, he met an
actual Churchill relative, and the old political warhorse couldn't resist
trotting the story out once more and, as it turned out, for the last time.

The relative was Anita Leslie, the daughter of Churchill's first cousin,
Shane Leslie, and the granddaughter of Jennie's younger sister Leonie.
Randolph Churchill excerpts in the first volume of his father's biography
a letter to him from Anita passing on Stevenson's story, which dramatically illustrates the lasting impression Cockran left on Churchill:

> It is just a week since I was sitting in the pavilion at Syon with
> Adlai . . . Learning I was Winston Churchill's cousin, he suddenly
> started to reminisce about his last meeting with him in the early
> 1950s. He said: "I asked him something I'd always wanted to know –
> I asked on whom or what he had based his oratorical style. WSC
> replied 'It was an American statesman who inspired me when
> I was 19 & taught me how to use every note of the human voice like
> an organ'." "You'd never have heard of him" said AS. "He wasn't
> a great statesman, just an Irish politician with the gift of the gab, but
> Winston called him a statesman – his name was Bourke Cockran."
> I couldn't help interrupting with "He married my mother's sister
> Anne & darling Uncle Bourke left us every penny we have!" AS
> looked amazed and said "Well he never said there was a family
> connection, how strange . . ." Nor was there really, for Bourke
> married the sister of Marjorie Ide who married Winston's first
> cousin, my father. But who else in England would have known all
> about Bourke! Such a character – I adored him – I was twelve when

7

he died, his great voice & thickset shoulders & granite ugly deeply hewn face came back to me. How Bourke would have loved to have known what a lot he could give to that young man. That his own talent for oratory, wasted on tiresome American financial problems, should in the end help a voice that would hold fortunate Europe through its most terrible hour.

Adlai was surprised at my interjections but went on, "Winston then to my amazement started to quote long excerpts from Bourke Cockran's speeches of sixty years before." Of course AS couldn't check the absolute accuracy but there was Winston pouring out to him this tremendous impact on his youth – saying, "He was my model – I learned from him how to hold thousands in thrall" and quoting with terrific force.

Within twenty-four hours of telling me all this – which moved him greatly – Adlai Stevenson was dead. I have quoted his words verbatim while they are still distinct in my memory . . .[6]

Perhaps, on the eve of his death, Stevenson can be forgiven for describing Cockran as 'not a great statesman, just an Irish politician with the gift of the gab'. It fit a stereotypical view of Irishmen, and of course, it made for a better story to have Churchill so dramatically influenced by an Irish nobody. But Cockran, a seven-term Congressman from New York City, who was fluent in French, Italian and Greek where Stevenson was not, was much more than just another Irish politician. Stevenson's grandfather and namesake, Grover Cleveland's vice president during his second term, certainly knew him well as Cockran was one of President Cleveland's closest economic advisers. From 1884 to his death in 1923, Cockran was a national figure as honoured for his wisdom as for his eloquence.

'A grand gentleman and the greatest orator in the land, but . . . he's not a dependable politician'

Born in County Sligo, Ireland, in 1854 of well-to-do parents, Cockran was sent at age nine to France, where he studied for five years under the Marist Brothers at their school near Lille. At age seventeen, he travelled to America on holiday and decided to stay. He became a lawyer five years later in 1876 and developed a lucrative law practice representing corporations as well as criminal defendants and labour leaders. A political reformer, he was a sometime member of Tammany Hall and a prominent public speaker who initially made a national reputation with a speech at the 1884 Democratic National Convention opposing the unit rule. He was first elected to Congress in 1886; skipped two terms after a fall-out with Tammany Hall; and returned for two more terms from 1891 to 1895 before once more falling into disfavour with Tammany. He served in Congress again from 1904 to 1908 and from 1920 until his death in early 1923.

The colourful New York politico, George Washington Plunkett, who coined the phrase 'honest graft', explained in a 1901 interview why Cockran was never held in high regard by Tammany:

> I'll admit he's a grand gentleman and the greatest orator in the
> land, but take it from me, he's not a dependable politician. He calls
> himself a Democrat but his heart was never in Tammany Hall. One
> look at him will tell you that he's as much of an aristocrat as Old
> Lord Salisbury himself . . . and while he was in Congress he never
> darkened the door of a Tammany clubhouse.[7]

Indeed, the hard-money Cockran bolted the Democratic Party in 1896 to oppose its nominee, William Jennings Bryan, because of his support for 'free silver' and to campaign actively at his own expense across the country for the Republican William McKinley.

Cockran already was a prominent New York legal and political fixture with well-appointed homes on Fifth Avenue and Sands Point, Long Island, when he and Churchill first met in November 1895. When Cockran died in 1923, Republican Congressman Hamilton Fish, Jr., said of his Democratic colleague that, except for Theodore Roosevelt, Cockran was the ablest man he had ever met; that he was without a rival as a public speaker; that he had more knowledge of the history of the world than anyone in his generation; and that 'none saw more with the eyes of the prophet or the vision of the seer . . . . He predicted events with almost uncanny or superhuman divination'. Fish said that Cockran embodied all the qualities of oratory 'such as has not been seen since the days of Webster, Clay and Calhoun'.[8]

Even the British were openly impressed by Cockran, notwithstanding his well-publicized support of Home Rule for Ireland. Lord Ripon once wrote of Cockran:

> When I was a young man we used to regard Carlyle as the greatest
> conversationalist of his time. Well, I heard Carlyle and Gladstone

many times and I am quite convinced that, in wit, wisdom and elegance of expression neither of them approached the American statesman Bourke Cockran.[9]

'I [had] great discussions with Mr. Cockran on every conceivable subject from Economics to yacht racing'

Churchill was en route to cover the Cuban rebellion as a correspondent in the fall of 1895 when he stayed with Cockran at his home in New York City while on temporary leave from the Army, where he had recently received a commission as a cavalry officer. As Anita Leslie wrote in her biography of Churchill's mother:

> Jennie talked a great deal about Winston to Bourke Cockran who, having no son of his own, wistfully enjoyed helping the young to find their feet . . . When Bourke returned to America, he casually asked Jennie to send her son, should he ever visit New York, to stay in his apartment. If Winston was interested in politics he could give him a few tips. She promised to keep the eventuality in mind, for indeed she did not want Winston to forget his American heritage.[10]

Churchill was twenty years old on his first visit to America. A lifetime of adventure and fame awaited him, but the next five years were some of the most adventurous times in his life as he became a war hero, a best-selling author and a member of Parliament (MP).

The five years of Churchill's life after that were as filled with political conflict as the previous five were military conflict. He became a rising political star and an accomplished public speaker who was ostracized by his father's Tory Party over the issue of free trade and switched to the Liberal Party where he achieved his first government office.

Churchill and Cockran had an extensive correspondence between 1895 and 1907, which took Churchill from the age of twenty to thirty-three, arguably the most important years in a young man's life. Though twenty-one years older than Churchill, Cockran was both a mentor and a role model for the young Churchill during those formative years. By the end of that time, Churchill had firmly launched his political career, one in which he would eventually assume the duties of every major British cabinet position over the next half century.

Churchill's son Randolph writes in his biography of his father that:

Bourke Cockran must certainly have been a man of profound
discernment and judgement of character. As far as we know, he was
the first man or woman Churchill met on level terms who really saw
his point and his potentialities. At this time Churchill had few friends
among his contemporaries and almost none among his elders; his
correspondence with Cockran was the first that he entered into with
a mature man. Cockran in some ways fulfilled a role that Lord
Randolph should have filled if he had survived.[11]

The study of adult development is a twentieth-century phenomenon.
Begun by Carl Jung (1875–1961) and expanded by Erik Erikson
(1902–1994), it blossomed in the final quarter of the twentieth century
with Yale psychologist Daniel Levinson (1920–1994) and his ground-
breaking studies, *Seasons of a Man's Life* (1978) and *Seasons of a
Woman's Life* (1996). Levinson's work provided new insight into how
mentor relationships affect adult development and offers support for
Randolph's observation on Cockran's role in Winston's life.

The period in a young man's life from age seventeen to thirty-three on
which we focus in this book is called 'The Novice Phase' by Levinson, the
time where a man makes the transition from childhood to the adult world.
During this time, a mentor's primary function is to be a transitional figure
in this process, 'a mixture of parent and peer; he must be both and not
purely either one'.[12]

All young people, in varying degrees, have a vision of what their life might
become, what Levinson terms 'The Dream'. A major task of the transition
from childhood to the adult world is to give definition to that vision and find
ways to live it out. Though only twenty years old when he met Cockran and
having not done much to distinguish himself up to that point, Churchill
already had his 'dream' – achieving a career in politics like his father.
Cockran was the first and, for some time, the only man to support and then
facilitate the realization of the young Churchill's dream of a life in politics.

His first impressions of Cockran in a letter to his mother in November 1895
foreshadow the relationship which was to develop between the two men:

I & Barnes are staying with Mr. Bourke Cockran in a charming and
very comfortable flat at the address on this paper . . . Mr. Cockran is
one of the most charming hosts and interesting men I have met . . . I

have great discussions with Mr. Cockran on every conceivable
subject from Economics to yacht racing. He is a clever man and one
from whose conversation much is to be learned.[13]

Especially telling, in understanding the foundation of their enduring
friendship and Cockran's growing influence, are their early letters in 1896.

On 29 February 1896, Churchill enclosed a copy of an article of his
on Cuba from *The Saturday Review* and solicited Cockran's opinion.
Cockran's return letter did so and passed on a speech of his on Ireland.
Churchill wrote back on 12 April 1896 agreeing with Cockran's views
on Cuba but not Ireland, nevertheless praising Cockran's eloquence.

Cockran promptly replied to the 12 April letter, and its content
illustrates how Cockran is assuming the role of a mentor to the young
man and facilitating Churchill's realization of his 'Dream', a life
in politics.

To Churchill, 27 April 1896

Do not My Dear Winston feel that I am troubling you with this long
letter merely to air my views. I was so profoundly impressed with
the vigor of your language and the breadth of your views as I read
your criticisms of my speech that I conceived a very high opinion of
your future career, and what I have said here is largely based on my
own experience. I give it to you for what it is worth, firmly convinced that your own judgement may be trusted to utilize it if it be
of any value or to reject it if inapplicable to your plans or your
surroundings.[14]

Winston Churchill was twenty-one years old when he received this letter
from the man who was even then acclaimed as America's greatest orator.
The young Churchill already had a high opinion of his abilities, notwithstanding his late father's belief that his son was not 'clever' enough
to be a lawyer and hence was only suited to a military career. Still, how
could Churchill not help but be captivated by the first adult who shared
the young man's own views on his future prospects?

In August 1896, Cockran had broken with his party and gave the
greatest speech of his life in Madison Square Garden, several weeks after
William Jennings Bryan, the Democratic presidential nominee, had
spoken there in favour of free silver. Bryan had not managed to fill the

Garden, whereas Cockran – opposing his own party's nominee – had 15,000 people hanging from the rafters. Cockran naturally sent a copy of the speech to his young friend who promptly replied:

To Cockran, 31 August 1896

You know how keenly I regret that I was not there to see – still more to hear.

I hope we shall meet again soon – if possible within a year . . . so perhaps I shall once more eat oysters and hominy with you in New York. Please send me press cuttings of your speeches.[15]

Another letter from Churchill to Cockran, in late 1896, commenting on Cockran's nationwide speaking tour against Bryan and free silver while Churchill was on his first tour of duty in India shows that Cockran was firmly planted in the young man's mind as a role model, a master orator who had showed him principle was more important than party:

To Cockran, 5 November 1896

Your tour of political meetings must indeed have been interesting and I regret so much that I had not the opportunity of accompanying you and listening to your speeches. From what I have seen – I know that there are few more fascinating experiences than to watch a great mass of people under the wand of a magician. There is no gift – so rare or so precious as the gift of oratory – so difficult to define or impossible to acquire . . .[16]

'You have powerfully influenced me in the political conceptions I have formed'

How much did Cockran influence Churchill's political thought? We shall explore this question in more detail later but, taking Churchill at his word, quite a bit, enough to cause him sixty years later to say that he was still a strong supporter of 'the principles . . . Bourke Cockran inculcated into me on my youthful visit'. Cockran was the first adult with whom the young Churchill seriously discussed politics and economics, and free trade was certainly one of those principles Cockran 'inculcated into' him.

Free trade, the legacy of the England of Cobden and Bright, was widely accepted as the foundation of the island's prosperity. In the ten years after Cockran and Churchill met, however, free trade would come under attack in England from protectionists within the Tory Party of Churchill's father. Fortunately for Churchill, Cockran was unusual for an American politician in that he and many Democrats at that time were a free trade minority in a country dominated for nearly a half century by protectionist Republicans and their big business allies. More importantly, Cockran could advocate and defend free trade in words which ordinary people would understand.

In a July 1903 speech on free trade to the Liberal Club in London, Cockran explained why war is a misleading metaphor for trade.

> The essential object of war being to injure your neighbor, while the essential object of commerce is to serve him, it surely ought to be self-evident that the terms applicable to the one must become ludicrously misleading when applied to the other.[17]

Churchill made the same point as Cockran five months later in a speech in Birmingham, where the influence of his mentor is apparent:

> [C]ommerce is utterly different from war, so that the ideas and the phraseology of the one should never be applied to the other; for in war both sides lose whoever wins the victory, but the transactions of trade, like the quality of mercy, are twice blessed, and confer a benefit on both parties.[18]

Free trade was a central political bond between Cockran and Churchill but not the only one. As Churchill wrote his wife in 1909, Cockran 'influenced my thought in more than one direction'.[19] They were both nineteenth-century classical liberals who had to adapt their values to the challenges of a new century, both of them supporting the early stages of the welfare state or the minimum national standard as Churchill called it. Looking back at the careers of both men, however, it is readily apparent that a deep devotion to individual liberty was the sturdy foundation on which each man erected what Churchill called 'a complete scheme of political thought', one which enabled them both 'to present a sincere and effective front in every direction according to changing circumstances'.[20]

Both men were ardent advocates of free markets and free trade, who recognized that economic freedom and political freedom were two

sides of the same coin. As Cockran's political biographer, Florence
Bloom, wrote:

> Cockran interpreted democracy as that climate which allows each
> man to choose between alternatives, freely and competitively, but
> not to the unfair detriment of others . . . He rejected as tyrannical
> any proposals, such as prohibition, to regulate moral behavior.[21]

The same was said of Churchill by his political biographer Paul Addison:

> Churchill . . . detested all peacetime plans for the regulation and
> control of the economy. They smacked to him of regimentation and
> dictatorship. Churchill was often dismissed as an adventurer but it
> was, of course, this quality of individualism for which, above all
> else, he stood.[22]

In *Churchill's Political Philosophy*, Churchill's official biographer Martin
Gilbert describes the essence of Churchill's political values with a quote
from Eric Seal, who was Churchill's Principal Private Secretary from
September 1939 to mid-1941. Seal made the following observation about
Churchill in private notes not intended for publication:

> The key word in any understanding of Winston Churchill is the
> simple word "Liberty". Throughout his life, through many changes
> and vicissitudes, Winston Churchill stood for liberty. He intensely
> disliked, and reacted violently against, all attempts to regiment and
> dictate opinion. In this attitude, he was consistent throughout his
> political life.[23]

The same has been said of Cockran. Robert McElroy, the editor of
In The Name Of Liberty, the only collection of Cockran's speeches
(published posthumously in 1925), wrote this about Cockran and liberty
in the Introduction:

> Whether [Cockran's] subject was political, racial or religious . . . the
> theme, Liberty, was ever on his tongue; and to him America was the
> apotheosis of Liberty . . . In almost every speech he uttered,
> Mr. Cockran emphasized the fact that the greatest lessons taught
> by American history are lessons, not for Americans alone, but for

all mankind; for all those whose aim is liberty and whose need
is light.[24]

It should come as no surprise, therefore, that Cockran's young English
protégé staked-out a series of positions in Parliament from 1900 to 1906
based on classical liberal principles which mirrored those of his mentor on
a wide range of issues. Churchill opposed increased military expenditures,
jingoism, the conduct of the Boer War by the British military and the use
of indentured Chinese labourers in South Africa. He supported open
immigration, racial and religious tolerance, restoring legal rights to trade
unions and maintaining free trade.

Free trade was Churchill's main battle during this period, a scorched-
earth campaign for the soul of the Conservative Party over the issue of
protectionism. His chief adversary, Joseph Chamberlain, sought preferential treatment for imports from throughout the British Empire,
something Churchill, never the arch-imperialist portrayed by his
detractors, strongly opposed.

Churchill supported unilateral free trade and was convinced that
protection meant the end of the old Conservative Party. He predicted
in early May 1904 that if they turned their backs on free trade, the
Conservatives would become like the Republican Party Cockran had
told him about: 'a party of great vested interests, banded together in a
formidable federation; corruption at home, aggression to cover it up
abroad; the trickery of tariff juggles, the tyranny of a party machine;
sentiment by the bucketful, patriotism by the imperial pint; the open
hand at the public exchequer . . .'[25]

Less than three weeks later, Churchill left the Conservative Party
of his father and crossed the floor of Parliament to join the Liberals.
Significantly – and overlooked by many biographers – he wrote a long
letter to Cockran the same day.

To Cockran, 31 May 1904

I shall look forward immensely to having some long talks with you.
You are in some measure responsible for the mould in which my
political thought has been largely cast, and for the course which
I have adopted on these great questions of Free Trade. It is in different spheres we are fighting in a common cause, and there can be
no doubt that a democratic victory in America resulting in the

reductions of the tariffs through the deliberate convictions of
the American people, would utterly smash once and for all the
Protectionist movement here . . .[26]

In those early days of Churchill's parliamentary career, he freely cribbed
from Cockran's free trade speeches to formulate his own. In a letter to
Cockran later that year, Churchill wrote:

To Cockran, 16 July 1904

I beg you to send me as much of your political literature as you can –
particularly your own speeches. As I have told you before you have
powerfully influenced me in the political conceptions I have formed
and I like to think that under different skies and different lands we are
fighting in one long line of battle for a common cause.[27]

Evidence that the mentor–protégé phase of their relationship had
concluded and had evolved into an enduring friendship can be found
in a long letter from Cockran to Churchill in 1905 where he offered –
for the first time – specific advice on Churchill's career, namely that he
announce publicly he would not accept office in a new Liberal government. Cockran did so because Churchill was being heavily criticized as
an opportunist who left the Tories in order to advance his own career
and used free trade merely as a convenient cover for his overreaching
ambition.

To Churchill, 6 June 1905

This then is very probably the crisis of your career. The judgement
which men fairly unbiased will form of you, now, is very likely the
one that will follow you through life.[28]

Cockran's advice was well intentioned and politically shrewd. It may
have had the effect on Churchill's enemies which he predicted. It was
certainly prescient because Churchill did accept an appointment in
December 1905 as Under-Secretary of State for the Colonies and his
party-switching and acceptance of office did in fact 'follow (Churchill)
through life' as his detractors today still hold it against him. A long
postscript to Cockran's letter, however, sufficiently hedged his advice so

that Churchill could have believed that his acceptance of office came within one of Cockran's exceptions: the office sought him, not vice versa.

The thirty-two-year-old Churchill again acknowledged Cockran's importance in a May 1906 letter to his first cousin, Shane Leslie:

> Tell [Cockran] that while our political views on the Irish question differ, I regard his as the biggest and most original mind I have ever met. When I was a young man he instantly gained my confidence and I feel that I owe the best things in my career to him.[29]

When he was President of the Board of Trade and married for less than a year, Churchill wrote a letter to his young wife Clementine in May 1909 telling her that Cockran was visiting him in London and asking her to come have lunch with the two of them and Cockran's 'pretty young wife'. In describing his mentor, Churchill wrote:

> Bourke Cockran – a great friend of mine – has just arrived in England from U.S.A. He is a remarkable fellow – perhaps the finest orator in America, with a gigantic C.J. Fox head – & a mind that has influenced my thought in more than one important direction.[30]

'Never did I detect any inconsistency'

Nine years after Cockran's death in 1923, Churchill wrote in his 1932 collection of articles and essays, *Thoughts and Adventures*, about the influence Cockran had on his early life. Churchill wished to illustrate, in mid-life, his own political consistency over the course of his thirty-plus years in the public arena despite his twice switching parties from Conservative to Liberal in 1904 and back again in 1924. Churchill's enemies saw it as evidence of his inconsistency and unprincipled opportunism. But to Churchill, consistency was to principle, not party, and he wanted to credit his mentor, Cockran, who had taught him that by word and deed.

The book's third essay 'Consistency in Politics' conveys Churchill's thoughts on this subject, using examples drawn from Emerson, Burke and Gladstone. Churchill also cites his own experience advocating naval preparedness in the years before the Great War when he was First Lord of the Admiralty and then urging naval retrenchment in the 1920s when he was Chancellor of the Exchequer. He contrasts that example with his old turn-of-the-century nemesis, Joseph Chamberlain, who supported free trade in 1884 and opposed it in 1904.

At the essay's conclusion, Churchill rebuts the oft-repeated charge of his own inconsistency stemming from his having left the Conservative Party to join the Liberals in 1904 over the issue of free trade and rejoining the Conservatives in the 1920s after the Liberals had abandoned free trade and the Conservatives had adopted a more neutral view:

> A change of Party is usually considered a much more serious breach of consistency than a change of view. In fact as long as a man works with a Party he will rarely find himself accused of inconsistency, no matter how widely his opinions at one time on any subject can be shown to have altered . . . To remain constant when a Party changes is to excite invidious challenge . . . Still, a sincere conviction, in harmony with the needs of the time and upon a great issue, will be found to override all other factors; and it is right and in the public interest that it should.[31]

Churchill learned this from Cockran, whom Churchill introduces in the book's next essay, 'Personal Contacts', where he describes the origins of his own approach to political thought. Churchill first pays brief homage to his distant father's posthumous influence and then turns immediately to Cockran and recounts the 'strong impression' the Irish-American lawyer made on him thirty-seven years earlier:

> When I first went to the United States in 1895, I was a subaltern of cavalry. I was met on the quay by Mr. Bourke Cockran, a great friend of my American relations who had most kindly undertaken to look after me during my stay in the city. I must record the strong impression which this remarkable man made upon my untutored mind. I have never seen his like, or in some respects his equal. With his enormous head, gleaming eyes and flexible countenance, he looked uncommonly like the portraits of Charles James Fox. It was not my fortune to hear any of his orations, but his conversation, in point, in pith, in rotundity, in antithesis, and in comprehension, exceeded anything I have ever heard.[32]

Churchill next gives a short history of Cockran's career, specifically referencing Cockran's opposition to his own party's candidate for president in 1896:

Originally a Democrat and a Tammany Tiger, he was affronted by Mr. Bryan's Free Silver campaign. He took sides against his party and delivered from Republican platforms a memorable series of speeches. Later on when the Currency issue was – for the time being – disposed of, he rejoined his old friends. This double trans-ference of party loyalties naturally exposed him to much abuse.[33]

Churchill quickly absolves his old mentor of inconsistency just as he did for himself and explains why:

I must affirm that never during our acquaintance of twenty years did I detect any inconsistency in the general body of doctrine upon which his views were founded. All his convictions were of one piece . . . . Cockran . . . had evolved a complete scheme of political thought which enabled him to present a sincere and effective front in every direction according to changing circumstances. He was a paci-fist, individualist, democrat, capitalist, and a "Gold-bug". Above all he was a Free-Trader and repeatedly declared that this was the underlying doctrine by which all the others were united. Thus he was equally opposed to socialists, inflationists and protectionists, and he resisted them on all occasions. In consequence there was in his life no lack of fighting. Nor would there have been had he lived longer.[34]

In their more honest, albeit private, moments, even Churchill's political detractors conceded his consistency. The protectionist MP Leo Amery wrote in his diary the following about Churchill in 1929: 'On essentials, he is still where he was 25 years ago, in intellectual conviction at least . . . He just repeats the old phrases of 1903.'[35] Had he known, Cockran would have been pleased.

Out of office himself after the war in 1946, Churchill journeyed to America to deliver in Fulton, Missouri, what has become one of his most memorable and controversial speeches, 'The Sinews of Peace'. During this speech in which he introduced the term 'Iron Curtain', he again publicly acknowledged the influence Cockran had upon him:

> I have now stated the two great dangers which menace the homes of the people: War and Tyranny . . .
>
> I have often used words which I learned fifty years ago from a great Irish-American orator, a friend of mine, Mr. Bourke Cockran. "There is enough for all. The earth is a generous mother; she will provide in plentiful abundance food for all her children if they will but cultivate her soil in justice and in peace."[36]

During his second term as prime minister in 1954, the State University of New York awarded Churchill a Doctorate of Law. Accepting the degree *in absentia*, Churchill once more publicly honoured his old mentor, concluding with the words with which this chapter began:

> Still, I remain, as I have said, a strong supporter of the principles which Mr. Bourke Cockran inculcated into me on my youthful visit before most of you were born.[37]

Ironically, when Churchill's mother Jennie introduced the two men, she was looking only to introduce a strong male influence into her young son's life in the wake of his father's death. Jennie had a knack for staying on good terms with her former lovers and frequently used them to benefit her son and his career. While Lady Randolph was politically astute, it is unlikely that she could have foreseen that her son would still be acknowledging some sixty years after their Parisian fling the central role her old lover had played in Churchill's political career. Having once chosen Cockran as a lover, Jennie was surely pleased by the relationship the two men established and the enduring effect it had on her son and his life.

It is an interesting story.

Chapter 2
'One of the President's Most Trusted Advisers'

Bourke Cockran loved the light in Paris, especially at sundown. Parisians called it 'le heure bleue', when the buildings seemed to soften at the edges and blend into the blue-grey light of dusk. Cockran looked back at the Eiffel Tower and then turned on to Avenue Kléber, the trees on the street framing the Arc de Triomphe, hazy in the distance. Cockran's heart was lighter than it had been in months, and he was looking forward to the evening ahead. He was a religious man and believed that life unfolded according to God's plan. Much had happened to him in the past year – the worst year of his life – and it had certainly tested his faith.

A year ago, Cockran and his pretty thirty-one-year-old wife, Rhoda, had dined more than once in the family quarters of the White House with President Grover Cleveland and his own pretty young wife, Frances, only two years younger than Rhoda. He had been a member of Congress, on Ways and Means, the most powerful committee in Congress. He was a close friend and even closer adviser to the president on monetary policy and free trade. He had good friends on both sides of the aisle, and he and his wife had entertained frequently at their home on 16th Street in Washington's fashionable northwest section, a mecca for Washington's literary and political lions from Mark Twain and Henry Adams to Henry Cabot Lodge and William Jennings Bryan. Friends from New York would frequently drop by as well, including his friend Charles Dana from the New York Sun *and his equally good friend and client, Joseph Pulitzer of* The New York World.

Life had been good. If a bill important to the president was before the House, he asked Cockran to lead the debate, not the Democratic Majority Leader or the chairman of Ways and Means. It spoke well of the president, Cockran thought, that he and Cleveland had become such good friends when he had, in fact, opposed Cleveland's nomination at the Democratic Convention of 1884 and again in 1892. But, once he was nominated, Cockran had both times campaigned vigorously for Cleveland and the president had not forgotten.

*Yes, a year ago, there were no clouds on Cockran's horizon and
he and Rhoda had every reason to look forward to a long and happy
life together. Now, Cockran had nothing, no seat in Congress and his
beautiful wife had been taken before her time. He knew losing Rhoda
had been God's will, and Cockran had accepted that with a heavy heart.
While he believed in and accepted God's will, he didn't have to like it nor
did he pretend that it was all for the best. It damn well wasn't.*

*As for losing his seat in Congress, that was a different matter entirely
and well within his control. Richard Croker, the boss of Tammany Hall,
had wanted Cockran to use his friendship with the president to gain
patronage for Tammany even though there was no love lost between
Cleveland and Tammany Hall. In fact, in contrast to Cockran, Tammany
had sat on its hands during the last presidential election and done little
for Cleveland in New York City. So Cockran had turned Croker down
flat, explaining to him that Cleveland owed nothing to Tammany and
would not give Tammany so much as a village postmaster in patronage.
Croker had coolly replied that he knew all of this. That wasn't his point.
While Cleveland would not do it for Tammany, he would do it for his
good friend Cockran.*

*Perhaps Cockran should not have laughed in Croker's face and called
him a damn fool for thinking that Cockran would trade upon a personal
friendship for political advantage. That had not been wise. Worse,
Cockran knew that Croker believed him responsible for the break-up of
Croker's marriage. Cockran shook his head at the thought. How did
a man become so self-centred? So blind? It was no secret Croker was
notoriously unfaithful to his wife. How long had he expected her to
suffer such humiliation in silence? Especially when their own parish
priest had given a thinly disguised sermon attacking Croker's infidelity.
It was perfectly natural for Mrs. Croker to seek to retain the man
many called the best trial lawyer in New York. But Cockran had turned
her down.*

*Not that it helped. Cockran knew Croker would deny him renom-
ination to his Congressional seat no matter what. So, as he had done
before with an earlier Tammany Boss, Cockran beat him to the punch
and announced that he would not stand for re-election. After that came
Rhoda's illness and death. The grey, cold winter in New York depressed
him further. It was good that he was no longer a drinking man because he
certainly would have sought solace in a bottle last winter had he been so
inclined.*

People have different ways of dealing with grief and sadness. For Cockran, it was travel. To Ireland, where he was born. To England, where he had many friends. And to France, where he had gone to school. So, in mid-March, Cockran had bought a first-class steamship ticket and sailed for Southampton. Indeed, it was due to an English friend, Moreton Frewen, that he was in such a good mood this evening. By now Moreton was back out in Colorado attending to his latest mining investment, but his wife, Clara, was in Paris with her two younger sisters. They had rented a large, comfortable home where, at Moreton's suggestion, he was now bound for dinner. He had only met Clara on a few occasions because she and her husband lived in England. Or, rather, Clara lived in England where Moreton occasionally joined her. Clara was pretty and pleasant enough, but they had never talked at length, certainly not at a dinner party. He had never met her sisters.

The sisters were the daughters of the American financier, Leonard Jerome, a true American original who had made and lost several fortunes and had substantial ownership interests in both the New York Times *and Belmont Park. His daughters had all married Englishmen. Clara, the oldest, marrying Frewen and Leonie, the youngest, marrying Sir John Leslie. But it was the middle daughter, Jennie, who held the most interest for Cockran. Lady Randolph Churchill. The most famous and the most beautiful of all Leonard Jerome's daughters and whose husband, barely ten years earlier, was talked of as a future prime minister.*

Like many Irishmen, Cockran had two weaknesses: strong drink and beautiful women. Strong drink had nearly done him in fifteen years ago, but he had mastered that, an occasional glass of champagne or wine was all that he permitted himself, which he certainly intended to do tonight. One glass of champagne stirs the imagination and braces your nerves. As Napoleon had said, 'In victory, you deserve champagne. In defeat you need it.'

As for beautiful women, he had married two, only to see them both perish, Mary in childbirth and dear Rhoda from a sudden, unknown affliction. His grief was too fresh to think of it seriously now, but Cockran knew, if he found the right woman, he would marry again. A vigorous forty-one years old, he could still have the children that fate had thus far denied him.

Cockran stopped to check his pocket watch as he arrived at the doorstep of 34 Avenue Kléber. He was frequently late but not tonight. Lady Randolph Churchill. Imagine that. A boy from County Sligo having

dinner with the woman whose late husband had coined the infamous
slogan: 'Ulster will fight; Ulster will be right.' Cockran shook his head.
There would be no need tonight to raise the unpleasant thought of Ireland
and the fading prospects for Home Rule. He had seen photographs of
the Jerome sisters in the New York newspapers. They were all attractive
enough but Lady Randolph – Jennie – was spectacular. She was reputed
to have had many lovers, possibly including, if you believed all you heard
which Cockran did not, the Prince of Wales himself.

A few years ago, Cockran had been dining at a London club with
friends and had been introduced to Sir Edgar Vincent, a tall, handsome
man, taller than Cockran, who had known Lady Randolph when she
and her husband had resided in Ireland in the latter part of the 1870s.
The image of Vincent's description of first seeing her had stayed with him
to this day.

> I have the clearest recollection of seeing her for the first time . . .
> [A] dark, lithe figure, standing somewhat apart and appearing to be
> of another texture to those around her, radiant, translucent, intense.
> A diamond star in her hair, her favourite ornament – its lustre
> dimmed by the flashing glory of her eyes. More of the panther than
> of the woman in her look, but with a cultivated intelligence
> unknown to the jungle.[1]

'More of the panther.' Cockran had been somewhat shocked. He had
never heard a man describe a woman in public like that. He was not
surprised when he learned later that the man was reputed to be one of
Lady Randolph's lovers, but he nonetheless thought it bad form.

Now, nearly twenty years on, Frewen said Jennie was still the most
beautiful woman he had ever seen. Frewen had told him many stories
about Lady Randolph, but the one that most captivated Cockran was
how she had campaigned for her husband in the 1886 elections, which
brought the Tories to power and Lord Randolph to Leader of the House
of Commons and Chancellor of Exchequer, nearly to the top of the
greasy pole, as Disraeli had termed it. Only being prime minister could
top that.

She could charm the birds out of the trees and into her hands, Frewen
had told him. Once, while campaigning, Frewen said she had been confronted by a butcher who, in front of his wife, advised Lady Randolph
that men did not appreciate being asked by a beautiful lady for

something as important as their vote. Jennie only smiled. 'But sir, you
have something I want very much' she said, her voice dripping with
innocence. 'However am I to get it if I don't ask?'[2]

However, indeed, Cockran thought. Here was a woman he wanted
to meet, a woman to take his mind off of himself and his sorrows. An
evening of sparkling conversation, good food, fine wine and the beautiful
Jerome sisters, Jennie especially, as his dinner companions.

Cockran reached for the heavy brass knocker at 34 Avenue Kléber.
Yes, he was certainly looking forward to meeting Lady Randolph
Churchill.

1884

Bourke Cockran became a national figure in the summer of 1884, the
nineteenth-century equivalent of a rock star, when he was first recognized
by the national press as a great orator at the Democratic Convention
in Chicago, Illinois. He was only thirty years old. Soon, he would be
acclaimed as the greatest orator in America and, some said, the world.
He occupied that position for nearly forty years until his death in 1923.

Cockran had come to America only thirteen years earlier in 1871 on
holiday. While in America, he visited Washington, D.C., where he
attended sessions of the Senate and House of Representatives. Already
an accomplished public speaker in several Dublin debating societies,
Cockran had wanted to study for the bar, but Dublin barristers were not
well paid in those days and his mother suggested he study for the Indian
Civil Service. Cockran said no thanks. She arranged a position for him
with a London stockholder, but Cockran said he wanted to visit America
first. His mother indulged him, bought him first-class passage on the
steamship *England* and gave him £125 for expenses.

Cockran was from a well-to-do Irish-Catholic family and had been
schooled for five years in France from age nine by the Marist Brothers at
the Institut des Petits Fréres de Marie at Beauchamp and later at St. Jarlath
College and Summerhill College in Ireland. He was fluent in French, Latin
and Greek. Once his money ran out, he was faced with returning to Ireland
and becoming a London stockbroker or staying in America and finding
a job. Cockran stayed. He taught language at St. Theresa's Academy, a
private Catholic girls' school, for a year. Then he became the principal and
sole teacher at a public school in Tuckahoe, New York, in Westchester

County. While in Tuckahoe, he studied for the bar under Abraham Tappan, a Crown Court judge in New York, and was admitted to the bar in September 1876 in the King's County Courthouse in Brooklyn.

Cockran opened a small law office in Mount Vernon and married a local girl, Mary Jackson, who had been a pupil of his at St. Theresa's Academy. She died in childbirth within a year of their marriage, leaving him a widower at the age of twenty-three. Thereafter, Cockran opened a law office in Manhattan at 178 Broadway in the spring of 1878 upon the advice of Judge Tappan.

That same spring, William M. Tweed, the infamous 'Boss Tweed' of Tammany Hall, died and was replaced by 'Honest John' Kelly, who was the antithesis of Tweed. When Kelly died eight years later, he was eulogized by the crusading journalist Charles Dana, for 'his unswerving and incorruptible honesty'.[3] Formed originally as a fraternal organization, Tammany Hall was the dominant organization in the Democratic Party in New York City and maintained its power and the loyalty of its members through patronage from the many political office-holders it helped elect. Wary of its reputation, however, Cockran steered clear of Tammany Hall and joined the Democratic faction known as 'Irving Hall' and campaigned widely for its New York mayoral candidate in 1878 and its gubernatorial candidate in 1879.

In 1880, the Democratic National Committee commissioned Cockran and others to tour the Midwest to support the Democratic nominee General Winfield Scott Hancock, who lost to Republican James Garfield of Ohio. During this period, Cockran continued to build his law practice, his reputation mounting as a trial lawyer, both in criminal and in civil litigation, and his clients included Joseph Pulitzer and his newspaper, *The New York World*. He was once retained by the infamous financier, Jay Gould, 'for any jury trials that may come up in my business for the next year'. The amount was $5,000, well over $100,000 in value today. Gould had no jury trials during the duration of the retainer, and Cockran declined to renew the contract.[4]

At the 1882 New York State Democratic Convention, Irving Hall opposed Tammany's nominee for governor, Buffalo Mayor Grover Cleveland. Cockran gave a well-received speech from the floor supporting the Irving candidate, but Cleveland received the nomination. After that, Boss Kelly arranged a private meeting with Cockran and invited him to join Tammany Hall. Cockran declined, but he agreed to make several campaign speeches for Cleveland under Tammany auspices.

In gratitude, Cockran was appointed Counsel to the Sheriff of New York County, a part-time position which did not interfere with his law prac- tice. More importantly, he was invited to give the major speech at Tammany Hall's Fourth of July celebration that summer. At age twenty- nine, Cockran was the youngest speaker ever selected to do so.

In 1884, Grover Cleveland was the leading candidate for the Demo- cratic nomination for president. He had been elected Governor of New York in 1882 by a wide margin of almost 200,000 votes. By 1884, however, Cleveland had fallen out with Tammany Hall because, although he had won with the support of Tammany Hall, he believed the margin of his victory entitled him to ignore Tammany when it came to patronage. Worse, with his eye understandably on the White House, Cleveland openly took on the machine bosses throughout the state, proposing the abolition of many state offices, reforming the primary system and extending Home Rule to local government. As a consequence, Tammany and the twenty-five delegates from New York City to the 1884 Demo- cratic National Convention – including Cockran – opposed their own governor's nomination for president.

The preliminary battleground on which both Cleveland and Tammany chose to fight was the so-called 'unit rule', which, if upheld, would require a state to cast all of its votes for the nominee favoured by a majority of the delegation. Speeches were made on both sides. The closing argument in favour of the unit rule was given by US Senator James Doolittle of Wisconsin, the primary speech against the rule coming from former US Senator Thomas Grady, who Governor Cleveland had denied renomination to the Senate.

Grady's speech was hostile and uninspired, and he clearly had been bested by Doolittle. But before the Cleveland forces could call for the question, Cockran stood up in the middle of the New York delegation and was recog- nized by the Chair. He was, according to the *New York Herald*, 'a tall, impressive looking young man with a well-shaped massive head, a handsome intellectual face, large blue eyes with heavy drooping eyelids and gifted with a peculiarly delightful and melodious voice'.[5] The thirty-year-old Cockran declined an invitation to speak from the platform saying, 'No, my friends, my place is on the floor and from here I hope to address a few words to the delegates on the resolution before the Convention'.[6]

It was a lost cause for Tammany Hall with, at that point, no more than 200 votes opposing the unit rule. Then Cockran began to speak, reminding the delegates that four years earlier the hated Republicans had rejected the unit rule in their convention, thereby denying President Grant a nomination for a third term.

> I am stating here, sir, nothing that the history of our State Convention will not justify and I desire to remind you again that the unit rule has always been the unholy device by which unscrupulous political engineers have sought to throttle the voice of democracy.

* * *

> When the Secretary of this Convention proceeds to record me in a way that my lips deny, he performs an outrage on free speech and reduces representative bodies to a comedy and a farce to which I hope they will never descend in this council of the free and enlightened Democracy.[7]

Cockran was the last to speak before the vote was called. Four hundred sixty-three delegates voted in favour of the unit rule, but a surprising 332 voted against it, whereas, before Cockran spoke, barely 200 were thought to oppose it. One speech by Cockran had changed the minds of over 100 delegates. The *New York Herald's* correspondent was clearly captivated by Cockran and said as much in the report. It was the first but not the last time that Cockran would be compared, both as a thinker and as an orator, to one of his heroes, Edmund Burke:

> I could have touched him [Bourke Cockran] with my pencil as I sat at his feet. I could feel his presence. I could see his Irish blood suffusing his great neck and face and his fiery Irish soul leaping from his wonderful eyes. And then there burst forth the burning words of eloquence from the glowing lava bed of his heart. Yet he had perfect self-control. And then something within me said, "this man is really great. Here indeed is another Burke." His rapidly spoken words fell clear-cut from his lips and could be heard to the uttermost parts of the auditorium. The yells and hisses subsided and finally gave way to wild cheering. His victory was complete – a victory of intellect, of speech, of personality over organized hostility. When he had finished, we all felt that a great orator had come upon the scene.[8]

The next day, Cockran again addressed the Convention, seconding the nomination of Senator Allen Thurman of Ohio. The delegates were looking to be entertained once more. James McGurrin, Cockran's principal biographer, wrote that Cockran's second appearance before the Convention occasioned a 'storm of cheers and the waving of hats' from 'friends and foes alike'. Cleveland was nominated on the second ballot, but Cockran, McGurrin wrote, 'was, next to Cleveland, the most talked of man in Chicago'.[9] Cockran and Tammany strongly supported the victorious Cleveland in the national campaign which followed, and Cleveland carried New York's electoral vote that fall.

An interesting footnote to Cockran's ability in 1884 to influence others is found in Patrick Paxton Hibben's biography of William Jennings Bryan, subsequently a sometime adversary of Cockran and three times his party's nominee for president. The young Bryan attended his first Democratic National Convention in 1884 as a delegate pledged to Cleveland:

> The highlight of the whole affair for Bryan was the exquisite beauty of Bourke Cockran's speech! He listened enraptured to a type of oratory he had never heard before, a diction, a phrasing, an elegance, a passion that might have belonged to Pitt or Fox . . . There was something terrible and divine in the power of the spoken word to move men as Bourke Cockran first arrested their attention and then held them enthralled.[10]

1885–1888

On 27 June 1885, Cockran married Rhoda Mack, the daughter of the New York merchant and financier, John Mack, whose fortune was estimated to be in excess of $2 million ($46 million in current value).[11] The next year, Cockran was first elected to Congress in 1886 with substantial financial support from his new client, Joseph Pulitzer. After Cockran's election, an editorial in Pulitzer's *New York World* said that:

> Mr. Bourke Cockran is a young man of remarkable gifts as a speaker and political leader. He is a natural orator of extraordinary power. Even those who do not agree with his political ideas will have to admit there are few men in our public life today who are

endowed with his rare intellectual equipment. He has talent, courage, honesty and culture.[12]

Cockran's influence was indeed felt at an early time, and it symbolized his career. Democrats controlled the House of Representatives, and they were determined to unseat a Republican representative from Indiana, James White, who had been narrowly elected. A Civil War veteran and native of Scotland, White was unable to produce a copy of his naturalization certificate. With their majority, the Democrats had every reason to expect that White would not be seated and that his Democratic opponent would be seated giving them one more vote in the House.

Then, Cockran rose to speak, opposing his own party. The *Louisville Courier Journal* described Cockran's appearance as he made his maiden speech in the House of Representatives:

> In physical appearance Bourke Cockran of New York has not an equal on the floor. He stands fully six feet, symmetrical in form and weighing nearly two hundred pounds. He has small feet and hands and on top of a magnificent pair of shoulders rests a great, large, well-shaped leonine head covered with a heavy suit of dark-brown hair which sometimes falls gracefully over his forehead. He has a strong nose and large, blue, deep-set eyes with a wide space between them. He is friendly and unaffected and his conversation is brilliant and fascinating. He moves about the floor with grace and energy and his whole appearance denotes intellectual as well as physical power.[13]

As they had in the 1884 Convention, Cockran's words changed minds. Many other Democrats opposed their party, and Captain White was seated by a vote of 186 to 105.

The new Tammany Boss, Richard Croker, who had succeeded John Kelly when he died in June 1886, was not pleased. He complained to a colleague that Cockran's speech was 'a terrible disappointment' and that he did not 'talk like a Tammany Democrat'. Croker did not go public with his complaint, telling a colleague 'No, no, he will calm down after a bit and take his orders like the rest of them'.[14] The Brooklyn Democratic boss, Hugh McLaughlin, was not so reticent and publicly attacked Cockran: 'Cockran's speech has cost us a seat in Congress that we need badly. If every Democratic Congressman acted that way, where would our party be?'[15]

If the bosses were not pleased, others were. Cockran made a good impression in Washington and was quite popular on both sides of the aisle. Two of his good friends were the Republicans Thomas B. Reed of Maine and Henry Cabot Lodge of Massachusetts, himself a newly elected Congressman and already an historian of note. They met as dinner guests at the home of former presidential candidate, James Blaine, whose cousin, Gail Hamilton, was present at the dinner and wrote in her diary: 'Bourke Cockran's talk was enchanting. He is an extraordinary young man, so brilliant, yet so gracious and considerate. His comments on the Webster book [Henry Cabot Lodge's biography of Daniel Webster] delighted everyone, especially the author.'[16]

Cockran biographers appear to accept at face value that he chose not to run for re-election in 1888 in order to return to his law practice.[17] It is more likely that Cockran chose not to run because he was not prepared to take orders 'like the rest of them' from Boss Croker. Cockran may have wanted to stay in Congress, but he most certainly did not *need* to. Cockran was a wealthy lawyer married to a wealthy woman. On three occasions he did not stand for re-election to Congress despite his popularity with voters: 1888, 1894 and 1908. He was out of favour with Tammany each time. Yet even though Cockran wouldn't take orders, Tammany was soon to need him again.

No longer in Congress, Cockran became involved in a landmark criminal case in 1889, the echoes of which are still being heard today. He agreed to represent *pro bono* William Kemmler, the first man to be sentenced to death by electrocution in the new and untested electric chair. Cockran secured a stay of execution pending appeal based on his argument that death by electrocution was cruel and unusual punishment in violation of the Eighth Amendment to the United States Constitution. Extensive hearings were held with expert testimony on both sides. Cockran's argument was that human resistance to electricity varied greatly from person to person and that it was scientifically impossible to determine whether a given individual would die instantly or suffer grievous pain as increasing voltages were applied.

Thomas Edison, the inventor of direct current (DC), was locked in a titanic struggle at the time with George Westinghouse, who was the US license holder on the alternating current (AC) invented by Nicholas Tesla. Only AC, properly applied, could kill. Edison saw that executing Kemmler with an electric chair powered by AC would be a great public relations coup for DC. So, Edison, who personally opposed the death penalty, volunteered to be the state's chief expert witness and, under Cockran's cross-examination, admitted that electrocution would mutilate a victim by burning him up, 'carbonize him' in Edison's phrase, which he later changed to 'mummified'.[18] He took care at all times to emphasize that these infernal devices were powered by Mr. Westinghouse's AC.

Cockran lost the case, the US Supreme Court holding death by electrocution to be constitutional. In the event, Kemmler's death was as horrific as Cockran had claimed – burning hair and flesh, witnesses fainting and vomiting at the scene, Kemmler's coat bursting into flame.[19] Electrocution didn't improve with practice so that few American states today permit electrocution as a means of carrying out death sentences, Florida being among the few. As recently as 2001, the Georgia Supreme Court held that:

> [D]eath by electrocution, with its specter of excruciating pain and its certainty of cooked brains and blistered bodies, violates the [constitutional] prohibition against cruel and unusual punishment.[20]

These were the same factual and legal arguments made by Cockran over 100 years earlier before the first person had been subjected to such state-sanctioned torture.

1891–1895

Tammany needed Cockran to stand for Congress in a special election in 1891 to replace the late Representative Spinola because Boss Croker initially had chosen a crony with a less than savoury reputation for probity to replace Spinola – John Scannell. A public outcry arose, forcing Croker to retreat. Croker may not have liked Cockran (he almost certainly did not), but a man of principle was what the beleaguered Tammany Hall boss needed to offset the scandal resulting from investigations into Tammany corruption earlier that year by the Republican-controlled New York state legislature. Cockran had enjoyed his first term in Congress and agreed to return, no more prepared to take orders than before.

Once again in Congress, Cockran made national headlines the following summer at the Democratic National Convention where former President Cleveland, defeated four years earlier by the Republican Benjamin Harrison, attempted an unprecedented comeback. As before,

Cleveland was without the support of Tammany Hall, which backed the favourite son candidacy of New York Senator David Hill. As he had done eight years earlier, Cockran rose to second the nomination of one of Cleveland's opponents. The circumstances, however, were very much different from what they were in 1884.

It was 2:00 A.M. Like the other delegates, Cockran was tired. He wanted nothing more than to go back to his hotel room and sleep. But Cleveland forces controlled the Convention just as they had in 1884 and 1888, and they were not going to give a 'prime time' slot to Cockran. Who knew how many delegates might be swayed by that golden voice? Far better to make him talk now when most delegates either were already asleep or, if not, were in a decidedly surly mood. They rejected his request to adjourn until 10:30 A.M. the following morning.

Cockran knew what they were doing and, he confessed later, it made the normally even-tempered Cockran angry. As he stood at the podium looking out over the sea of faces, it seemed to him like 'a wall of darkness punctured with white spots'. In the New York delegation, he later said, 'The only person I recognized was Governor Flower of New York. Rain was constantly coming through the roof, and he sat on the back of a chair to keep his feet from the wet floor, with an umbrella over his head. I remember that I thought he looked like a huge turtle'.[21]

Cockran shook his great head, paused, waited for silence and then began to speak, echoing his theme of eight years ago. As in 1884, he did not attack Cleveland personally because Cockran believed Cleveland had been a good president. Instead, he again suggested that Cleveland could not win, a not unreasonable proposition given Cleveland's narrow loss four years earlier.

> Let me say to you in no spirit of disparagement to Mr. Cleveland and t
> o his history, to his record as an administrative officer, to his patriotism
> as a man, to his virtue as a citizen . . . I have said that I believe that
> Mr. Cleveland is a popular man . . . Let me say a man of extraordinary
> popularity . . . [*cheers*]

Cockran paused at this point and waited for the cheering of Cleveland's supporters to subside. When they had, he continued:

> . . . on every day of the year except one and that – Election Day. It is
> a popularity which may be described as tumultuous, but it will not

produce votes. It is calculated to arouse enthusiasm four months before election and produce disappointment for four years after.[22]

The impact on the sleepy and surly delegates was electrifying. The *New York Herald* wrote:

> Cockran's walk back to his seat was attended by an ovation such as few men could draw from a friendly audience and none probably has ever before forced from one so large and hostile.[23]

Clark Howell, the editor of the *Atlanta Constitution*, wrote:

> Bourke Cockran made the greatest speech ever delivered in a political convention. His achievement was nothing short of sensational.[24]

Cockran's friend, Charles Dana, was equally extravagant in his praise in the *New York Sun*:

> Bourke Cockran was the leading, the most admirable, the most imposing and most powerful figure at the Chicago Convention.[25]

For sheer drama, however, nothing can top the story in the *Toledo Sunday Journal*:

> Consider for a moment: An audience of twenty thousand men and women. A hot, stuffy hall, close, leaky and uncomfortable. Hard wooden-seated chairs, none too large for a child, much too small for a grown person. An audience weary, hungry and thirsty, that had sat from 4:30 P.M. to 2 A.M. Imagine eight-tenths of those present opposed to the candidate whom the speaker espoused. Recall the fact that the great Virginia orator Senator John W. Daniel, had been utterly unable to hold the attention of those present.
>
> Merge all these conditions before you and think what it meant for one man to hold the crowd spellbound for nearly an hour and then decide that never before has there been in this land so dramatic a moment as when the imposing, heavy-browed lawyer from New York, bearing most evident signs of the terrific mental and physical strain he had been undergoing, faced the throng.

Group all these factors before you and then see the army there gathered, breathless and bewitched, maintain a silence almost painful, a silence so profound that the smallest cadence of his voice reached past the delegates and penetrated the furthermost recesses of the great wigwam, and that the mellow flow of his matchless arraignment of the man who eighteen out of twenty there present delighted to honour, reached each ear and penetrated to every heart, and that when he concluded he received an ovation the like of which was never before accorded to a speaker at a political convention.

Then you will perhaps comprehend what Bourke Cockran did in Chicago on last Thursday morning.[26]

Notwithstanding his opposition to Cleveland at the convention, Cockran campaigned extensively across the country for the former president, who prevailed in the fall election. In contrast, Tammany Hall's support for Cleveland was tepid at best. Cockran was re-elected to Congress as well.

Cleveland never took Cockran's convention criticisms personally, and the two men continued to hold each other in high regard. The Washington press routinely referred to Cockran as 'one of the President's most trusted advisers'. An 1893 article in the *Philadelphia Press* referred to 'the warm friendship that has lately sprung up between the President and Bourke Cockran . . . The political gossipers are still discussing the private dinner given by the President and Mrs. Cleveland at which Mr. and Mrs. Cockran had the seats of honour'.[27]

It is likely that the president was publicly acknowledging his gratitude to Cockran for the role he played early in 1893 in the first great legislative initiative of the second Cleveland administration – repeal of the Sherman Silver Purchase Act, named after the Ohio Senator who sponsored it. The president had asked Cockran to take the lead in the House of Representatives, where he squared off against the young pro-silver Democratic Congressman, William Jennings Bryan, who eight years earlier had been inspired by Cockran's oratory.

It was a star turn for Cockran. The galleries were packed with Senators, Supreme Court Justices, and citizens alike because a Cockran speech was known to be as enlightening as it was entertaining. Even Vice President Adlai Stevenson, the grandfather of the 1952 Democratic presidential nominee, had come over from the Senate to occupy a seat beside the Speaker of the House.

Cockran did not disappoint his audience because the issue of silver versus gold – or, as Cockran saw it, inflation versus monetary integrity – was of critical importance to him. The Sherman Silver Purchase Act required the US Treasury to purchase 4,500,000 ounces of silver each month and to issue certificates redeemable in either gold or silver. The effect was predictable. People were selling the government silver and taking away gold in return, thus jeopardizing the nation's gold reserves as the price of silver dropped in the open market to forty-six cents an ounce while the government continued to pay ninety-six cents an ounce.

Both major parties were split over the issue of 'free silver' and 'sound money'. Democrats and Republicans alike from western states supported 'free silver'. Cockran and other Democrats from the East meanwhile stood side by side with 'sound money' Republicans like Cockran's good friend (and future Speaker of the House) Thomas Reed of Maine.

The last day of the debate on the repeal of the Sherman Silver Purchase Act was Saturday, 26 August 1883, and Cockran was the last speaker. Cockran proceeded to conduct a seminar on the history of money. He covered coinage in England from the 1600s; England's civil wars; free banking in Scotland; the attempted indictment of Jonathan Swift for attacking a proposed debasement of coinage; the panic in England of 1793; and the suspension of specie payment by the Bank of England in 1797. He concluded by saying:

> I think it safe to assert that every commercial crisis can be traced to an unnecessary inflation of the currency, or to an improvident expansion of credit. The operation of the Sherman Law has been to flood this country with paper money without providing any method whatever for its redemption. The circulating medium has become so redundant that the channels of commerce have overflowed and gold has been expelled. No power is conferred on any officer to secure sufficient gold to redeem the notes which the Treasury is compelled to issue.[28]

The House voted 239 to 108 to repeal the Sherman Silver Purchase Act. The Senate then did the same. The *New York Sun's* story on Cockran speech reported that:

> When Mr. Cockran finished his historic speech he was overwhelmed with congratulations, while a whirlwind of applause which lasted several minutes swept the floor and galleries. He was followed to the

cloakroom by more than a hundred cheering members of the House and there felicitations continued to be showered on him for nearly an hour.[29]

Cockran delivered an equally impressive speech as an encore a year later in January 1894. William Wilson, the new chairman of the Ways and Means Committee, introduced legislation in December 1883 to remove all tariffs from raw materials imported into the United States. This time, Cockran's friend Thomas Reed was on the opposing side along with almost all the other protectionist Republicans. Cockran treated the House of Representatives to the same economic seminar he would commence in 1895 with his soon-to-be young protégé, Winston Churchill.

In many ways, Cockran was a supply-sider before his time when it came to the subject of taxes in the form of tariffs. Lower taxes, he argued, would produce more revenue.

A low tariff will not only increase the revenues of the government, it will increase the opportunities of American labor. For every dollar that goes into the Treasury hundreds of dollars are collected by the processes of consumption and trade all over the country.[30]

Cockran concluded by charging that large standing armies in Europe inevitably led to protectionism and that America could and should do better.

In 1870 Germany entered upon a war of conquest and then began the day of large standing armies. That explains the protective revival in Europe. Protection is the logical result of a policy that maintains in idleness the flower of the youth of the country. As one vice breeds another, so the government that ceases to encourage production and sustains a powerful military establishment naturally drifts toward the protective system.

In seeking to find the freest market for our products, we seek the welfare of the whole human race; we seek to establish a commercial system which will make this land the fountain of civilization – this people the trustees of humanity – which will make the flag of freedom in the air above us the emblem of freedom in our fields, freedom in our mines, freedom on the seas, freedom through all the world for all the children of men.[31]

As before, Senators had come over to the House to hear Cockran speak. The House galleries erupted in cheers three times. The *New York Times* reported that Cockran had roused 'the House and its visitors to a pitch of enthusiasm perhaps never before reached in the history of Congress'.[32] The *New York World* echoed this, saying that Cockran had 'dazzled the House'.[33] Indeed, the *New York Times*, which three years earlier made a slighting reference to a 'windy Bourke Cockran' defending Tammany Hall with his 'erstwhile whole potato voice', now said in an editorial on 15 January 1894:

> He is one of the few men in public life who unite brilliant orator-ical power with solid reasoning and careful study, and he handles a subject on the floor with the art of an advocate and the breadth and penetration of a statesman . . . But to apply that [economic] truth to the individual cases, to test the plausible pretexts for a departure from it by quick and searching analysis, and to maintain good temper in a process essentially cruel is a gift that few men possess as does Mr. Cockran.[34]

It was not readily apparent at the time, but 1894 would mark the high point of Cockran's political career. He had become a close friend and adviser to a Democratic president whose economic views on sound money and free trade mirrored his own. He was a member of Ways and Means, the most powerful committee in the House, and was widely respected on both sides of the aisle. He and his wife Rhoda had just purchased the year before a grand house on 16th Street, N.W. in Washington, D.C., where they entertained on a grand scale. As Thomas Reed once wrote to their mutual friend, the New York lawyer James Carter:

> Things have changed dreadfully in this town since the days of your early visits . . . Will you ever forget the open-handed hospitality, the merry combats, the scintillating, unwounding raillery in which we reveled at Bourke Cockran's fireside?[35]

Guests at the Cockran dinner parties were a who's who of political and literary figures including Mark Twain, Henry Adams, Thomas B. Reed, Senator Eugene Hale of Maine, James C. Carter, William C. Whitney, Stanford White, General Lloyd Bryce, Augustus Saint-Gaudens, Charles A. Dana, William Dean Howells, Julian Hawthorne, Richard Harding Davis and Joseph Pulitzer.[36]

By the following January 1895, a year after his famous tariff speech in the House, Cockran had lost the two things in life most dear to him: his wife, Rhoda, and his seat in Congress. The former an Act of God, the latter an act of man, one man in particular – a fellow Irish immigrant named Richard Croker. Boss Croker of Tammany Hall.

Cockran's break with Boss Croker was of a public variety, at least from Croker's side, the culmination of which was a bitter *ad hominem* attack on Cockran delivered by him to the press on Christmas Day 1894 after he had denied Cockran renomination to Congress in the 1894 election:

> I have become satisfied that certain vicious newspaper attacks on
> Tammany Hall and myself, made since the last election, have been
> inspired by Bourke Cockran. I have no hesitancy in saying that
> I believe he has been going around talking about me in a way that
> sometimes leads men to be termed informers.[37]

Cockran refused to descend to Croker's level, calmly telling the press:

> A man's utterances are usually infallible tests of his character.
> I decline to be drawn into any controversy with the author of such
> stuff or to notice it in any way.[38]

Cockran never explained what was behind Croker's attack. The fact is that Croker and Cockran had been on the outs since the fall of 1893, and the events of 1894 only made things worse. The break with Croker had two causes: one political, the other personal.

Politically, Croker tried to take advantage of Cockran's friendship and influence with President Cleveland and his unquestioned stature in Congress. Croker wanted Cockran to persuade Cleveland to deliver federal patronage to Tammany. Cockran, who valued his friendship with the president and his reputation in Washington, declined to do so. His reasons were quite practical. Tammany Hall had sat on its hands in 1892 and had done little to secure Cleveland's election. Consequently, Cleveland owed Tammany nothing and Cockran explained that to Croker. Croker did not care. He believed Cleveland owed something to Cockran both for his speeches during the 1892 campaign and for his taking the lead on the repeal of the Sherman Silver Purchase Act. As Cockran was from Tammany Hall, loyalty to Tammany Hall dictated that Cockran use whatever influence he had with the president to secure federal patronage. Cockran refused once again and did not stand for re-election. Matthew P. Breen, a long-time observer of the New York political scene, wrote about this in his book *Thirty Years of New York Politics*:

> One of the most brilliant men who ever occupied the attention of the entire country was W. Bourke Cockran, who . . . assumed to think and act for himself . . . Croker runs a great political circus and gets all the gate money. Like P. T. Barnum he never permits any of his exhibits to get too frisky. When one of them forgets the ringmaster's whip and begins to caper as if he were an indispensable feature of the show, Dick turns him out to forage on the highway.[39]

There was a personal reason as well for Croker's hostility to Cockran. Croker was a notorious womanizer, openly unfaithful to his wife, Elizabeth, a deeply religious woman with whom he had nine children. In fact, one priest, Reverend Thomas Ducey, the pastor of St. Leo's Church in Croker's own parish, even devoted a Sunday sermon to Croker's infidelity.[40] By May 1894, the long-suffering Mrs. Croker had had enough and was determined to sue for divorce, writing a letter to the man she believed to be the best trial lawyer in New York City, Bourke Cockran, and asking him to represent her.[41]

Cockran politely declined to do so, claiming he was soon to leave for Europe, perhaps concluding that he had done enough already to alienate Dick Croker. The fact that she had consulted Cockran at all, however, goes a long way toward explaining the vehemence of Croker's attack on Cockran that December, especially as Mrs. Croker had obtained a separation decree in October 1894.

Shortly after Croker's attack, Cockran was in mourning for his wife, Rhoda, who died on 20 February 1895, from an internal haemorrhage. After her will was probated on 8 March 1895, Cockran decided he needed a change of scenery and embarked for London on 19 March and from there to Paris, where his good friend Moreton Frewen had suggested that he visit Frewen's wife, the former Clara Jerome, who had, along with her two younger sisters, Jennie and Leonie, leased a large home at 34 Avenue Kléber in Paris to cheer Jennie up in the aftermath of her husband Lord Randolph's death in late January. Cockran agreed.

Unknown to Cockran, however, Jennie Churchill was not in mourning for her husband, Lord Randolph. Indeed, that was why she had left London for Paris because society dictated at the time that she spend a half year in mourning. Those rules did not apply in Paris, and the sadness Jennie felt was not over her husband's death, which came as a relief, but over the recent wedding of her long-time lover, Count Charles Kinsky.

Chapter 3

'I Have Been Paid Out For All My Own Iniquities'

Paris
April 1895

Lady Randolph Churchill was not looking forward to tonight's dinner party as she sat at her vanity table, looking at her reflection in the mirror. The only new face was some obscure American politician, a friend of Clara's husband who apparently shared Frewen's incomprehensible interest in monetary policy. Jennie shook her head. It was cruel but true that Clara was the least clever of the three Jerome sisters and certainly the one who had made the worst match. Jennie had little use for her brother-in-law, Moreton Frewen. Even his friends called him 'Mortal Ruin' for the many failed commercial ventures in which he had persuaded others to invest.

Jennie had agreed to invite this friend of Frewen's to placate her sister. After all, Clara's husband was rarely around and cheated on her like most men. But Clara was as unlucky in lovers as she was in husbands. Poor Clara was having an affair with the odious King Milan of Serbia, who was also coming to dinner tonight. He was royalty from a minor country in the Austro-Hungarian Empire, far from the throne in Vienna. Royalty or not, King Milan had never been taught how to properly use a knife and fork. Her sister deserved better.

Jennie sighed and continued putting on her make-up. For as long as she could remember, she had always known she was the most beautiful woman in the room. At forty, however, she knew that, no matter how artful her make-up, she would soon no longer be the most beautiful woman in the room. But, not now. Not tonight.

Jennie had come to Paris early in March to escape the social dictates of London society. Her husband, Lord Randolph, had died in January shortly after they had completed an around-the-world journey undertaken at her insistence. She had known her husband was dying, even if he had not, and she had been a loyal wife if not a faithful one. Most of her female friends had active and healthy sexual relationships both with and without their husbands, many of whom were frequently away on excursions to the far-flung regions of the British Empire, on whom, it was justly said, the sun never set. In the last ten years, however, Jennie's sexual relationships had not included her husband. They had not lived together as man and wife since1885. Ironically, that was the year Lord Randolph's career began, what many termed, its meteoric rise, only to flame out in December 1886 with his resignation as Chancellor of Exchequer.

At first, Jennie had suspected another woman. She knew it was hypocritical, but the thought of Randolph with another woman bothered her greatly. She had been with other men before then of course, but that was only because her husband was so frequently away. What was a girl to do when all those strong and attractive men were attempting to seduce her and her husband was nowhere to be seen? Especially in Ireland where they had effectively been exiled soon after their marriage and horse riding was one of the few pleasures afforded her. If she and her riding companion came back an hour later than expected with a rosy glow on their faces, it was simply put down to an exceptionally vigorous ride, which it frequently had been.

After Randolph resigned, Jennie had learned from him that there was no other woman and that Randolph had withdrawn from their marital bed because he had been diagnosed with syphilis. He explained he did not wish the woman he loved to share the same fate. Jennie had been both touched at his love and relieved there was no other woman. She had loyally rededicated herself to her husband's career in which she still believed but no one else did. She vowed to become more discreet in her affairs and she had. Limiting herself mostly to Charles Kinsky, a tall, handsome Austrian Count and a noted equestrian whose sure manner and strong hands were as renowned in horse shows as they were in boudoirs throughout Europe.

And, of course, her good friend, the Prince of Wales with whom she continued to be as discreet in their affair as she was with Kinsky. He held no physical attraction for her, far too fat for Jennie's taste. But what woman would say no and what husband could object to his wife being bedded by the future King of England? No one she knew of. Besides, it served Lord Randolph right, a payback by the Prince for Randolph's heavy-handed attempt to blackmail him with his love letters to a well-travelled matron in their circle. 'I have the future king of England in my pocket', Randolph had unwisely boasted. But the boast was hollow, and Lord and Lady Randolph had been effectively banished to Ireland for five long, boring years. When at last they were allowed back into the Prince's social presence, the Prince wasted no time in completing his revenge. The Prince could have boasted that he had cuckolded the

Chancellor of the Exchequer whose accommodating spouse was comfortably settled in <u>his</u> pocket. But it was enough for the Prince that Randolph knew his wife was sleeping with him, as evidenced by the jewellery and other gifts he had lavished upon Jennie.

In the days after Randolph's resignation, Jennie had come to rely strongly upon Count Charles Kinsky and had fallen in love with him and he with her. But their love notwithstanding, they could never marry as long as Lord Randolph was still alive. The around-the-world tour with Randolph had taken half a year. She had talked with Kinsky before they left and told him how poor Randolph's health was and how little time the doctors thought he had to live. Kinsky had been understanding; he pledged his love to her and promised to wait.

The thought of Kinsky could still make her cry. He had not waited. Under pressure from his parents, he had become engaged to a young and very Catholic Austrian princess before Jennie could return to London with Randolph. It had ruined her last months with Randolph because all she could think of was Kinsky. She had written her younger sister, Leonie, begging her to do what she could to break up the pending marriage but to no avail. In part, she blamed herself because of the brief affair she had enjoyed with an Englishman in the months before her departure on the world tour with Randolph at a time when Kinsky was on Austrian army manoeuvres. Kinsky moved in the same social circles as she did in London, and she assumed, in her grief, that Kinsky had learned of her indiscretion and that was why he had reneged on his promise to wait for her.

Whatever the reason, the fact was that Jennie had found herself in January without a husband and without a lover. She could not bear facing the six months of mourning Lord Randolph that was dictated by London's society, six months without dinner parties, new gowns, sparkling conversation and, perhaps, even romance. The solution was simple. Contact her two best friends in the world, her sisters, Clara and Leonie; cable their adoring papa to come up with the rent to lease a spacious home in the heart of Paris for his darling daughters; and cross the channel where she could permanently put away the black clothes required in London.

Unfortunately, tonight did not promise to be one of those gay occasions to which she had been looking forward. Politics had ruined her husband and ruined her life. Her son, Winston, now twenty years old and freshly graduated from Sandhurst, talked incessantly of a life in politics, emulating his father. But what did Winston know of the world? While *she had a much higher opinion of his abilities and prospects than her late husband, the fact was that the poor boy had started at the bottom of his form at Harrow and had stayed there. It took him three tries before he finally passed the entrance exam at Sandhurst. He had done well there, better than anyone had expected, but after all, it was only a military academy, not Oxford or Cambridge. Maybe the Churchill name could count for something in Winston's career, but the sons of great men rarely reached the heights of their fathers'.*

Jennie sighed again. Dinner with an American politician. It was a good thing she loved her sisters so much. She hated politics and she hated politicians.

Jennie looked at herself in the mirror and liked what she saw. The deep blue velvet of her gown, its décolleté daring but not risqué for Paris, contrasted sharply with the pale skin exposed above. It was a shame to waste such beauty on the eyes of an oily Balkan King and a boring American politician. She checked her watch. All the guests should have arrived by now. Time to make her entrance. She walked out of her room and down the long hallway, pausing at the top of the grand staircase.

Jennie heard a voice below, fluently passing from French to English, then back again. That in itself was not unusual at their dinner parties but this voice was. It was striking. Deep, masculine but mellow at the same time. She could hear every syllable as if he were standing next to her, yet he was a full floor away and not speaking loudly. Jennie knew all the men invited tonight, save one, their guest from America. Clara's congressman. As she walked down the stairs, Jennie wondered if the man would match the voice.

She paused ten steps from the bottom of the stairs. Before her, talking in French to her sisters and King Milan was a veritable bull of a man, easily six feet tall and she reckoned nearly 200 pounds. He had small feet and hands for such a big man, and his movements as he talked were marked by grace and energy. His shoulders were simply magnificent. And on them rested a great, well-shaped leonine head. His dark brown hair streaked with grey was longish and fell gracefully in a comma over his forehead. He had a strong nose, large, blue, deep-set eyes with a wide space between them and that long Irish upper lip. He was not handsome but striking as if his face had been hewn from a block of wood.

This could be interesting, Jennie thought, and she smiled as she descended the final ten steps, joined her sisters and extended her hand. 'Mr. Cockran, I presume?'

1884–1887

9 March 1884 was an important day for Lady Randolph Churchill, the former Jennie Jerome. She and her husband, Lord Randolph Churchill, the Tory MP from Woodstock, had been invited to a dinner party hosted by his good friend the Attorney General, Sir Henry James, where the Prince and Princess of Wales would be guests, as would Prime Minister Gladstone and his wife. It had been nearly ten years, ten long years, when last she and her husband were invited to a social event attended by Prince Edward. At long last, to her joy and relief, the social ostracism of Lord Randolph Churchill and his beautiful, young American wife was coming to an end.

It was, for Lord Randolph, at least, a well-deserved ostracism stemming from a Victorian melodrama, where his older brother had been having an affair with a former married lover of Prince Edward whose twice cuckolded husband was a close friend of the Prince. His brother refused to break the affair off, and Lord Randolph unwisely sought to dissuade the Prince from applying Royal pressure by threatening to release love letters of the Prince to the charming, bed-hopping matron. Repeating the threat directly to the Princess of Wales only compounded Lord Randolph's offence. The Prince was outraged. All this happened shortly after Winston's birth, and as a consequence, the young family spent the next five years more or less living in social exile in Ireland.

Jennie was determined to make the evening successful and she did, comforted by the sure knowledge that she was always the most beautiful woman in the room. Jennie was at her most sparkling and charming best, so much so that she and the future King of England were to remain close, if not intimate, friends over the course of the next ten years, ten years which would see her mercurial husband rise rapidly to the top of English politics – Chancellor of the Exchequer and leader of the Tory Party in the House of Commons. His fall, however, was to be equally precipitous. By the first month of 1895, he would be dead from a debilitating illness, a brain tumour diagnosed at the time as syphilis.

But for now, the future looked bright. After the March 1884 dinner party with the future King, Lord and Lady Randolph were invited to another dinner party that summer attended by the Prince and Princess of Wales. In the summer of 1885, Lord Randolph received his first Cabinet position – Secretary of State for India. Everyone said it was only a matter of time before he became prime minister.

The eighteen months from Lord Randolph's first Cabinet position in the summer of 1885 to his sudden and unexpected resignation in December 1886 should have been the high point of Jennie's life. But they were not. They were, in truth, among the most miserable months of her life.

It was in the summer of 1885, Anita Leslie writes in her biography of her great-aunt, that Randolph first withdrew from physical relations with Jennie. Jennie was crushed and, throughout the eighteen months that followed, believed there was another woman. In truth, it may have served Jennie right to be labouring under this misapprehension because she had taken lovers of her own, many of whom were physically more imposing than her husband. But Jennie loved Randolph nonetheless, and an appreciation of what Jennie saw in him can be found in a description of him by his friend, Lord Rosebery, a prominent Liberal MP who wrote of him during the summer of 1885 after Randolph became Secretary of State for India:

> His demeanour, his unexpectedness, his fits of caressing humility, his impulsiveness, his tinge of violent eccentricity, his apparent daredevilry, made him a fascinating companion: while his wit, his sarcasm, his piercing personality, his elaborate irony, and his effective delivery, gave astonishing popularity to his speeches. Nor were his physical attributes without their attraction. His slim and boyish figure, his moustache which had an emotion of its own, his round protruding eyes, gave a compound interest to his speeches and his conversation.[1]

Randolph did not share with Jennie at the time why he had ceased marital relations. Notwithstanding any affairs she may have had during Lord Randolph's frequent absences, the couple by most accounts had a close and affectionate, if not loving, relationship for most of their lives. Their correspondence reflects this. Yet during the eighteen-month period at the peak of Lord Randolph's career, that suddenly changed and the two were no longer close and Jennie no longer his confidant.

Notwithstanding their estrangement, Jennie remained a loyal political wife throughout. During the summer of 1885, after the Tories regained power, Lord Randolph, upon assuming a cabinet position, had to stand for re-election and it was Jennie who did almost all of the campaigning and speech giving. Even the Prince of Wales congratulated Lord Randolph on Jennie's speeches.

Jennie was privately unhappy throughout this eighteen-month period and did not even tell her closest friends, her sisters Clara and Leonie, that she and Randolph were no longer intimate and 'for a long time she kept her mortification to herself'.[2] The best evidence of Jennie's anguish is found in a remarkable series of letters between Jennie and her mother-in-law, the Duchess of Marlborough. Remarkable because there was no love lost between the two women and Jennie, in fact, believed that the Duchess hated her as she had once written to her mother during a month-long stay at Blenheim.

Theirs was not a relationship which improved with age. Hence, it is all the more astonishing that Jennie would seek out her mother-in-law for marital advice. But, commencing in September 1886, she did just that. Jennie's letters do not survive, but the ones to her from the Duchess do. Jennie's anguish is reflected in them just as is, between the lines, the disapproval of the Duchess for Jennie's prior conduct.

On 24 October 1886, she wrote to Jennie:

It will bring you a blessing if you accept patiently this trial & look on it as a sort of retribution for indiscretions or errors——[3]

On 19 November 1886, after Jennie and Lord Randolph spent a weekend with Prince Edward at Sandringham, her mother-in-law once more wrote to her:

Dearest Jennie

My heart aches for you but I feel you intensify Matters and worry yourself in vain. If you could only be quiet and calm – I feel sure everybody at Sandringham saw your jealousy – & I know there is just as much talk abt. it as abt. the Brooke affair . . . you have been too successful & prosperous not to have made Enemies.[4]

After Lord Randolph's sudden resignation as Chancellor of the Exchequer in late December 1886, the gossip and whispers about their marriage were openly discussed. The American magazine *Town Topics* wrote that Lord Randolph had resigned because of an affair he had with Lady Brooke, who was suing her husband for divorce (and to whom the Duchess had referred in her 19 November letter to Jennie).

Arthur Brisbane, the London correspondent for the *New York Sun*, had the audacity to write to Jennie about these rumours on 14 January 1887:

> An article furnished me this week for enclosure in my Saturday cable to the New York Sun, deals with the details of a separation which the writer alleges to be pending between yourself and Lord Randolph.[5]

Jennie gave the letter to her husband, who was enraged and wrote back to Brisbane the same day:

> It passes my comprehension how such rumours could have been started, how anyone of position or respectability; could pay the smallest attention to such scandalous gossip, & how an American gentleman could write such enquiries as you have written to a lady & to one moreover who is a compatriot of his.[6]

Thereafter, a reconciliation occurred between Jennie and Lord Randolph, who left for a long holiday in February and their correspondence once again became warm and affectionate.

Jennie and Randolph continued to be close for the remainder of his life, including memorable holidays of extended duration to the Russian and German courts as well as their last cruise together around the world.

1894–1895

Lord Randolph's condition continued to deteriorate, but as late as 1894 Jennie had not told her sons how serious his condition was. Lord Randolph spoke for the last time in the Commons in June 1894, and it was not pleasant. He was halting and repetitive and frequently lost his train of thought. Two of his close colleagues saw Jennie afterwards, entreating her to spare Lord Randolph any further public humiliation. 'He died by inches in public' his close friend, Lord Roseberry, was to later write.[7]

Jennie had been conducting a discreet affair with Count Charles Kinsky of Austria since at least 1884, an affair which intensified after Lord Randolph's resignation in December 1886. Kinsky was a large, handsome man, intelligent and outgoing, as were so many of Jennie's lovers, men who appealed to her mind as well as her body. With

Lord Randolph's health rapidly growing worse and his refusing to adhere to his doctor's orders for rest, Jennie believed that travel would be best for him and persuaded her husband to commence an around-the-world holiday in 1894. It was to last nearly six months. Before she did so, however, she advised Kinsky of her plans and, it is believed, advised him then, if not earlier, of how grave her husband's condition was. There had never been a question of a marriage between the handsome and very eligible bachelor Kinsky and Jennie, not while Lord Randolph was alive. A divorce in Victorian times was not common and Jennie was a loyal if not especially faithful spouse. Kinsky promised to wait for her, a promise he was not to keep.

Jennie and Lord Randolph travelled from New York to Bar Harbor, Maine, and then by train across Canada to Victoria and down to San Francisco. From there, they sailed for Yokohama, Japan, on 24 August 1894. From Japan, the couple went on to Hong Kong and then Mainland China, Singapore and Burma. In Rangoon, Jennie received a telegram from Charles Kinsky telling her he was engaged to be married. In a letter to her sister, Clara, Jennie wrote:

> I had a telegram from Charles at Rangoon telling me of his engagement. I *hate* it. I shall return without a friend in the world & too old to make any more now.[8]

In a letter written from Rangoon at the same time, Jennie opened her conflicted heart even more to her sister Leonie:

> Leonie my darling I am ashamed of myself at my age not to be able to bear a blow with more strength of character. I feel *absolutely mad* . . . it hurts me so. I really think if I have, I have been paid out for all my own iniquities.[9]

By early December, en route to Egypt from India, Jennie again wrote to Leonie. She did not want to give up Kinsky without a fight and asked her sister to help:

> Oh Leonie darling do you think it is *too late* to stop it? Nothing is impossible you know. Can't you help me – for Heaven's sake write to him . . . I am frightened of the future all alone – & Charles is the only person on earth that I cd start life afresh with . . . Leonie

darling use all yr cleverness & all yr strength & urge him to put off his marriage .... *Don't breathe* what I have written about Charles to anyone———.[10]

It was to no avail. Kinsky married on 9 January 1895, and Lord Randolph died two weeks later.

Jennie's letters to Leonie about Kinsky reflect her state of mind in the days after her husband's death and leading up to her initial meeting with Bourke Cockran. The details of the romance between Cockran and Jennie are not well documented. Jennie's principal biographer, the American writer Ralph Martin, imagines at length all that Bourke and Jennie 'must have' experienced in Paris during the spring of 1895. It is well written and certainly plausible. But it is *imagined*, much like the fictional narratives that begin each chapter in this book.

By contrast, Anita Leslie's recounting of the romance in her biography of her great-aunt is at once more intimate and revealing because her source, either directly or once removed, is Jennie's sister Leonie, her grandmother and both Jennie's and Bourke's closest confidant about their romance. It is well worth repeating verbatim, especially as Anita knew both lovers personally, being Cockran's niece as well as Jennie's grand-niece.

> Then, as the chestnut trees blossomed and bright parasols enhanced the boulevard, Mr. Bourke Cockran came to dinner. It was Clara who brought him to the Avenue Kléber, vaguely describing "a friend of Moreton's from Washington who knows something about bi-metallism." Thus she described the Democrat Irish-American orator who three years previously delivered what one American paper called "the greatest speech ever made at a political convention."

* * *

But American politics meant nothing to the Jerome sisters. Jennie expected some old bore of a Congressman, hipped on financial theory. She felt a tremor of surprise when Mr. Cockran entered her drawing room – for he was extraordinary-looking, a heavy-boned bull of a man, wide-shouldered, with a huge head and the long Irish upper lip. His features looked hewn rather than chiseled, and bright blue eyes shone incongruous as forget-me-nots stuck in a mask of granite. He was ugly – but in a magnificent way. No man looked like Bourke Cockran and no man could speak like him. The perfection of his French and the musical intonation of his English, his memory for poetry and his flair for extemporizing, the whole style of the man astonished. When taken to Seymour's room the child laughed at his big head and asked to try on his hat. He spoke French with the little boy and gave him as a present, *Les Vieilles Chansons*, by Boutet de Monvel.

Sitting beside Jennie at dinner, Bourke delighted her with droll stories, the first of which concerned an Irishman he had overheard at her father's race course, Jerome Park. Surveying the fashionable throng in the grandstands, this Mick swaggered away, snorting in the Cork accent which Bourke could well reproduce, "And what's yon to Mallow races!"

The Jerome sisters worked hard at their parties; guests were expected to invigorate each other. And here was a man who could charm in two languages – and several dialects! A man who could make you laugh and cry in the same instant.

* * *

Jennie captured him for her dinner parties and then an amusing friendship sprang up between these two hot-blooded individuals. Bourke had recently lost his second wife and he was nursing a raw heart. He had come to Paris for a change of scene. Jennie on the rebound *was* a change of scene. The two of them could not but be mutually attracted, but their relationship entailed the clash of broadswords rather than the handing of bouquets. Two beings of violently tempestuous nature, they each complained about their "romance" to Leonie. Bourke said that Jennie wore him out – she was so overcharged with energy, and Jennie said it was exhausting to be alone with Bourke; they quarreled unless she had a table of guests where he could "show off." Jennie and Leonie never dominated the conversation, but they were past masters at the art of starting up subjects when men who could talk were at their disposal – an art not to be despised, though somewhat corresponding to that of ball boy at tennis.

Battered Jennie needed to be helped to her feet and here was the man to do it. Bourke needed diversion and here was the cleverest hostess in Europe. So the sun shone again and the blows of winter were forgotten. Clara just looked pretty and admired all the contestants. She was busy having a very discreet love affair with King Milan of Servia. Jennie was horrid to her about it, and said that Milan didn't know how to use a knife and fork!

Unselfish Leonie, the quietest but also the wittiest of the sisters, immediately recognized the calibre of Bourke Cockran. He was a man after her own heart, so erudite, so humorous, with that prodigious memory for literary quotation. He could be as versatile in Greek as in French and English, but few dinner tables could appreciate this, and he dropped his knowledge sparingly. In a way Leonie fell in love with Bourke as she had with Charles Kinsky, but she left him to "poor darling Jennie" who wanted to drive around in his open landau and do all those expensive things which Mr. Cockran was well able to afford. After all, she was happily married and poor Jennie was "unhappily unmarried." The consolation must be hers. So the exuberant Jennie drove and flirted with Bourke Cockran and introduced him to *le beau monde* while Leonie became his confidant.

* * *

She and Bourke Cockran parted none too soon. Their duet was that of two pairs of cymbals. But both had been stimulated and Jennie returned to England mightily pleased with a summer which had "restored her health" and served Charles Kinsky right![11]

Chapter 4

'A Startling Letter'

Hounslow, England
4 October, 1895

When he was at Sandhurst, Winston Churchill had never imagined that being a soldier in peacetime could be so boring. There were no wars and few skirmishes to be found anywhere in the British Empire. Difficult to make a name for yourself simply playing polo. Of course, playing polo was certainly not boring, but there were no medals for polo! There was also fox hunting in the winter, but like polo, fox hunting was frightfully expensive. And no medals! Besides, Churchill knew he had already spent far too much money on his own polo ponies. Almost as much money as his mother spent on dresses and ball gowns.

Churchill paced back and forth in his small room at the barracks of his regiment, the Fourth Hussars, and looked out over the parade ground, pen in hand, waiting for the words to come to him. They always did.

The newly commissioned second lieutenant in the Cavalry knew he was being impatient, but he was easily bored. When he had to and when he wanted to, however, he could put his mind to and succeed at whatever he chose. And he had chosen not to prepare for a winter of fox hunting. He didn't have the time or the money. He had more important things to accomplish which he couldn't do on a subaltern's wages. He may have been only twenty years old, but he wasn't going to let life pass him by. The Churchill men were not long-lived. His father hadn't made it out of his forties.

Churchill was a soldier now, but he had always known that he was not going to make a career in the military. His heart was set on a career in politics. That was the game he knew he would enjoy above all others, even polo. But how to get into politics? There was the rub. Would his famous name be enough? Ten years ago, it might have been because his father was the most-talked-about politician in England. But his father was gone and even his enemies mentioned him now only in tones of sorrow and pity. Churchill wanted neither emotion to be the foundation of his political career. He would vindicate his father's memory and the treacherous way in which his own party had turned on him, but he would

do it on his own terms and as his own man, not his father's son. He knew
all too well the gaps in his education. Sandhurst was essentially a trade
school, not university. But he would close that gap. That wasn't his
problem.

Churchill's problem was that he lacked two important things: money
and fame. Churchill's new plan, one he had quickly conceived and
fine-tuned over the past few days, began to address both aspects of
the problem. He had persuaded his good friend and fellow Sandhurst
graduate, Reggie Barnes, to accompany him to Cuba during their ten
weeks of leave that fall. With luck, he would find fame and if not fame,
then possibly the beginnings of fortune because he had been engaged
by the Daily Graphic *to send back dispatches from the bloody insurrec-*
tion the Spanish were attempting to put down in Cuba. For that, he would
receive the tidy sum of £5 an article.

Only one obstacle remained in his plan to insert himself into the thick
of military action so he could begin to carve out his own public identity:
his mother, the formidable Lady Randolph Churchill.

Churchill loved his mother dearly and he knew she loved him.
Unfortunately, they were in an awkward period of adjustment after
his father's death. He knew she still thought of him as the troublesome
boy he most certainly had been. He felt, however, that his father's death
had made him the head of their family, solidified by his graduation
from Sandhurst and his commission in the Cavalry. Unfortunately, his
mother did not quite see it that way, and for now, she controlled the
family's income, £2,000 a year settled on her by his grandfather, Leonard
Jerome. His father had left nothing behind but debts. Two-thousand
pounds was not a large sum but it certainly was compared to the £150
a year Churchill was making as a second lieutenant, supplemented by
a £300 annual allowance from his mother, paid monthly. Still, Churchill
had made his calculations carefully and he believed that he could
scrape by in relative comfort during the two-month sojourn in Cuba for
under £100.

How best to approach his mother? Churchill smiled. Not a flank
attack, that would never do. His darling Mamma would easily deflect
that. No, a full frontal assault was the only answer. Overwhelm her with
his enthusiasm, followed by a gentle reminder that it would be less
expensive and certainly safer than riding to the hounds.

*Churchill stopped pacing, sat down at the small campaign table and
began to write:*

4 October [1895]   *Hounslow*

My dearest Mamma,

*I daresay you will find the content of this letter somewhat startling.
The fact is that I have decided to go with a great friend of mine – one
of the subalterns in the regiment to America and the W. Indies.
I propose to start from here between the Oct 28 & November 2 –
according as the boats fit. We shall go to New York & after stay there
move in a steamer to the W. Indies to Havana where all the
Government troops are collecting to go up country and suppress the
revolt that is still simmering on: after that back by Jamaica and Hayti
to New York & so home. The cost of the Ticket is £37 a head return –
which would be less than a couple of months at Leighton Buzzard by
a long way. I do not think the whole thing should cost £90 – which
would be within by a good margin what I can afford to spend in 2
months. A voyage to those delightful islands at the season of the year
when their climate is at its best will be very pleasant to me – who has
never been on sea more than a few hours at a time. And how much
more safe than a cruise among the fences of the Vale of Aylesbury....
    Please send me a line.*

Your ever loving son
WINSTON[1]

1884–1887

Eighteen eighty-four was not a good year for nine-year-old Winston
Churchill. He was nearing the conclusion of the two years he spent at the
St. George's School in Ascot, two of the most miserable years in his life.
As Churchill wrote in *My Early Life*:

My teachers saw me at once backward and precocious, reading
books beyond my years and yet at the bottom of the Form. They

were offended. They had large resources of compulsion at their disposal, but I was stubborn. Where my reason, imagination or interest were not engaged, I would not or I could not learn.[2]

Churchill's unhappiness at St. George's was compounded by the discipline administered by the headmaster – flogging. Churchill did not appear to be intimidated by this punishment and on one occasion even kicked the headmaster's favourite straw hat to pieces in retaliation.[3] In the fall of 1884, Churchill transferred to a small private school near Brighton which was close to the Churchill's family doctor and run by the Thomson sisters. Churchill found Brighton much more to his liking:

> At this school I was allowed to learn things which interested me: French, History, lots of Poetry by heart, and above all Riding and Swimming. The impression of those years makes a pleasant picture in my mind, in strong contrast to my earlier schoolday memories.[4]

Notwithstanding Churchill's benign portrait of Brighton, he continued to be an unruly child. In December 1884, immediately prior to the Christmas holiday, he was stabbed in the chest with a penknife during an altercation with another student in an art class. This confirmed Lady Randolph's belief that Winston was an impossible little boy, and she told her husband in a letter that she could not possibly under-take to manage ten-year-old Winston without the help of his nanny, Mrs. Everest.

During Winston's time at Brighton, from late 1884 to 1888, his father, Lord Randolph, reached the peak of his career. As a ten- and eleven-year-old boy, Winston was well aware that his father was a prominent member of Parliament and knew he was being spoken of as a future prime minister. Writing to his father from Brighton on 5 May 1885, Churchill told him how men in the street were speaking of him as someone who should be prime minister.

The Liberal government fell in June 1885, and Lord Salisbury formed a caretaker Conservative government in which Lord Randolph became Secretary of State for India. An election was held in November 1885, but the results were inconclusive. The Liberals had an eighty-six seat majority, 335 to the Tories' 249, but the Irish Nationalist Party had

eighty-six members, thus holding the balance of power. Salisbury's
government hung on for a few months but fell at the end of January
1886, and the Liberal Party leader William Gladstone once more became
prime minister. But the Liberal Party was soon to split over Home Rule
for Ireland, where, that February, Churchill's father coined the inflam-
matory phrase 'Ulster will fight; Ulster will be right'. Gladstone resigned
in June when his Home Rule bill was defeated by the defection of Liberal
Unionists. A general election was held in July 1886, where the Tories and
their Liberal Unionist allies achieved a 100-plus seat majority in the
House of Commons. The Tories attributed this victory in large part to
Lord Randolph.

Winston had been following his father's political fortunes closely,
and in a letter on 27 July 1886, two days before his father was appointed
Chancellor of the Exchequer, he wrote to his mother, his yearning for his
father's attention quite apparent:

> I received Papa's letter this morning, it was so kind of him to write
> to me when he was so busy. Do you think he will be Secretary of
> State for India, or that he will have a new post?[5]

After his father became Chancellor of the Exchequer and Leader of the
House of Commons, Winston continued to keenly follow his career. Lord
Randolph made a speech at Dartford, where he called for closer links
between Germany and Austria as a means of countering Russian influence
in the Balkans, a position at odds with his own government's foreign policy.
Winston refers to this in a 19 October 1886 letter he wrote to his father:

> I received your kind letter, and the Autographs and stamps . . .
> I am trying for the Classical Prize and hope I shall get it. I am also
> getting on well in my swimming. The weather is gradually settling
> down. I hope you will [be] as successful in your speech at Bradford
> as you were at Dartford, and regularly "cut the ground from
> under the feet of the Liberals". I trust that you will have a
> pleasant crossing.[6]

Two months later, Lord Randolph offered his resignation to Lord Salisbury
over the failure of his Cabinet colleagues to cut military spending for 1887.
It was not the first time Lord Randolph had offered his resignation in order

to get his way, but to his immense surprise, the prime minister accepted. Lord Randolph was never to hold office again.

His father's fall from grace clearly affected Winston greatly as Jennie noted in a postscript to her 15 February 1887 letter to Lord Randolph:

> Winston was taken to a pantomime at Brighton where they hissed a sketch of you – he burst into tears – & then turned furiously on a man – who was hissing behind him – & said 'Stop that row you snub nosed Radical'!![7]

Lord Randolph was pleased and sent Winston a sovereign to reward his loyalty.

1888–1894

In March 1888, Winston passed the entrance examination for Harrow by a narrow margin. Once there, young Winston quickly became his own worst enemy. A 12 July 1888 letter to Lady Randolph from Henry Davidson, the assistant master at Harrow, helps explain why more than one psychotherapist has diagnosed the young Churchill as having had what is today termed attention deficit disorder.[8] After explaining that the school had decided to promote her wayward son to the next level, Davidson went on to write that:

> [B]ut I must own that he has not deserved it. I do not think, nor does Mr Somervell, that he is in any way wilfully troublesome; but his forgetfulness, carelessness, unpunctuality, and irregularity in every way, have really been so serious, that I write to ask you, when he is at home, to speak very gravely to him on the subject.
>
> When a boy first comes to a public school, one always expects a certain amount of helplessness, owing to being left to himself so much more in regard to preparation of work &c. But a week or two is generally enough for a boy to get used to the ways of the place. Winston, I am sorry to say, has, if anything got worse as the term passed. Constantly late for school, losing his books, and papers and various other things into which I need not enter – he is so regular in his irregularity that I really don't know what to do; and sometimes think he cannot help it . . . As far as ability goes he ought to be at

the top of his form, whereas he is at the bottom. Yet I do not think he is idle; only his energy is fitful, and when he gets to his work it is generally too late for him to do it well . . .[9]

The fact is the young Churchill made little effort to do well in subjects in which he had no interest, but he did do well in areas – like history – which interested him. Indeed, Davidson concluded his letter to Lady Randolph by writing: 'I ought not to close without telling you that I am very much pleased with some history work he has done for me.'[10]

Shooting, fencing, history and, of course, English were among the things Churchill liked and did well at. It sometimes goes unnoticed, but Churchill only received a technical education at Harrow where he spent three years in the Army class consisting of boys who were being prepared to take the examination for the British military academies at Sandhurst (infantry and cavalry) or Woolwich (artillery and engineers).

In the summer of 1890, two years after the unfavourable report from Davidson, Churchill was scheduled to take the preliminary examination for Sandhurst. At the last moment, however, Harrow's headmaster, James Welldon, decided Churchill was not ready. His parents were disappointed, and his mother's letter to him on 12 June 1890 shows that she believed the fifteen-year-old Churchill had not changed much in the intervening two years and the symptoms of attention deficit disorder were still very much with him.

Your report which I enclose is as you see a very bad one. You work in such a fitful inharmonious way, that you are bound to come out last – look at your place in the form! Yr Father & I are both more disappointed than we can say, that you are not able to go up for your preliminary Exam: I daresay you have 1000 excuses for not doing so – but there the fact remains! If only you had a better place in your form, & were a little more methodical I would try & find an excuse for you . . . but your work is an insult to your intelligence. If you would only trace out a plan of action for yourself & carry it out & be determined to do so – I am sure you could accomplish anything you wished. It is that thoughtlessness of yours which is your greatest enemy.[11]

In March 1892, Churchill won the Harrow fencing championship. Many Churchill biographers have focused more attention on his slight build and childhood illnesses and less on his considerable athletic abilities, into which he channelled the restless hyperactivity which so frequently accompanies attention deficit disorder. His father wrote and congratulated him but added: 'I only hope fencing will not too much divert your attention from the army class'.[12]

Churchill was very much focused on fencing, however, and went on the next month to win the fencing championship at a tournament of all the public schools. As his father had feared, Churchill failed his first entrance examination for Sandhurst that summer. He returned in the fall term to Harrow with nothing to do but study for the next Sandhurst entrance examination to be conducted in November. That September, Lord Randolph wrote to his mother, the Duchess of Marlborough, that if Winston failed the entrance examination a second time, 'I shall think about putting him in business'.[13]

In the event, Churchill did fail his second entrance examination for Sandhurst in November, but Lord Randolph did not follow through on his threat to put Winston into business. Instead, he engaged the foremost 'crammer' in England, Captain W. H. James, who specialized in preparing young men to pass the entrance examination for Sandhurst.

Churchill's self-esteem was not diminished in the least by having twice failed the entrance examination for Sandhurst nor being sent to a crammer. What Captain James found was an eighteen-year-old boy with a much higher opinion of himself than his accomplishments to date would warrant. Shortly after Churchill arrived, Captain James wrote a letter to Lord Randolph which captures the essence of the boy who had so frustrated his parents and his Harrow masters and who was to so greatly impress Bourke Cockran only two years later:

> . . . I had to speak to him the other day about his casual manner. I think the boy means well but he is distinctly inclined to be inattentive and to think too much of his abilities . . . [H]e has been rather too much inclined up to the present to teach his instructors instead of endeavouring to learn from them, and this is not the frame of mind conducive to success. I may give as an instance that he suggested to me that his knowledge of history was such that he did not want any more teaching in it! . . .
>
> The boy has very many good points in him but what he wants is very firm handling.[14]

Notwithstanding, Churchill narrowly passed his third entrance examination for Sandhurst in the summer of 1893, finishing 95th out of 389 and scoring 6,309 points out of a total of 12,000. He actually placed first among all candidates in the English and history sections. Churchill was delighted to have passed and wrote his parents in Switzerland. His mother wrote back and warned him that his father was not pleased:

> . . . I am glad of course that you have got into Sandhurst but Papa is not very pleased at yr getting in by the skin of yr teeth & missing the Infantry by 18 marks. He is not as pleased over yr exploits as you seem to be! . . . I don't write more about Sandhurst as I know Papa intends to let you know his views![15]

Lord Randolph certainly did let his son 'know his views'. Read in isolation, it is an exceptionally cruel letter, but within the context of the seemingly never-ending stream of poor reports from Winston's tutors and masters, it is clearly the eruption of a frustrated father deeply disappointed in his son's lack of success:

My dear Winston,

I am rather surprised at your tone of exultation over your inclusion in the Sandhurst list. There are two ways of winning an examination, one creditable the other the reverse. You have unfortunately chosen the latter method, and appear to be much pleased with your success.

The first extremely discreditable feature of your performance was missing the infantry, for in that failure is demonstrated beyond refutation your slovenly happy-go-lucky harum scarum style of work for which you have always been distinguished at your different schools. Never have I received a really good report of your conduct in your work from any master or tutor you had from time to time to do with. Always behind-hand, never advancing in your class, incessant complaints of total want of application, and this character which was constant in yr reports has shown the natural results clearly in your last army examination.

. . . I am certain that if you cannot prevent yourself from leading the idle useless unprofitable life you have had during your school-days & later months, you will become a mere social wastrel one of the hundreds of the public school failures, and you will degenerate into a shabby unhappy & futile existence. If that is so you will have to bear all the blame for such misfortunes yourself.[16]

Surprising his parents, Churchill did quite well at Sandhurst, something his father began to notice early on. In a letter to Jennie on 24 October 1893, Lord Randolph wrote:

> . . . I took Winston to Tring on Saturday. He had to leave at 4.30 afternoon to get back to Sandhurst. He has much smartened up. He holds himself quite upright and he has got steadier. The people at Tring took a great deal of notice of him but [he] was very quiet & nice-mannered. Sandhurst has done wonders for him. Up to now he has had no bad mark for conduct & I trust that it will continue to the end of the term.[17]

'Tring' was Lord Rothschild's country home and Churchill described these visits in *My Early Life*:

> Once I became a gentleman cadet I acquired a new status in my father's eyes. I was entitled when on leave to go about with him, if it was not inconvenient . . . He took me also to important political parties at Lord Rothschild's house at Tring, where most of the leaders and a selection of the rising men of the Conservative Party were often assembled. He began to take me also to stay with his racing friends; and here we had a different company and new topics of conversation which proved equally entertaining. In fact to me he seemed to own the key to everything or almost everything worth having.[18]

During this period, Churchill began to be interested in girls like any other teenage boy, primarily Molly Hacket from late 1893 through most of 1894. This did not stop Churchill, however, from paying attention to other girls as well. Indeed, after leaving Miss Hacket a present of sugar plums, he apparently asked her for the address of a mutual acquaintance, Alexandra Ellis. On more than one occasion thereafter, Molly would write Winston inquiring as to whether he had seen 'Alex' and reminding him in one letter on 28 March 1894: 'I am so sorry not to have answered yr letter before, but I have been waiting for yr photograph which you promised and I want so much.'[19] During this same period of Molly and Alex, Winston also managed to make the acquaintance of a showgirl, Mabel Love, who had appeared in the Follies Bergeré. She autographed photos Churchill sent to her and wrote back to him saying: 'I shall look forward to seeing you when you come to town.'[20]

1895

Eighteen ninety-five was a year of dramatic change in Churchill's life. He graduated Sandhurst in the top 15 percent of his class; suffered the death of his father in January; received his commission in the Cavalry in February; saw the death of his grandmother Jerome in March and his surrogate mother and nanny, Mrs. Everest, in July; and, by year's end, had been a war correspondent covering the Cuban rebellion. He also met and began to forge a friendship with his mother's recent lover, Bourke Cockran.

Over the next twelve years, Churchill would pass through three distinct periods of adult development described by Daniel Levinson. They began at age seventeen when Churchill entered Sandhurst and concluded at age thirty-three when Churchill was married. Bourke Cockran's influence would span and play an important role in all three periods.

The first was the 'early adult transition', roughly age seventeen to twenty-two, when a young man begins to form the foundation for an adult life.[21] This period saw Churchill through Sandhurst, followed by an intensive self-education in political and economic thought, his initial assignments as a war correspondent and his first book as well as his first taste of combat.

The second was 'entering the adult world', age twenty-two to twenty-eight, when a young man begins to build a first, provisional life structure upon the foundation created earlier.[22] In this period, Churchill established himself as a first-class writer who could support himself with his pen; a brave and heroic, albeit frequently reckless, soldier who became a household name in England for his daring escape from a Boer prisoner of war (POW) camp; and a rising political star in Parliament with a decided flair for public speaking.

The third was the 'age thirty transition', age twenty-eight to thirty-three, when a young man re-evaluates his initial life structure and decides what parts, if any, need to be changed.[23] In this period, Churchill became

estranged from his father's political party, the Conservatives, over
the issue of free trade versus protectionism. While Churchill fought
within the party for free trade for a number of years, party leaders made
it abundantly clear that he was expected to toe the party line or be
ostracized – which, in fact, he was. As a consequence, Churchill left the
Conservatives for the Liberal Party in May 1904 and became one of its
leading free trade spokesmen, being rewarded for his efforts with his first
junior ministerial position in December 1905. He married in 1908.

Each of these three periods has its own particular tasks, but in addition, a young man has four common tasks to work on throughout his
twenties and early thirties.[24] The four tasks are as follows: (1) forming a
dream and giving it a place in the life structure; (2) forming mentor
relationships; (3) forming an occupation; and (4) forming love
relationships, marriage and family.[25]

As we will see, the young Churchill's progress on all four tasks by age
thirty-three was substantial, if not remarkable, and formed a foundation
which made possible everything that followed in his life.

After his father died in January 1895, Winston promptly set about
creating a new relationship with his mother. As he wrote in *My Early Life*
about the death of his father:

> All my dreams of comradeship with him, of entering Parliament at
> his side and in his support, were ended. There remained for me only
> to pursue his aims and vindicate his memory.
>
> I was now in the main the master of my fortunes. My mother was
> always at hand to help and advise; but I was now in my 21st year
> and she never sought to exercise parental control. Indeed she soon
> became an ardent ally, furthering my plans and guarding my inter-
> ests with all her influence and boundless energy. She was still at
> forty young, beautiful and fascinating. We worked together on even
> terms more like brother and sister than mother and son. At least so
> it seemed to me. And so it continued to the end.[26]

Churchill wasted no time soliciting his mother's assistance in arranging for
him to go into the Cavalry, The Fourth Hussars, rather than the Infantry,
The 60th Rifles, which his father had arranged for him because it was less
expensive to do so. Jennie sent a telegram to Colonel John Brabazon, the
Commanding Officer of The Fourth Hussars, for his advice. Reputed to be

one of Jennie's former lovers, Brabazon promptly replied and gave her specific advice, virtually writing the letter for her to the Commanding Officer of The 60th Rifles, the Duke of Cambridge and the Queen's first cousin. The Duke replied on 6 February giving his permission.

Shortly thereafter, Churchill joined his regiment at Aldershot, while Jennie was off to Paris with her sisters, soon to meet Bourke Cockran. Churchill wrote faithfully to his mother, several times a week, recounting for her his first days in the Army. During this time, and for the next five years, the subject of finances was frequently a topic covered in almost all of Churchill's letters to his mother and hers to him. They weren't brother and sister when it came to money. She was the mother and she had the money, although Churchill did not always appear to appreciate or recognize this.

In July, Churchill's life-long nanny Mrs. Everest died. Churchill was devoted to her and made all the arrangements for the funeral, including ordering a wreath from his mother, telling her he had done so because 'I thought you would like to send one'. He concluded the letter by telling his mother he felt 'very low' and 'never realized how much poor, old Woom was to me', adding as the final line 'I don't know what I should do without you'.[27] On 30 September 1895, Churchill wrote to his mother commenting on current events in China, Armenia and Africa. He closed the letter by telling her he was required to take his two-and-a-half month leave from 24 October to 8 January. 'Do try and arrange some common rendezvous for us.'[28]

Imagine Jennie's surprise four days later to receive Churchill's letter with which this chapter began, grandly advising her of his spur-of-the-moment decision to travel to Cuba. To Jennie, the impulsive decision must have reminded her of the harum-scarum boy she had so frequently had to deal with in the past ten years. At this point in their lives, Churchill to the contrary, they were still more like mother and son than sister and brother. Her 11 October 1895 reply makes this all too clear:

Friday [11 October 1895]   Guisachan

My dearest Winston,

You know I am always delighted if you can do anything which interests & amuses you – even if it be a sacrifice to me. I was rather looking forward to our being together & seeing something of you. Remember I only have you & Jack to love me. You certainly have not the art of writing & putting things in their best lights but I understand all right – & of course darling it is natural that you shd want to travel & I won't throw cold water on yr little plans – but I'm very much afraid it will cost a good deal more than you think. N.Y. is fearfully expensive & you will be bored to death there – all men are . . . Considering that I provide the funds I think instead of saying 'I have decided to go' it may have been nicer & perhaps wiser – to have began by consulting me. But I suppose experience of life will in time teach you that tact is a very essential ingredient in all things.

I leave here tomorrow & go to 'Minto House Hawick N.B.' Write to me there & tell me more – you have ignored my long letter over yr future career.

Yr loving Mother
JRC[29]

Winston may have ignored his mother's earlier 'long letter over yr future career', but he was clearly taking steps during the summer of 1895 to prepare for that career. Churchill was more determined than ever to go into politics and revive his father's reputation. Indeed, he would write a well-received biography of his father before he was thirty years old. At age twenty, Winston was on his own and on the cusp of meeting a gifted man who had the biggest and most original mind Churchill ever met. A man who would instantly gain Churchill's confidence and influence him for the rest of his life. It was Winston's beautiful and heartsick mother Jennie who made it all possible.

Chapter 5
'I Have Great Discussions With Mr. Cockran'

Bourke Cockran felt a chill wind whip in from the Hudson River and he pulled the collar of his Chesterfield topcoat higher around his neck. The sky was grey and a light mist was falling as he watched two tugboats nudge the Cunard Lines Royal Steamship Etruria *into the pier. It was a big ship, well over 500 feet long with two stacks amid ship and three tall masts sporting no sails. A far cry from the* SS England *which had brought him to America over twenty years earlier, with only a single stack and a full complement of sails.*

Ten minutes later, the gangplank was down, and the first-class passengers were beginning to debark. He thought he would recognize Winston because Jennie had shown him a photograph of her son when they were in Paris. Jennie. Paris. Had their love affair really been six months ago? He shook his head. In May, after their mother's death, he had agreed to accompany the three Jerome sisters back to America along with their mother's body, as Clara's husband was already in America and John Leslie could not spare the time to accompany his wife Leonie.

Cockran had been surprised when Jennie, at the last minute, begged off. It had surprised her sisters as well when she told them she was not returning to America. At first, Cockran had feared that it was because of him, but Leonie had assured him that was not true. She told him that he had done wonders to revive Jennie's spirits and that returning to America on such a sad occasion might undo all the good Cockran had done. Cockran had been encouraged by this and so continued to hold hope that he still had a chance with Jennie, notwithstanding some of the spirited arguments between them.

Cockran had never met a woman like Jennie Churchill. In fact the only one to compare was his own Rhoda, but she had known little of politics and could not have cared less. Jennie professed not to care about politics also, but her familiarity with all the political issues of the day and the personalities behind them belied that notion.

Upon returning to America, Cockran had spent some time researching the career and reading the speeches of Jennie's late husband, Lord

Randolph, for whatever insight that might afford him in wooing her. Randolph was quick enough in debate and he had possessed a withering tongue, but he appeared to Cockran to be more of an opportunist than a principled statesman. Lord Randolph's speeches on Ireland alone convinced him of that. In a speech in the late 1870s, Randolph had showed remarkable empathy for the situation in Ireland when he attacked Gladstone's proposal to suspend Irish civil liberties, including habeas corpus. In doing so, Randolph had isolated himself from his own Conservative Party and Cockran had admired what he thought was Randolph's political courage.

However, once he read that infamous incitement to rebellion in 1886 – 'Ulster will fight; Ulster will be right' – when Lord Randolph had opposed any Home Rule for Ireland that included Protestant Ulster, he found he didn't have much respect for Lord Randolph. Pure politics. Opportunism. An election was coming and Randolph had played the 'orange card' to attract the Liberal Party Unionists who opposed Home Rule. To Cockran, he was no better than a Tammany Hall hack dancing to Boss Croker's tune, something Cockran had never done.

Still, Cockran was looking forward to meeting Jennie's son. If he had half the ambition and brains of his mother, then he might have a bright future in politics, brighter even than his father's. The question was what kind of politician would he be? Jennie's son would have political courage. Of that he was certain. Would Lord Randolph's son? He didn't know.

Cockran had often wished for a son, but the Good Lord obviously had other plans. In time, he knew, they would be revealed. Cockran hoped that Winston would be amused and entertained by what he had planned for him during his time in New York. He was determined to do everything in his power to ensure that Winston made a favourable report to his mother of Bourke Cockran's hospitality. A dinner party tonight was only the beginning, an assembly of the leading lawyers of the New York City Bar and Judiciary. At Cockran's suggestion, Judge Ingraham had agreed to invite the young Churchill to attend an especially sensational society murder trial over which he was presiding. Next Wednesday, Cockran had arranged with the Commandant for Churchill and his travelling companion to visit West Point so they could see the American equivalent of Sandhurst.

Cockran watched the first passengers walk down the Etruria's gangplank. Cockran stood a good head taller than most of the people around him and he quickly spotted his two charges, Lieutenants

Churchill and Barnes, when they were half way down the gangplank. He recognized Winston from the photograph, a trim, good-looking, sandy-haired youth, maybe five feet, seven inches, give or take an inch or two. The dark-haired lad beside him must be Reggie Barnes.

'Winston Churchill! Over here!' Cockran's voice easily carried over the crowd and Churchill acknowledged it with a wave of his hand. Moments later, the three were together.

'Delighted to meet you, Mr. Cockran', Churchill said as he introduced Reggie Barnes.

'Please, call me Bourke', Cockran said as he directed a porter to follow them with the Englishmen's baggage. 'I have a carriage waiting for us.'

What may well have prompted Jennie's 'long letter over yr future career' to Churchill mentioned at the close of Chapter 4 were passages like this one in a 16 August 1895 letter to his mother:

> It is a fine game to play – the game of politics and it is well worth waiting for a good hand – before really plunging.
>
> At any rate – four years of healthy and pleasant existence – combined with both responsibility & discipline – can do no harm to me – but rather good. The more I see of soldiering – the more I like it – but the more I feel convinced that it is not my *métier*. Well, we shall see – my dearest Mamma.[1]

If Churchill was to have a life in politics, however, he knew he needed to learn more than he had so far. The young Churchill who two years earlier had confidently advised his Sandhurst crammer that his knowledge of history was such that he needed no more teaching in it had been left in the past. In his place was a young man who knew he was easily bored and who believed he needed more education than he had received. Responding on 31 August 1895 to a letter from his mother suggesting that he commence a study of the supply of army horses, Churchill politely declined. Churchill then displayed in his letter a mature self-awareness of the deficiencies of his formal education as he explained to his mother why he was not going to study horses:

> Besides if one hears 'horse' talked all day long – in his every form & use – it would seem a surfeit to study his supply as one of

the beaux-arts. No – my dearest Mamma – I think something more
literary and less material would be the sort of mental medicine I
need . . . You see – all my life – I have had a purely technical education. Harrow, Sandhurst, James's – were all devoted to studies of
which the highest aim was to pass some approaching Examinations.
As a result my mind has never received that polish which for
instance Oxford or Cambridge gives. At these places one studies
questions and sciences with a rather higher object than mere
practical utility. One receives in fact a liberal education.[2]

Indeed, Churchill had started to give himself such a liberal education and
told her:

> . . . I have now got a capital book – causing much thought – and
> of great interest. – It is a work on political economy by Fawcett.
> When I have read it – and it is very long, I shall perhaps feel inclined
> to go still farther afield in an absorbing subject. But this is a book
> essentially devoted to "first principles" – and one which would
> leave at least a clear knowledge of the framework of the subject
> behind – and would be of use even if the subject were not
> persevered in.
>
> Then I am going to read Gibbon's *Decline and Fall of the Roman
> Empire* & Lecky's *European Morals*. These will be tasks more
> agreeable than the mere piling up of sloppy statistics.[3]

Fawcett and Lecky, largely unknown today, are two early influences
on Churchill overlooked by many biographers. They are indispensable,
however, for those who wish to understand how Churchill developed
his political and economic thought; why Cockran was impressed with a
relatively uneducated twenty-year-old boy; and how Cockran was able to
gain Churchill's confidence so quickly.

Henry Fawcett was a classical liberal economist who was appointed
professor of political economy at Cambridge University in 1863, the same
year he published his major work, *Manual of Political Economy*, which
Churchill was reading when he wrote to his mother. Fawcett was only
thirty-one years old when the book was published, and more remarkably,
he had been blinded in a shooting accident at the age of twenty-five. He
was a colleague and strong supporter of John Stuart Mill. *Manual of
Political Economy* is considered a classic in the field and was based

squarely on Mill's work. In 1865, Fawcett was elected to Parliament as a Liberal, where he joined a group of radical MPs whose leader was Mill.

William Lecky was a protestant Irish historian whose *History of European Morals from Augustus to Charlemagne* was published in 1869 and was also considered a classic in the field. It was one of Mark Twain's favourite books. Like Fawcett, Lecky was a strong believer in capitalism as a great agent of change. Lecky was also a member of the Liberal Party and was elected to Parliament in 1895 as a Unionist Liberal who opposed the Liberal Party's policy of Home Rule for Ireland. Lecky's book went through fifteen editions and was popular on both sides of the Atlantic. When he died in 1903, a statue of him was placed outside the University of Dublin in Ireland, which still stands today.

It would be surprising if Cockran had not read or was unaware of Fawcett's and Lecky's classical works. Bourke Cockran was a widely read man with a library of over 5,000 books. He was not a collector, he once said, but someone who accumulated books for general reading. He kept them all and they included Mill, Hume, Locke, Burke and Adam Smith as well as Bryon, Tennyson, Bacon, Gibbon, Macaulay and Thackeray. His tastes were eclectic and wide ranging and also included the poets Yeats, Whitman and Longfellow as well as Thomas More, James Russell Lowell, Ralph Waldo Emerson, Leo Tolstoy, Henry Longfellow and Henry Thoreau. Fiction was not neglected either. Fifty volumes of Victor Hugo as well as Dumas, Balzac and Dickens, not to mention all of Oscar Wilde's plays and the collected works of Mark Twain. On politics, there was Thomas Paine, Jefferson, Lincoln, Karl Marx and Richard Wagner. Sir Horace Plunkett and Theodore Roosevelt even sent him proof copies for his comments on, respectively, *Ireland in the New Century* (1905) and *An Autobiography* (1913).[4]

The significance of what Churchill was reading in the months before his travel to America and his first meeting with Bourke Cockran is that the classical liberal, free market ideas and principles Churchill found in those books by Fawcett and Lecky would have been reinforced in his conversations with Cockran. As Churchill confessed to his mother, he had no liberal education and few political preconceptions, except his father's 'Tory Democracy' which was more a political slogan than anything else. Therefore, when it came to political economy, Churchill was a blank slate on which Fawcett and Lecky had barely begun to write when he met Bourke Cockran, and under his guidance, Churchill began to fill in the spaces.

Churchill's first crossing of the Atlantic Ocean was not a pleasant one. In a shipboard letter to his mother on 8 November 1895, Churchill wrote, 'We had it rough and stormy – with the spray covering the whole ship & the deck almost underwater.' Nevertheless, he and Reggie Barnes were eager to get to the action in Cuba. They had planned to spend only three days in New York, but he wrote to his mother that it was possible they would cut down their stay in New York to only a day and a half. Then Churchill met Bourke Cockran as he left the *Etruria* and everything changed. Under Cockran's spell, the visit in New York was extended to a full week and the mentoring relationship began.

On Saturday, 9 November 1895, Cockran held a large dinner party in Churchill's honour, attended by prominent judges before whom Cockran practiced. Churchill wrote to his mother the next morning about his first day in New York and about Bourke Cockran:

I & Barnes are staying with Mr Bourke Cockran in a charming and very comfortable flat at the address on this paper.

Everybody is very civil and we have engagements for every meal for the next few days about three deep. It is very pleasant staying here as the rooms are beautifully furnished and fitted with every convenience & also as Mr. Cockran is one of the most charming hosts and interesting men I have met. Last night we had a big dinner here to 10 or 12 persons all of whom were on the Judiciary. Very interesting men – one particularly – a Supreme Court Judge – is trying a "cause célèbre" here now – and so we are going to hear the charge to the Jury on Wednesday and in all probability the capital sentence.

* * *

I have great discussions with Mr. Cockran on every conceivable subject from Economics to yacht racing. He is a clever man and one from whose conversation much is to be learned.[5]

On Tuesday morning, Churchill wrote a long letter to his Aunt Leonie. It contains the first evidence of Cockran's influence on Churchill's thinking, his mind already primed by Fawcett and Lecky. After observing how extraordinary was the 'comfort and convenience' of the various modes of transportation – tramways, cable cars and ferries – which 'harmoniously

fitted into a perfect system accessible alike to the richest and poorest',
Churchill made an insightful political and economic observation which
belied the fact he had no formal education in either field. It was the first but
not the last time Churchill would echo the words of Bourke Cockran:

> So far I think the means of communication in New York have struck
> me the most. The comfort and convenience of elevated railways –
> tramways – cable cars & ferries, harmoniously fitted into a perfect
> system accessible alike to the richest and the poorest – is extra-
> ordinary. And when one reflects that such benefits have been secured
> to the people not by confiscation of the property of the rich or by
> arbitrary taxation but simply by business enterprise – out of which
> the promoters themselves have made colossal fortunes, one cannot
> fail to be impressed with the excellence of the active system.[6]

Churchill, however, was not impressed with paper currency in America
and offered this explanation to his aunt, one in which he compared
government unfavourably to the market:

> I wondered how to reconcile the magnificent system of commu-
> nication with the abominable currency for a considerable time and
> at length I have found what may be a solution. The communication
> of New York is due to private enterprise while the state is respon-
> sible for the currency: and hence I come to the conclusion that the
> first class men of America are in the counting houses and the less
> brilliant ones in the government.[7]

While Churchill had written his mother he would be going to court
on Wednesday to hear the charge to the jury after visiting West Point
on Tuesday, it would appear from his letter to Leonie that the order
was reversed and he went to court on Tuesday, 12 November 1895,
undoubtedly because the jury was ready to be charged a day earlier
than the judge who had invited Churchill had anticipated. By this time,
Cockran had come up with another way to keep Jennie's son entertained:
a visit to New York fire stations where they sounded the alarm so that
Churchill could see firemen sliding down the pole and galloping off in
their engine towards the fire, apparently unaware that it was only a dry
run arranged for the young Englishmen's entertainment.

Churchill described all three occasions in a letter to his brother Jack on Friday, 15 November 1895 discussing Cockran and closing with a paragraph vividly recounting his initial impressions of America.

I am still staying with Mr Bourke Cockran, whom you met in Paris, in his very comfortable and convenient flat in 5th Avenue. We have postponed our departure from New York for three days as there was lots to see and do.

Mr Cockran, who has great influence over here, procured us orders to visit the Forts of the Harbour and West Point – which is the American Sandhurst.

* * *

The other night Mr Cockran got the Fire Commissioner to come with us and we alarmed four or five fire stations. This would have interested you very much. On the alarm bell sounding the horses at once rushed into the shafts – the harness fell on to them – the men slid half dressed down a pole from their sleeping room and in 5-1/2 seconds the engine was galloping down the street to the scene of the fire. An interesting feat which seems incredible unless you have seen it.

* * *

A great, crude, strong, young people are the Americans – like a boisterous healthy boy among enervated but well bred ladies and gentlemen. Some day Jack when you are older you must come out here and I think will you will feel as I feel – and think as I think today.[8]

Churchill and Barnes left New York that Sunday by train for Key West, Florida, in a private stateroom secured for them by Cockran, which, as he informed his mother in a letter from Havana, Cuba, made 'the 36 hours we passed there . . . not as unpleasant as if we had to travel in a regular compartment'.[9]

The first letter in the Churchill–Cockran correspondence was written on 20 November 1895 after Churchill had arrived in Havana. Churchill was to say later in life that his tastes were simple, 'easily satisfied with the best'. His tastes were certainly in evidence now as Churchill told Cockran they were returning on Monday, 16 December 1895 and asked him to once more arrange a private stateroom for them.

20 November [1895]   Havana, Cuba

My dear Cockran:

We had a very comfortable journey which was entirely due to your kindness in getting us a state room. The food all along was execrable but the passage was good and the weather perfect. Early this morning a violent rain storm woke me up and I went on deck as soon as it cleared up. There, on our port under the towering and stormy clouds lay the shores of Cuba. We got into the harbour without incident and live in a convenient hotel – we remain.

We start tomorrow for Santa Clara where are rumours of great things doing. The route is by rail and an additional interest will be lent to it – by the fact that the insurgents do all they can to wreck the trains and occasionally succeed. As to our return we propose to leave the island on Monday 16th prox. (three boats a week in December). Can you get us a state room from here to New York? If you can – will you? I cannot tell you what a difference it made on our journey here and we shall be quite spoiled going back by the ordinary method.

I must reiterate my thanks to you for your kindness and courtesy in putting us up all the time we were in New York. We had many delightful conversations – and I learned much from you in a pleasant and interesting way. I hope in England to renew our discussions and though I can never repay you for your kindness I trust you will take the hospitality of the 4th Hussars "on accounts", as we say.

Yours Ever
Winston S. Churchill[10]

There is no record whether Cockran secured another stateroom for the two men, but by the time they returned to New York on Tuesday, 11 December 1895, Cockran had already left for Europe. To resume courting Jennie? No record remains. Nevertheless, Cockran put his apartment at Churchill's disposal and he and Barnes stayed there for four days, sailing for England on Friday, 14 December 1895 on the same ship, the *Etruria*, which had brought them to America.

During their time in Cuba, both Churchill and Barnes were awarded the Spanish military decoration of the Red Cross for gallantry displayed during an engagement between government and rebel troops where Churchill came under fire for the first time in his life. Elements of the English and American press were critical of this, including the *New Castle Leader* in England, which wrote that 'spending a holiday in fighting other people's battles is rather an extraordinary proceeding even for a Churchill'.[11] The *New York Herald* was equally critical. Consequently, upon arriving back in America, Churchill denied having been a combatant. The *New York World*, owned by Cockran's client, Joseph Pulitzer, had not been critical of Churchill's conduct in Cuba and published a tongue-in-cheek article poking fun at their competitors the day after Churchill sailed:

> The young warriors were Winston Leonard Spencer Churchill, son of the late Lord Randolph Churchill, and R.W.R. Barnes. Both are in the Fourth Hussars. When the hunting season began in England they tossed up a penny to see whether they should chase foxes this winter or watch Gen Campos chase rebels. The rebels won, and they obtained a two months' leave of absence and started for Cuba.
>
> The Bungtown Bird of Freedom and the Kalamazoo Daily Celery Stalk printed many flaming editorials on the conduct of these gentlemen in going to Cuba, declaring that they were emissaries of the British Government sent to teach Campos how to whip the secessionists, and that England was throwing more bricks at the Monroe doctrine. Of course this was nonsense. Churchill is not yet twenty-one years old, and knows only the amount of strategy necessary for the duties of a second lieutenant. He and Barnes went on the trip actuated only by youthful enthusiasm.[12]

Churchill's adventure in Cuba was the first – but not the last – time over the next five adventure-filled years where he was to experience the exhilaration of being shot at without result.

Chapter 6

'A Very High Opinion of Your Future Career'

London
April 1896

Winston Churchill pushed back from his writing desk where he had been drafting a new article and lit one of the fine Havana cigars he had brought back with him from his adventure in Cuba. He and Barnes had enjoyed a ripping good time, both in New York and in Cuba. It was a shame he had not been able to come up with enough to write a book about his adventure in Cuba, but there simply wasn't a story there. Something with a beginning, middle and end with a dashing young hero, himself of course, right in the thick of things. Still, he was pleased with the initial literary output afforded him by Cuba. Five letters from the field for the Daily Graphic *had been well received. And £5 for each of the five reports was equal to a month's allowance from his Mamma, a tidy sum. Upon his return to England, the* Saturday Review *commissioned three articles, further advancing the cause of the Churchill name and coffer. The first two articles had been well received also, and now he was working on the third.*

Churchill smiled. The eight articles had persuaded him that he might make a name for himself as a journalist as well as a soldier. But his compensation as a writer paled by comparison to what he had made the previous month as a litigant. Four hundred pounds to be precise, and all because the father of an officer cadet who had been forced to resign from the Fourth Hussars had publicly accused Churchill of committing 'acts of gross immorality of the Oscar Wilde type'. Churchill's first reaction had been to laugh it off as an absurd accusation. After all, weren't Molly Hacket and Mabel Love proof enough of his sexual preferences? But a discussion with his Mamma and the family solicitors quickly persuaded him that false accusations of this sort could not go unanswered. So he authorized filing the action and within a month the accusation had been withdrawn without reservation, accompanied by a cheque to the tune of £400.

Churchill's dilemma now was in finding a way to duplicate his journalistic success in Cuba. He was scheduled to leave for India at the end of the summer. India . . . Nothing was happening there. No newspaper would hire him to file dispatches from such a tranquil land where trouble did not loom on the horizon. But Egypt? South Africa? Trouble did loom there. He and Cockran had talked about it earlier this year when the older man had called to his attention the fact that the majority of the British population in the Transvaal paid 90 percent of the taxes yet had no representation in the Boer Parliament. Cockran reminded Churchill that the American as well as the French Revolutions had arisen from just such unfair and inequitable taxation.

Cockran's conversations with Churchill, initially in New York and then in London, had opened a new world to Churchill. Economics. It moved everything. Cockran had brought to life for him what he had only read about in Fawcett and Lecky. It certainly explained Cuba. As he had written for the Daily Graphic, *'There is no doubt the island has been overtaxed in a monstrous manner for a considerable period. So much money is drawn from the country every year that industries are paralysed and development is impossible.'*

Churchill once more picked up Cockran's letter, impressed by the man's prophecy. It was the economic condition of Cuba and not the passions on either side that would dictate the outcome of the rebellion. Sugar and tobacco were all the wealth which Cuba possessed, and those industries had been destroyed by the rebels. Soon, famine would follow and when that happened, Cockran had written, America would have to act.

At least Cockran would be pleased with what Churchill had written about Cuba in his final Saturday Review *article. As for Ireland, however, nothing he could say or write would meet with Cockran's approval. Cockran's case was persuasive, and Churchill had imagined the rich timbre of the older man's voice as he read the copy of the speech which Cockran had sent him on Home Rule. He was rather pleased with the reply he had posted to Cockran earlier today. He'd used Cockran's own logic. Economics. He wondered how Cockran would reply to his having used the example of Scotland as a country whose wealth increased after its union with England. Why should Ireland be any different now that England recognized the sins of the past and had done its best to correct them? 'Everything that can be done to alleviate distress and heal the wounds of the past is done – and done in spite of rhetorical attempts to keep them open' was how he had phrased it in his letter to Cockran. Let him reply to that, he thought.*

Churchill hoped Cockran would return soon to England. There were more things than Ireland that he wanted to discuss.

Churchill's first assignment as a journalist was a success. The *Daily Graphic's* editor wrote that his dispatches 'had been extremely interesting and were just the kind of thing we wanted'.[1] Further, the newspaper had illustrated Churchill's letters with ink drawings based on sketches Churchill had submitted.

Upon his return from America, Churchill renewed his relationship with Cockran, as the American had been in England since early December and stayed through much of February, seeing Jennie and Leonie during his nearly three-month visit. How often the two men saw each other during this time is not known, but in the next letter in the correspondence Churchill apologizes for not having come to see him 'as I promised' before Cockran sailed for America.

Churchill enclosed in this letter to Cockran a copy of his article on Cuba in the 15 February 1896 issue of the *Saturday Review,* which was even-handed and critical of both sides, even though Churchill was more sympathetic to the cause of the Cuban rebels, if not to the rebels themselves.

29 February [1896]   Bachelor's Club
                                                     Hamilton Place W.

My dear Cockran:

You must think me a very faithless and unreliable person – for I never – as I promised, came to see you before your departure from these shores. I suppose you are now comfortably installed in that most convenient & commodious of flats – at the Bolkenhayn. Thither – at any rate I direct this letter.

I am much interested in the action of the United States as respecting Cuban belligerency. I enclose you a copy of an article of mine in the *Saturday Review* which will show you the line I think is sensible.

I should very much like to know what your opinion is upon the whole question and particularly as regards the recent & future actions of the Senate. Please if you can find the time write me a letter – as I want so much to keep myself really well informed on the whole subject. Of course I won't think of giving you away.

I hope the United States will not force Spain to give up Cuba – unless you are prepared to accept responsibility for the results of such action. If the States care to take Cuba – though this would be very hard on Spain – it would be the best and most expedient course for both the island and the world in general. But I hold it a monstrous thing if you are going to merely procure the establishment of another South American Republic – which however degraded and irresponsible is to be backed in its action by the American people – without their maintaining any sort of control over its behaviour.

I do hope that you will not be in agreement with those wild and I must say – most irresponsible people who talk of Spain as "beyond the pale" etc. etc. Do write and tell me what you think.

I have seen a lot lately of Lord Dunraven. He is quite unrepentant – and maintains all his charges – though in justice to him I must say that he always declares that he is convinced that none of the owners – or members of the Yacht Club were in any way cognisant of the alleged fraud. The whole matter is most unfortunate – and has probably caused much bad – one with you. I hope we have now heard the last of it. Speaking generally – I think international contests should be avoided. There is rivalry enough – without furthering it into actual expression.

I commend rather a good book to your notice "The Red Badge of Courage" a story of the Civil War. Believe me it is worth reading.

Now au revoir – do please be pacific and don't go dragging the 4th Hussars over to Canada in an insane and criminal struggle.

Yours ever
Winston S. Churchill[2]

This letter and Cockran's prompt reply is the first tangible evidence that a mentor relationship was in the process of being established on both sides. Not only is Churchill presenting his Cuban article for Cockran's review and approval, he is also seeking the older man's 'opinion . . . upon the whole question and particularly . . . the recent & future actions of the Senate.' He is clearly seeking Cockran's private views because he promised not to 'giv[e] you away'. The letter's closing lines further illustrate the breadth of their conversations and the easy relationship that had developed between them. Not only does he recommend a book to Cockran, but he closes with a jest about a US invasion of Canada, probably a reference to a diplomatic dispute at the time between the

United States and Great Britain over Venezuela. The United States' annexation of Canada, by force if necessary, was by no means a dead political issue in the 1890s.

No copy of Cockran's reply to Churchill's 29 February 1896 letter remains, but Cockran did give Churchill his 'views upon the Cuban question'. Reading between the lines in Churchill's next letter to Cockran on 12 April 1896, one can see that any disagreement between Cockran and Churchill does not involve the principle of ultimate independence for Cuba. Both support that goal, but Cockran is more sanguine that independence will restore order to the island and prosperity will follow in its wake. Churchill is at once more sceptical and less patient.

The most intriguing aspect of Churchill's long 12 April 1896 letter to Cockran, however, is the comments and opinions he offers on Ireland as Cockran had sent Churchill one of his speeches on Ireland and solicited his comments. Churchill disagreed with everything Cockran said on Ireland and told him so, but Churchill's letter also makes clear the deep regard he has formed for Cockran. Cockran's response two weeks later will assure the young Churchill that the feeling is mutual. With these two letters, the mentor relationship was solidly established and would continue over the next nine years. Ironically, by the time the mentor relationship had run its course – as all such relationships do – Churchill had almost entirely reversed his position on Home Rule for Ireland and had come to accept Cockran's views.

12 April [1896]   The Deepdene
                                                              Dorking

My dear Cockran:

I read with great interest both your letter and speech. With regard to the former – in which you were good enough to give me your views upon the Cuban question – I think that your principles are indisputable & unassailable. Undoubtedly in time all communities will learn that "that prosperity is the result of order & that misery is the production of shiftlessness and strife" and if the Cubans ever obtained independence I am sure that ultimately they would establish a settled government, and that order would be evolved from chaos. But what is a short time in the history of a people is a long time in the life of a human being. To a serene Providence a couple of generations of trouble and distress may seem an insignificant thing – provided that during that time the community is moving in the direction of a good final result. Earthly Governments however are unable to approach questions from the same standpoint. Which brings me to the conclusion that the duty of governments is to be first of all practical. I am for makeshifts and expediency. I would like to make the people who live on this world at the same time as I do better fed and happier generally. If incidentally I benefit posterity – so much the better – but I would not sacrifice my own generation to a principle – however high or a truth however great. This will explain to you the state of mind which induced me to write the articles in the *Saturday Review*, which I will send you as soon as I go back to London.

Now to turn to your speech. It is one of the finest I have ever read. You are indeed an orator. And of all the gifts there is none so rare or so precious as that. Of course – my dear Cockran – you will understand that we approach the subject from different points of view and that your views on Ireland could never coincide with mine. You invited me in your letter to comment on the opinions you then expressed. I do so without reserve. I consider it unjust to arraign the deeds of earlier times before modern tribunals & to judge by modern standards. No one denies – no one has ever attempted to deny – that England has treated Ireland disgracefully in the past. Those were hard times; – death was the punishment of every crime; & the treatment of the Irish by the stronger power was in harmony with the treatment of the French peasantry – the Russian serfs & the Hugenots. Mercy and economics were alike unknown. Wherefore I think it unfair to depict the English government of today as part and parcel of Mountjoy's ravages and Cromwell's massacres.

Again you allude to the rejection of the demand for the release of the dynamite prisoners. I had the opportunity of talking to Mr. Asquith on this subject and I said that I would have released them in deference to the opinion of the Irish people – like Barabbas. He said "We are all agreed that in fifteen months they will be released in the ordinary course of reconsidering sentences." In other words the problem is nearly solved. So it is with the question of Home Rule. There is no tyranny in Ireland now. The Irish peasant is as free and as well represented as the English labourer. Everything that can be done to alleviate distress and heal the wounds of the past is done – and done in spite of rhetorical attempts to keep them open. Your contention that a government from a "foreign" city cannot produce prosperity – is not borne out by other instances. Take for example – Scotland, whose population and wealth have increased manifold since the Act of the Union.

Six years of firm, generous, government in Ireland will create a material prosperity which will counteract the efforts which able and brilliant men – like yourself – make to keep the country up to the proper standard of indignation. Not for twenty years could a Home Rule bill pass the English people – so sick and tired are they of the subject – and by that time the necessity for one will have passed away. Home Rule may not be dead but only sleeping – but it will wake like Rip Van Winkle to a world of new ideas. The problems & the burning questions of today will be solved and Home Rule for Ireland as likely as not will be merged in a wider measure of Imperial Federation.

Nor will the civilised world compel us as you suggest to a prompt settlement. How could they with justice. Does Russia give up Poland? Does Germany surrender Alsace and Lorraine? Does Austria give up Hungary? Does Turkey release Armenia – or Spain grant autonomy to Cuba? One more instance shd the United States accede to the demand for Confederate independence? And one more argument. You may approve of Home Rule on principle. But I defy you to produce a workable measure of it. He will be a bold man who will rush in where Mr. Gladstone failed.

Finally, let me say that when I read your speech I thought that Ireland had not suffered in vain – since her woes have provided a subject for your eloquence. Do write me again. I am in hope of going to Egypt in the autumn and in the meanwhile Polo fills my mind and time. Aunt Leonie is very well and flourishing – but my mother has been rather ill and is gone to Monte Carlo. Barnes begs me to send you messages from him.

Yours ever,
Winston S. Churchill[3]

Cockran's reply to Churchill on 27 April 1896 continues Cockran's effort to apply the economic principles they both shared to practical problems, of which none was more important to Cockran than Ireland. More importantly, it is in this letter that Cockran formally takes it upon himself to become Churchill's mentor: 'I hope you will allow me to assume the privilege of my years and advise you strongly to take upon the study of sociology and political economy . . .' But Cockran is not just giving advice to the young man in this letter, he is doing precisely what Levinson says is the most crucial function a mentor can perform, supporting his protégé's dream 'by believing in him, sharing the youthful Dream and giving it his blessing'.[4] Cockran does this right after advising Churchill to study sociology and political economy.

April 27/96   763 Fifth Avenue

My Dear Winston

I was delighted to hear from you and especially gratified by your frank and sensible criticism of my speech. I hope to sail for Europe next week but as I will not be able to stay more than a day or two in London I do not think it possible that I will see you. I write therefore mainly to explain my purpose in devoting some part of my address to the oppressive legislation from which Irish industry has long suffered. I did not dwell on this subject merely to inflame passions or to awaken resentments as you suppose. I have long since concluded that revenge is the most expensive luxury known to man. Any one who pursues vengeance can generally attain it, but it is all that he is ever likely to accomplish. What is true of individuals is true of nations, and any man who would counsel or invite a people to seek revenge for its own sake is utterly unworthy of confidence. My object in reciting the story of Irish suffering was merely to account for the existing economic condition of Ireland. I pointed out at some length that capital is essential to production and that the industrial capacity of a country is proportioned to the volume of its capital. Ireland is today without manufacturing industries simply because she has been prevented from accumulating capital by the operation of those laws which you condemn so freely and so generously. If we meet on the other side I will go into this subject more freely and I am sure I will be able to convince you that in recalling that melancholy history I was actuated by a better purpose than a mere desire to inflame the anger of an audience. I can say with perfect sincerity that I have never in my life delivered an address in which I consciously used a sentence for any other purpose than to express the truth as I understood it. And now let me congratulate you on the good temper, the acuteness and excellent judgement which pervaded your whole letter. I do not think you and I are very far apart in our convictions. We differ more in phrases than in principle. If your idea of Imperial Federation be the solution of the Irish question nobody will rejoice at it more than the men who have struggled for the same result under the name of Home Rule. But whatever may be the ultimate outcome of the Irish agitation I hope you will allow me to assume the privilege of my years and advise you strongly to take upon the study of sociology and political economy. These two subjects are more closely interwoven than most people ever believe. They are considered dry and uninteresting by those who are not familiar with them, but they are two branches of inquiry which in the future will bear the most important fruits to the human family.

With your remarkable talent for lucid and attractive expression you would be able to make great use of the information to be acquired by study of these branches. Indeed I firmly believe you would take a commanding position in public life at the first opportunity which arose, and I have always felt that true capacity either makes or finds its opportunity.

Do not My Dear Winston feel that I am troubling you with this long letter merely to air my views. I was so profoundly impressed with the vigor of your language and the breadth of your views as I read your criticisms of my speech that I conceived a very high opinion of your future career, and what I have said here is largely based on my own experience. I give it to you for what it is worth, firmly convinced that your own judgement may be trusted to utilize it if it be of any value or to reject it if inapplicable to your plans or your surroundings.

Very sincerely yours[5]

What Cockran says in the last paragraph of the letter are words Churchill never heard from his father nor, by that time, had he heard anything comparable from his mother. By now, Churchill was making contacts and moving at high levels in political society because his father had died so young and his colleagues were still in office. For example, the Ambassador to Spain, Sir Henry Drummond Wolfe, was his father's old Fourth Party colleague who had been the one who secured letters of introduction on Churchill's behalf in Cuba. Churchill had also returned early in the year to the Rothschild estate at Tring, where he once more mingled with aristocrats and politicians alike, all eager to meet Lord Randolph's son. Still, there is no record that anyone else who knew Churchill had formed the same high opinion of his future prospects as Cockran.

While Churchill was always seeking his parents' approval as a young boy and a young man, its absence never appeared to affect his self-confidence, a self-confidence which his father found unwarranted based upon his son's lack of accomplishment. Churchill's self-confidence, therefore, might not have suffered without Cockran as a mentor, but it surely did it no harm when Cockran, both a principled man of the world and a great orator, validated Churchill's dream of a life in politics.

Levinson described how young men react to constructive mentors. They feel admiration, appreciation, gratitude and love for the mentor. The mentor has qualities of character, expertise and understanding that the young man admires and wants to emulate, excited and spurred on by the shared sense of his promise. So far, Churchill's reaction to Cockran fits this picture. Yet, Levinson wrote, the young man is 'also full of self-doubt: can he ever become all that both of them want him to be?'[6] Self-doubt is not a word which readily springs to mind as a characterization of the now twenty-one-year-old Winston Churchill. Indeed, Churchill probably had the same reaction to Cockran as his son Randolph would in writing his biography – 'a man of profound discernment and judgement', someone who confirmed Churchill's belief, held even then, that he was destined to do great things, a belief never shared by his father.

Cockran again travelled to Europe in May 1896 and stayed through the beginning of August 1896. He and Churchill apparently did not see each other during this time because Cockran only spent a few days in London. Their correspondence resumed upon Cockran's return to America with two letters between them before Churchill departed in October for India and two more letters once Churchill reached India. Cockran's letters do not remain, only Churchill's replies.

As we shall see, both men were active during this period. Cockran once more achieved national recognition when he bolted the Democratic Party in the summer of 1896 to support the Republican candidate William McKinley in a national speaking tour where he, and not McKinley, engaged the Democratic nominee William Jennings Bryan over the issue of sound money versus the free coinage of silver. Meanwhile, Churchill was desperately trying to find a conflict somewhere in the world to cover as a soldier and correspondent and duplicate his success in Cuba. Crete. South Africa. Egypt. Anywhere other than India, which, at that point in 1896, offered no prospect for glory to the young soldier-correspondent.

Chapter 7

'You Have Won a Glorious Victory'

New York City
18 August 1896

*It was a hot, muggy New York summer evening as Bourke Cockran
looked out the window of his library in the Bolkenhayn Apartments
over the vast green expanse of Central Park, sipping a tepid cup of tea.
The preparation was over. The battle would soon begin. He felt calm,
composed. He was rarely nervous before a major speech, no matter how
high the stakes. And tonight, the stakes were high.*

*People were sceptical when he explained to them that his speeches
were a hobby, a diversion. He made no money on them. Indeed, his
speeches were a drain on the Cockran exchequer because he accepted
no speaking fees, not even travel expenses. Besides, those who rode the
Chautauqua circuit made peanuts compared to what his law practice
brought him every year. Indeed, he had sometimes wondered how much
more he could make as a lawyer if he chose not to spend several months
each year in Europe. Cockran shook his head. He didn't care. There were
more important things in life than money.*

*Tonight was different. Tonight, nothing was more important than
money. Sound money. Cockran knew that some people blamed him and his
absence in Europe for William Jennings Bryan stampeding the Democratic
Convention in Chicago and capturing its nomination. Upon his return
from Europe less than three weeks ago, someone had given him a clipping
from the* Charleston News *which quoted a Sound Money Democrat
lamenting Cockran's absence.*

> *Oh, if we only had Cockran here! The one man who could have
> exposed the absurdity of the sublimated nonsense of the Cross of
> Gold exhortation was sojourning in Europe. And what a pity!
> How the scholarly, golden-tongued Bourke Cockran would have
> stilled the camp-meeting frenzy produced by the boy orator and
> brought the delegates back to their senses.[1]*

*Well, Cockran was back now and he was ready for battle. He was not
easily flattered, but there was some truth in what the disappointed
delegate had said. But he had got it wrong. It was common sense, not*

Cockran's golden tongue, that would have stemmed the tide of the Bryanites. Bryan was a good orator, and on more than one occasion when they were in Congress together, Cockran had heard him speak. Bryan had a voice and a command of language which was impressive. Bryan could speak. That wasn't his problem. It's just that he wasn't very bright. For all Bryan's good intentions, a voice was no substitute for a brain. The man actually believed the wild inflation in currency which would follow free coinage of silver was a good thing. That was because Bryan didn't understand the basic concept of money as a medium of exchange. He shook his head. Few politicians did.

Cockran paused, walked back to his desk and made a note on the writing pad in front of him. He took another sip of tea. That was the right tack to take tonight. He would portray Bryan not as a knave but a fool. He would not use that phrasing, of course. Something more diplomatic was called for. Cockran paused and then spoke the words aloud, testing them as he listened. 'Indeed, I believe it is doubtful if the candidate himself quite understands the nature of the faith which he professes. I say this not in criticism of his ability, but in justice to his morality. I believe that if he himself understood the inevitable consequences of the doctrine which he preaches, his own hands would be the first to tear down the platform on which he stands.'

Cockran smiled. Even if Bryan himself were present to hear the words, he was too full of himself to realize he was being called a fool.

Notwithstanding Bryan's nomination, Cockran had no regrets about spending the summer in Europe. He was no longer in public life, and he had needed the rest. Especially after his bicycle accident in Central Park in April which delayed his departure for nearly a month. He knew harm could befall you just as easily while horseback riding, but horses were more predictable than bicycles and he had already vowed to stick to them in the future. Another reason for going to Europe, of course, was to see Jennie. He knew now that things might not work between them, and he believed he understood why. They led separate lives, he in New York and she in London. Neither could give them up, and now that he had met her son, he knew why. Wholly apart from her beauty which had captured him at first sight, that woman understood politics like no other woman he had ever known and she was determined to use every bit of influence she had to see her son succeed where her husband had not. Cockran thought she would succeed and had told her so that summer, just as he had told her son in a letter he wrote before that damned bicycle betrayed him in Central Park.

It was interesting, Cockran thought, how much she had changed her views on her son's political career in only a year. When they had first met last spring in Paris, Jennie was not entirely pleased with the prospect of her son becoming a politician. She thought politics a cruel profession and Cockran had agreed. One of the few things they had agreed upon. But Winston had won her over just has he had won Cockran over. Winston was a man after Cockran's own heart. Barely twenty-one years old, he had an opinion on everything. Occasionally incorrect but rarely uncertain. Despite having less formal education than Cockran, Winston had a firm grasp of politics, history, war and, above all, economics. It was as if he had memorized Fawcett and Lecky and then applied it to everything he saw in Cuba. He was as intellectually voracious as Cockran himself.

Cockran pulled the gold pocket watch out of his vest pocket and checked the time. One hour to go. It was time to leave. He took a last sip of tea and walked to the elevator. His carriage was waiting downstairs. In the lobby, he greeted the doorman and stepped into his carriage. The venue for his speech originally had been Carnegie Hall, but that had proved too small, so he would be speaking tonight in the same place where Bryan had spoken six days earlier when he accepted the Democratic nomination for president. Madison Square Garden. He was pleased at the symmetry and symbolism.

Cockran had quietly slipped into the Garden to hear Bryan's speech and had been surprised at how poorly the boy orator had done. Cockran was disappointed because he knew from their days in Congress together that Bryan was capable of much better. Bryan had committed, however, what Cockran considered to be an unforgivable sin for an orator. He had read his speech. As a consequence, his delivery was jerky and halting and, combined with the intense heat and humidity that night, over a third of the audience had simply walked out during the speech, something which Bryan had noticed and that made him even more nervous. All in all, it had been an uninspiring performance.

By now, Cockran's carriage had turned onto Madison Avenue. The crowd waiting outside the Moorish architecture of the Garden was enormous. Why aren't they going in, he wondered. But, as he stepped down from the carriage, reporters were shouting questions at him.

'Why do you oppose your Party's nominee?'

'Isn't Bryan a friend of yours?'

'Are you going to become a Republican?'

Cockran decided to give them a small preview of his speech, so he stopped, his voice easily reaching the fringes of the crowd of twenty reporters gathered around him. 'Mr. Bryan is a former colleague of mine in Congress and an honourable man.' Cockran paused for effect and then continued. 'But he is a pawn of the Populists who have captured my Party and that I cannot abide. The movement launched at Chicago is an attempt to paralyze industry by using all the powers of government to take property from the hands of those who created it and place it in the hands of those who covet it.'[2]

'Well, are you going to sit on your hands during this campaign or actively oppose your own Party?' asked a reporter with a sharp, rodent-like face punctuated by a thin moustache. Cockran recognized him from the New York Times, a paper which had said unkind things about him in the past.

Cockran casually looked back and down over his shoulder as if to note his posterior's location, then held out his hands, palms up, as if to show his derrière was nowhere near them, drawing an appreciative chuckle from the reporters up front. 'I'm standing up tonight, not sitting, and that will remain my posture until the campaign is over.'

'In a contest for the existence of civilization no man can remain neutral. Whoever does not support the forces of order aids the forces of disorder. If I can do anything to thwart a movement the success of which I should regard as an irreparable calamity, not only to this country but to civilized society everywhere, I shall certainly do it.'[3] Cockran had spoken above the heads of the reporters in front so that his voice would carry to those in the rear but now he returned to the front row and fixed his gaze on the Times reporter. 'Your paper should do the same, for the likes of Mr. Hearst surely will not.'

Once inside the Garden, Cockran proceeded to the dais and stood there, hand over his heart as he listened to over 15,000 people sing the Star Spangled Banner. Cockran marvelled at the sight. The throngs of people he had seen outside the Garden weren't going in because they couldn't. The Garden was packed and there were as many still outside. The crowd for Bryan six days earlier had been announced as 15,000 also, but having been there Cockran knew it couldn't be true. Either that or tonight's crowd was well beyond the Garden's stated capacity of 15,000. Cockran had spoken to large crowds before. Over 20,000 at two Democratic Conventions. He had tamed them just as he would this one.

He stood there motionless at the podium waiting for the tumult to subside as he knew it would. These were his people. New Yorkers. Democrats. Irishmen. He was one of them. He knew that when he finished tonight, the Garden would still be as packed as it was at this moment. And he would have them.

'Ladies and gentlemen, fellow Democrats,' Cockran said and then paused as the cheering recommenced. When it subsided once more, Cockran continued 'With the inspiring strains of the National song still ringing in our ears, who could doubt the issue of this campaign? Stripped of all verbal disguise, it is an issue of common honesty; an issue between an honest discharge and a dishonest repudiation of public and private obligations. On this question, honest men cannot differ. It is a contest for civilization itself.

'Fellow Democrats, let us not disguise from ourselves that fact that we bear in this contest a serious and solemn burden of duty. We must raise our hands against the nominee of our Party itself. A Democratic Convention may renounce the Democratic faith, but the Democracy remains faithful to Democratic principles. Democratic leaders may betray a party convention to the Populists, but they cannot seduce the footsteps of Democratic voters from the pathway of honour and justice.'[4]

Again, Cockran was interrupted by cheering and shouts. He let the applause roll over him in waves. Oh yes, Cockran thought, no one was going to leave before he finished. Not tonight. He had them.

Winston Churchill believed that he had found the formula which would propel him into public life. Cuba was the prototype he followed tirelessly over the next four years until his election to Parliament in the fall of 1900. Unfortunately, he was not successful at duplicating in 1896 what he had done in Cuba the year before. It would not be until the latter part of 1897 that Churchill finally found another conflict to cover as a soldier-correspondent. In the interim, he began to fill in the gaps in his education so that when opportunity presented itself, he would be prepared.

In June, Churchill attempted to persuade London's *Daily Chronicle* to engage him as their special correspondent to cover the conflict in Crete. His offer was declined, but if Churchill went there at his own expense the *Chronicle* offered to pay him £10 a letter, twice the amount paid for his dispatches from Cuba. Churchill declined and next attempted to be sent to Sudan, where General Kitchener was organizing an expedition. But again he was unsuccessful. Undeterred, Churchill attempted to use his mother's influence to be sent to South Africa, where a native uprising had broken out in nearby Rhodesia. Once more, he was unsuccessful.

Churchill was desperately trying to avoid service in India because nothing was going on there. Churchill expressed his disappointment in a letter to his mother on 4 August 1896 accompanied by an unsubtle suggestion she was not trying hard enough to help him:

> [M]y dear Mamma you cannot think how I would like to sail in a few days to scenes of adventure and excitement – to places where I could gain experience and derive advantage – rather than to the tedious land of India – where I shall be equally out of the pleasures of peace and the chances of war.

* * *

> A few months in South Africa would earn me the S.A. medal and in all probability the [British South Africa] company's Star. Thence hot foot to Egypt – to return with two more decorations in a year or two – and beat my sword into an iron despatch box. Both are within the bounds of possibility and yet here I am out of both. I cannot believe that with all the influential friends you possess and all those who would do something for me for my father's sake – that I could not be allowed to go – were those influences properly exerted.[5]

Churchill was being unfair to his mother, who well knew how to exercise her influence, more so than her impatient twenty-one-year-old son.

It is likely that Bourke Cockran had not given up his pursuit of Jennie Churchill by the spring of 1896. Cockran had spent many months in Europe in 1895 romancing her. He entertained her son Winston in lavish style in November, and upon the young Churchill's departure for Cuba, he had promptly embarked upon another voyage to England, where he stayed through much of February 1896. The possibility that he did not see Jennie during this period, whether or not their romance resumed, is unlikely. He now intended to sail back to England in April 1896, less than two months after his return to America. That was delayed for a month by an unfortunate bicycle accident in nearby Central Park. But return to England he did in May, and the possibility that he did not visit with Jennie once more is remote. The short interval between these two extended visits to Europe by Cockran was uncharacteristic, but the fact that he soon moved on from England to France and subsequently to Italy seems to suggest that the romance with Jennie was beginning to run its course. Events in 1897, however, would offer evidence to the contrary.

By this time in his life, Cockran was financially secure. He didn't need a seat in Congress to fulfil himself. He enjoyed being a lawyer, and he knew people would line up to hear him speak whether he held political office or not. He was content to wait Boss Croker out. Tammany Hall bosses came and went, and eventually Boss Croker would go, as he in fact did. Bourke Cockran – his mind and his voice – would remain, and if a less corrupt regime came to power in Tammany, it would call on him again. So Cockran enjoyed himself in Europe for another three months, with politics far from his mind, unaware that when he returned home, he would be cast into the role of a lifetime: president-maker.

Cockran returned to a political firestorm in America in August 1896. Out of politics for nearly two years, he vaulted once more into national prominence over the issue of sound money versus the openly inflationary 'free coinage of silver'. Both major parties were split over the issue. 'Silver Republicans', mostly but not entirely from western states, bolted their party to support the Democratic candidate, William Jennings Bryan. Some 'Gold Democrats' formed a third party. Others supported the Republican candidate William McKinley, even though he was originally a free silverite who converted to a sound money supporter on the eve of his nomination.

Cockran was a Gold Democrat, and within a week of his return to America in early August 1896, Cockran had enthusiastically endorsed the protectionist McKinley for president based solely on the issue of sound money versus free silver. Cockran took great pains, however, to establish his independence from the Republicans. Cockran was met at the pier by a delegation of the Honest Money League headed by Major John Byrne. After ascertaining that the league was not a Republican front, he agreed to give speeches across the country opposing Bryan and free silver on the condition that he not be paid for his efforts. The league agreed and Cockran was as good as his word. Major Byrne later said that Cockran 'never cost the league a single dollar. Railroad fares, hotel expenses and everything else he paid out of his own pocket.'[6]

Cockran wasn't seeking a return to public life, and agreeing to support McKinley did not further that purpose. He was by far the most prominent Democrat to do so, and it did not endear him to Tammany Hall. Instead, it further cemented his reputation as an unreliable politician who put principle ahead of party just as he had done back in 1888 when he opposed his party over the seating of a Republican Congressman from Indiana. In fact, Cockran even turned down a Republican offer in September to run for a safe seat in Congress.

The Populists of the 1890s in the United States are often recalled today as the Have Not's versus the Have's. That is mostly inaccurate. The true 'have-nots' were hourly factory and mine workers who would be hit the hardest by the inflation engendered by free silver. Their wages would stay the same and their dollars would buy less. Populism was agrarian based, and farmers were largely credit based. Inflation through the free coinage of silver would allow them to repay their obligations with cheaper dollars, using the government to cheat their creditors. They found ready allies in Western silver mining interests who would happily supply the silver at a fixed gold exchange rate to make it all possible. Ponzi had nothing on the Populists. And one hot July day in Chicago in 1896, the mining and farming interests hijacked the Democratic Party in the person of William Jennings Bryan.

Cockran's opposition to free silver was based on principle, but politics played a role. Cockran saw the two as inextricably intertwined. Cockran's understanding of economics was acquired from Adam Smith, Cobden, Bright, Fawcett and other classical liberals. He understood the nature of money as a medium of exchange between men, apart from its intrinsic value. All debtors would understandably benefit from an inflationary money supply and creditors would suffer. That was important, but it was not Cockran's only or even primary concern. He was a New York Democrat and New York Democrats were largely working-class people who laboured for a living, more than a few of them union members. Cockran knew that while farmers would benefit from inflation, labourers wouldn't. They would be taking pay cuts as the purchasing value of their wages decreased. The same principles animated Cockran's support for free trade. Tariffs cut off competition, allowing farmers and manufacturers alike to charge higher prices than they otherwise could if forced to compete with imports. That meant Cockran's people, the labouring class, had to pay more for food and clothing than they otherwise would.

Cockran's appearance at Madison Square Garden on 18 August 1896 was a star turn for America's greatest orator. Cockran could convey economics principles in language which workingmen would understand, something his protégé Churchill would do one day as well. A few excerpts from Cockran's speech at Madison Square Garden illustrate this.

> The difference between the Populist who seeks to cut down the rate of wages and the Democrat who seeks to maintain it is that the Democrat believes high wages and prosperity are inseparable and interdependent, while the Populist thinks lower wages would diminish the cost of agricultural production, and he thinks he can carry this election by tempting the farmer to make war upon his own workingmen.[7]

* * *

> Money can never circulate freely and actively unless there be absolute confidence in its value. If a man doubts whether the money in your pocket will be as valuable to-morrow as it is to-day, he will decline to exchange his commodity against it. This extraordinary campaign against honesty, by raising a doubt as to the soundness of our money, has frightened trade from the market places, and has been the cause of the hard times from which this country is suffering . . .[8]

Cockran received congratulations for the speech from all over the country, and he understandably sent a copy of the speech to his young English friend. Churchill replied on 31 August 1896. This is Churchill's first letter to Cockran which he begins with 'My dear Bourke':

31 August 1896

My dear Bourke–

Very many thanks for the report of your great speech, which you so kindly sent me. I congratulate you most heartily upon what was not only a rhetorical triumph but also a moral victory. I hope that in advancing the cause of honesty and probity you have also brought yourself back to power and place. Fifteen thousand people forms a larger concourse than ever collects in England to hear political speeches. You know how keenly I regret that I was not there to see – still more to hear.

The question at issue is one about which I know very little &
hence my views are proportionately strong. It seems to me however that no sweeping changes in currency are possible – far less
expedient. Even if you prove to me that our present system is
radically bad – my opinion is unaltered. A man suffering from
dyspepsia might pray for fresh intestines but he would fare badly
while the alteration was being effected. How much more does this
apply to changes which affect the chief – the most delicate &
sensitive – organs which produce & on which depends our wealth –
Capital, Credit and Commerce. It may be that some reform &
readjustment are necessary – in the currency of the world, – but
those who endeavour to deal with so complicated and vital a subject
should approach it tentatively – feeling their way with caution. –
What Bryan has done is like an inebriate regulating a chronometre
with a crowbar. It is monstrous that such subjects should be made
the bagatelle of political parties and that issues so vast should
be handed over to excited & flushed extremists. At least so it
strikes me.

I sail for India the 11th September and my address will be the
4th Hussars Bangalore. Thither, if you will, you had better write:
I enclose you an article of mine on Cuba continued – for which
perhaps even amid the struggles for the president – you may find
a moment.

I hope we shall meet again soon – if possible within a year. I may
return to England via Japan after a little of India so perhaps I shall
once more eat oysters and hominy with you in New York. Please
send me press cuttings of your speeches.

Yours very sincerely
Winston S. Churchill

P.S. I am sending by this mail 2 vols. of my fathers speeches. They
will I am sure be interesting to you.

W.S.C.[9]

Cockran engaged in a whirlwind, cross-country tour after his Madison
Square Garden appearance. He spoke in Baltimore on 27 August 1896.
The *Baltimore Sun* carried this story the following day:

. . . It was not only in eloquence and logic that Mr. Cockran distinguished himself last night. His ready Irish wit never sparkled to better advantage than when some silver advocates in the audience tried to interrupt him. Had they thought for a moment they would not have made the attempt. They had forgotten that this was the man who four years ago at the National Convention in Chicago conquered a hostile audience of twenty thousand.[10]

After his triumph in Baltimore, Cockran headed west into Bryan country and delivered a speech on 5 September 1896 in St. Louis, turning a hostile crowd to a cheering one. Cockran moved further into Bryan country with a speech in Des Moines, Iowa, before a crowd of 10,000 on 8 September 1896. As he had in St. Louis, Cockran spoke before an initially hostile audience and had them cheering at the end.

Churchill sailed for India on 11 September 1896, while Cockran moved on to Nashville, Tennessee, where support for Bryan was also strong. Bryan supporters packed the hall in an effort to break up the meeting. One local newspaper predicted the meeting would break up in a riot. The following account of Cockran's Nashville speech appeared in the *Memphis Commercial Appeal*:

More than eight thousand people gathered into the old Auditorium. The inside of the building was as hot as a hard boiled egg just out of water. Hundreds of the Free Silver boys gathered down in front. One man had a cane the size of a baseball bat. The vast majority was for Silver.[11]

Cockran easily tamed the hostile crowd and by the end of his speech had them cheering for him, not Bryan. This was Bourke Cockran at his best. McKinley was not a stirring speaker, and having once supported the free coinage of silver himself before his convention-eve conversion, he was not a skilled advocate for sound money. After McKinley's decisive victory over Bryan, his campaign manager, Mark Hanna of Ohio, said that Cockran had done more to deliver the White House to McKinley than all the Republican orators combined.[12]

Despite the pressures of a national speaking tour, Cockran found the time to write Churchill in late September or early October 1896. The letter does not survive. Churchill mentions it in a letter to his mother on 26 October 1896:

Bourke Cockran writes me a long letter – describing his campaign against Bryan & is very pleased with himself indeed. He has had great audiences and much enthusiasm. He has received the volume [Lord Randolph's speeches] I sent him and is delighted. I shall endeavour to lure him out here: – India to an American would be the most interesting experience possible to a human being.[13]

Churchill's feeling of isolation in India and his desire to receive letters from England is apparent as he continues:

You can't think with what pleasure and excitement I look forward to the mail. Do persuade people to write. Aunt Clara, who writes such good letters or Aunt Leonie. Turn on the devoted Warrender – stimulate Jack and above all write yourself long, long, letters. Every word is thoroughly appreciated out here – in this godless land of snobs and bores.[14]

Cockran wrote Churchill another letter after the one referenced in his 26 October 1896 letter to his mother – which also does not survive and apparently was written close to the conclusion of the campaign. Churchill replied a day after receiving the letter, having already heard by telegram of McKinley's victory. In it, he attempts to lure Cockran to India much as Cockran later would repeatedly attempt to lure Churchill to visit America.

5 Nov. 1896
Telegrams

"Bolarum"
Trimulgherry,
Deccan

My dear Bourke,

I was very glad to get your letter last mail and to hear of your campaign. I congratulate you upon the issue. A telegram received here last night informed us of McKinley's election – which, as you say, – vindicates the common sense of an Anglo-Saxon democracy. You have passed through a great struggle and have won a glorious victory – but I suppose like all great triumphs it has been expensive. I wonder if you would care to calculate how much this year's Presidential election has cost you – in dollars – considering for the purpose not only the actual electoral expenses, but also the disturbance of business the fluctuations of capital. Of course I know you maintain that the contest is of great value as an educational institution, & I am prepared to willingly admit that no price was too much to pay to smash Bryan and display to the world on what firm foundation American credit and honour repose. But I am included to think if you consider one election with another – you will agree with me that your system of government costs you more than ours. You may rejoice, that it is better to be free than wealthy. That itself is a question about which discussion is possible: but I assert that the English labourer enjoys an equal freedom with the American workman & in addition derives numerous advantages from the possession of those appurtenances of monarchy – which make government dignified and easy – & the intercourse with foreign states more cordial.

I know what a stalwart democrat you are. But look at the question philosophically – cynically if you like. Calculate the profit and the loss. Consider the respect human beings instinctively and involuntarily feel for that which is invested with pomp and circumstance. As a legislator discard unbending principles & ethics and avail yourself of the weaknesses of humanity. Yours may be the government of gods – ours at least is suitable to men.

Your tour of political meetings must indeed have been interesting and I regret so much that I had not the opportunity of accompanying you and listening to your speeches. From what I have seen – I know that there are few more fascinating experiences than to watch a great mass of people under the wand of a magician. There is no gift – so rare or so precious as the gift of oratory – so difficult to define or impossible to acquire.

My Indian experiences have now lasted for over a month. Our voyage out was pleasant and prosperous – though of course in the Red Sea the heat was excessive. Bangalore – which is my permanent address while in this country – possesses a beautiful climate and is for many other reasons an agreeable place to live in.

This country would fascinate you. Indeed I imagine no more interesting experience than for an American to visit India. A more amazing contrast than that between the United States and this country – passes the wit of man to devise. I give you an invitation to come. My house is large and there is ample room for visitors. I need not say how delighted Barnes and I would be if you could. The expense of the trip & the time consumed would be well repaid by the value of the experience. You can't think how interesting this country is. I am staying here for the polo tournament which we now stand a good chance of winning. Ten miles away is the independent city of Hyderabad containing nearly 300,000 inhabitants and all the scoundrels in Asia. Alone among Indian Princes the Nizam has preserved by his loyalty in former days his internal independence and the consequence is that the natives assume a truculent air and all carry arms. Hence the presence of the 19th Hussars – whose guest I am – and who with nearly 14,000 European and native soldiers are assembled here in the great camp of Secunderabad to overcome the turbulent city. The spectacle is at least instructive. You must come out here – if only for a flying visit.

Yours very sincerely
Winston S. Churchill

P.S. I cannot tell you how much letters are appreciated out here – so do write. W.S.C.[15]

By the first anniversary of their relationship, Cockran had already fulfilled two of the functions Daniel Levinson describes for a mentor. From the very first Cockran acted as a teacher to enhance Churchill's skills and intellectual development.[16] Then, in April 1896, Cockran's letter to Churchill openly endorsed and expressed his belief in Churchill's dream of a life in politics. Now, with this last letter from Churchill, we can clearly see that Cockran had performed a third function Levinson attributes to a mentor: 'An *exemplar* that the protégè can admire and seek to emulate.'[17] Cockran's triumphant 1896 speaking tour had defeated Bryan, and Churchill had been impressed. He had found a mentor who believed in him and whose oratory and principled approach to politics he could emulate. As Churchill said in his 5 November 1896 letter 'there are few more fascinating experiences than to watch a great mass of people under the wand of a magician. There is no gift – so rare or so precious as the gift of oratory – so difficult to define or impossible to acquire.'

Tammany Hall was not pleased with Cockran after the election defeat of the Democrats. His political enemies circulated post-election lies about a 'deal' Cockran had made with McKinley's campaign manager, Mark Hanna, for a seat in the Cabinet after the election. Other lies were that the Republican National Committee had paid Cockran $5,000 a speech during the campaign. As he had with Croker in December 1894, Cockran ignored the lies. Nevertheless, Cockran was approached by grateful McKinley people to ascertain his interest in serving as Attorney General in McKinley's administration. Cockran rebuffed the overture just as he had declined a Republic nomination for a Congressional seat in New York, telling the McKinley people that he 'could not accept a position in the Cabinet since I am a Democrat and unalterably opposed to the Republican Tariff policies.'[18]

By the time he was twenty-one, Churchill had made more than moderate progress on two of the four common tasks of the novice phase. He had formed his dream of a life in politics and he had formed a strong mentor relationship with a man who supported his dream and would serve as both a teacher and a role model. He had yet to form an occupation, but that would come. Which left the fourth task: forming romantic relationships. Contrary to the impressions left by many biographers, he was not faring badly even if he did not measure up to Harry Flashman standards.

Churchill did not marry until 1908 when he was thirty-three years old. Some biographers have suggested Churchill's single-minded devotion to his career was to the exclusion of interest in the opposite sex. It's not true, just as his slight build and childhood illnesses have led biographers to downplay, if not ignore, his prowess as a first-class athlete in fencing and polo. From the first period of the novice phase through the third, Churchill avidly pursued romance and dated beautiful women throughout. He seriously courted and proposed marriage – four times – to beautiful women, the fourth time being the charm. He married a beautiful woman with whom he had five children and to whom, unlike contemporaries such as Lloyd George, he was ever faithful. Moreover, his interest in the opposite sex commenced in his teenage years like everyone else.

As a Sandhurst cadet, he had seriously dated and corresponded for over a year with Molly Hacket. Now, in India, Churchill met the first love of his life, Pamela Plowden, whom he was to see and woo over the next four years and with whom he would maintain a warm relationship for the rest of their lives. In a letter to his mother on 4 November 1896, the day before he wrote to Cockran, he told of meeting Pamela for the first time.

> I was introduced yesterday to Miss Pamela Plowden – who lives here. I must say that she is the most beautiful girl I have ever seen – "Bar none" as the duchess Lily says. We are going to try and do the city of Hyderabad together – on an elephant. You dare not

walk or the natives spit at Europeans – which provides retaliation leading to riots.[19]

Plowden eventually married Lord Lytton in 1902 after her father refused to give his consent to her marrying Churchill, but she and Winston remained close friends. In 1950, the ever-romantic Churchill responded affectionately to a letter from Pamela reminding him that fifty years ago he had proposed to her.[20] In 1905, upon Churchill's acquiring his first executive office, he had asked a friend of Pamela's family, Edward Marsh, to be his private secretary. Marsh, who didn't know Churchill, knew of their past romance and asked Pamela about her old flame. She replied that, 'The first time you meet Winston you see all his faults, and the rest of your life you spend in discovering his virtues.'[21] Churchill's wife, Clementine, knew of her husband's earlier romance but still became friends with Pamela as well, and even in Churchill's old age, she would refer to her in letters to her husband as 'your Pamela'.

Notwithstanding his attraction to Pamela, however, Churchill continued to focus on his dream and his future occupation because, in the next paragraph of his 4 November letter to Jennie, he lamented to her that he was not back in England at that time to stand for a vacant seat in Parliament and that he was not learning in India the kind of things he had in Cuba. Churchill was impatient to get on with his life, but it would be almost another year before he could do so in any meaningful way.

Chapter 8

'Ambition Was The Motive Force'

Bangalore, India
28 August 1897

Lieutenant Winston Churchill looked up from his writing desk and out the open window of his bungalow on South Parade. The windows opened to the long passages of the bungalow and a pleasant breeze. The air was filled with the noise from pigeons sitting on the windowsill and the occasional horse-drawn carriage. The mail should arrive soon, but he had little hope that it would contain what he so desperately desired – a letter or telegram from General Sir Bindon Blood, who had promised Churchill nearly a year ago that if ever he commanded another expedition on the Indian frontier, he would let Churchill come with him. Churchill had been home on leave in England barely a month earlier in the summer when he learned Blood was doing precisely that. So he had promptly sent Blood a telegram reminding him of his promise and then had cut short his leave by three weeks to return to India in the shortest time possible. In his haste to depart as quickly as he could, he even had forgotten to pack his polo sticks. At each port of call along the way, he checked at the telegraph office, but there was no word from Blood. Nothing at Aden. Nothing at Bombay. Nothing when at last he arrived at his quarters in Bangalore.

What was the British Empire coming to, he thought, if a General, a Knight of the Realm, could so casually ignore such a solemn commitment?

He looked at his pocket watch. The mail was not due for another two hours. No rest for the weary, he thought, as he looked down once more at his writing desk, took a sip from a weak whisky and water and picked up his pen to return to Affairs of State, *his political romance set in the mythical Republic of Lauranian located somewhere in the Balkans. He wasn't yet satisfied with Chapter 3, 'The Man of the Multitude', in which he introduced his hero, who was, of course, Churchill's alter ego. He read what he had written that morning, occasionally pausing to reread a passage he particularly liked. 'But for the present they must wait; and they could afford to wait, for the prize was worth winning. It was the most precious possession in the world – liberty.'[1]*

It was, he thought, one thing to be so open about himself in a letter to his Mamma and something else entirely to place it in a book for all the world to see. He supposed he could always publish the novel under an assumed name, but he knew he could not help telling his friends about the novel even if he did so. And, of course, Lady Randolph would tell all of her friends; and Aunt Clara and Aunt Leonie would tell all of their friends; and, very quickly, everyone in England, from the Prince of Wales on down, would know of his ambition and his high opinion of himself.

Churchill thought about this for awhile and then dismissed his concerns. What in bloody hell was he writing the book for other than to draw attention to himself and get noticed? Why had he sent the telegram to Blood except to get noticed; to get medals; and to be mentioned in dispatches? No, he decided, he would leave the passage exactly as he had written it because – precisely because – it described him just as he was.

He was a young man . . . but already he felt the effects of work and worry. Was it worth it? The struggle, the labour, the constant rush of affairs, the sacrifice of so many things that make life easy, or pleasant – for what? A people's good! That, he could not disguise from himself, was rather the direction than the cause of his efforts. Ambition was the motive force, and he was powerless to resist it . . . 'Vehement, high, and daring' was his cast of mind. The life he lived was the only one he could ever live; he must go on to the end . . . [2]

Yes, he thought with satisfaction, the novel really was far and away the best thing that he had ever written. He rummaged through the papers until he located Chapter 6 and found the passage that described his self-confidence and his philosophy just as the previous passage had detailed his ambition and his emotional make-up.

[T]here were many dangers ahead. Well, he did not care; he was confident in his own powers. As the difficulties arose, he would meet them; when dangers threatened he would overcome them. Horse, foot, and artillery, he was a man, a complete entity. Under any circumstances, in any situation, he knew himself a factor to be reckoned with; whatever the game, he would play it to his amusement, if not to his advantage.

He basked in the smiles of fortune, and shrugged his shoulders at the frowns of fate. His existence, or series of existences, had been agreeable. All that he remembered had been worth living. If there was a future state, if the game was to begin again elsewhere, he would take a hand. He hoped for immortality, but he contemplated annihilation with composure.[3]

Churchill stood up, satisfied. Someday soon there would be 'many dangers ahead' for him as well, especially if Blood would keep his word. He heard horses outside and looked once more at his watch, surprised that two hours had passed. The mail at last, he thought, and he once more let his hopes rise. He knew he shouldn't but he couldn't help it. He was an incurable optimist whose glass was always half full.

Churchill waited patiently for his Indian servant to bring in the mail. When he did so, Churchill quietly thanked the small, smiling man and, in response to his query, told him that nothing more was needed. The servant bowed and silently left the room while Churchill looked at the four envelopes he had been given. He recognized his mother's handwriting on the top letter and placed it down on the desk for reading later. He did the same with the next two letters, one from his Aunt Leonie and the other from his brother Jack. He didn't recognize the handwriting on the fourth letter and his heart skipped a beat as he quickly slit it open and read it, his excitement rising. It was even better than Cuba! Not only was he to join the Malakand Field Force, but Blood was personally inviting him to join as a press correspondent. The best of both worlds!

Churchill read the letter again to make sure that, in his enthusiasm, he had not misread its contents. No, he had not misread it and now he must arrange for another leave immediately. Reggie Barnes would help him there, he was certain. Then he would have to send a cable to his mother. Some newspaper had to actually hire him so he could get a special pass as a correspondent. Otherwise, he was out of luck. He wasn't worried. His mother had always come through for him, and he was certain she would do so again. Lady Randolph knew everyone.

Winston Churchill was a happy man. Adventure was once more on the horizon.

That time Churchill writes of in *My Early Life* where he and his mother were more like brother and sister than son and mother had not entirely arrived in early 1897, two years after his father's death. As always with Winston, the dispute with his mother involved money, a subject of discord between them until Churchill's success as a writer made him financially independent. Until then, Winston had to endure letters from his mother like this one of 26 February 1897 on the occasion of his overdrawing his account at Cox's bank.

Dearest Winston,

It is with very unusual feelings that I sit down to write to you my weekly letter. Generally it is a pleasure – but this time is quite the reverse. The enclosed letter will explain why. I went to Cox's this morning & find out that not only you have anticipated the whole of yr quarter's allowance due this month but £45 besides – & now this cheque for £50 – & that you knew you had nothing at the bank. The manager told me they had warned you that they would not let you overdraw & the next mail brought this cheque. I must say I think it is too bad of you – indeed it is hardly honourable knowing as you do that you are dependent on me & that I give you the biggest allowance I possibly can, more than I can afford. I am very bad up & this has come at a very inopportune moment & puts me to much inconvenience . . . If you cannot live on yr allowance from me & yr pay you will have to leave the 4th Hussars. I cannot increase yr allowance.

Money wasn't Jennie's only concern. She had not yet come to appreciate in the same way Cockran had that her son was preparing for a life in politics:

As for yr wild talk & scheme of coming home for a month, it is absolutely out of the question, not only on account of money, but for the sake of yr reputation. They will say & with some reason that you can't stick to anything. You have only been out 6 months & it is on the cards that you may be called to Egypt. There is plenty for you to do in India. I confess I am quite disheartened about you. You seem to have no real purpose in life & won't realize at the age of 22 that for a man life means work, & hard work if you mean to succeed. Many men at yr age have to work for a living & support their mother . . . . You cannot but feel ashamed of yrself under the present circumstances – I haven't the heart to write more.

Yr Mother
JRC[4]

Churchill was heading home come hell or high water. He informed his mother so in a letter on 6 April 1897. A week later, on 14 April 1897, he wrote her another letter telling her in detail how boring his life was in India.

> I am looking forward immensely to seeing civilisation again after the barbarous squalor of this country. I do hope you will sympathise with my desire . . . [M]y life here would be intolerable were it not for the consolations of literature. The only valuable knowledge I take away from India (soldiering apart) could have been gathered equally well in Cumberland Place.[5]

The key passage in that letter is Churchill's reference to 'the consolations of literature' and the fact that all he learned in India worth knowing could have been accomplished reading the same books in London. Before departing for India, he had already read Fawcett, Lecky and Gibbon. While in India, he asked his mother to send him twelve volumes of Macaulay (eight of history and four of essays) as well as Adam Smith's *Wealth of Nations*. He also asked her to send him twenty-seven volumes of the *Annual Register*, a detailed year-by-year parliamentary history first edited by Edmund Burke.[6]

A 31 March 1897 letter to his mother records for her the breadth of his scholarship:

> Many thanks for your letter of the 11th and for the two vols *Annual Register* & two *Wealth of Nations* – all of which have been safely received . . . Since I have been in this country I have read or nearly finished reading (for I read three or four different books at a time to avoid tedium) all Macaulay (12 vols) all Gibbon (begun in England 4000 pages) *The Martyrdom of Man – Modern Science and Modern Thought* (Laing) the *Republic* of Plato (Jowett's Translation) Rochefort's *Memoirs* Gibbon's *Life & Memoirs* & 1 Complete *Annual Register* on English Politics. I have hardly looked at a novel. Will you try and get me the *Memoirs* of the Duc de Saint Simon & also Pascal's *Provincial Letters* – I am very anxious to read both these as Macaulay recommends the one & Gibbon the other.[7]

With the possible exception of the *Annual Register*, there is no book Churchill read in India not found in Bourke Cockran's library. We

know, from what Churchill has written, the subjects he and Bourke
Cockran discussed during their long conversations in 1895 and 1896.
There is a passage in the 31 March 1897 letter to his mother which
suggests the strong influence of Cockran, who from his first speech
in Congress in 1887 to the recent presidential campaign in 1896
placed principle over party and consistency over partisanship. The
twenty-two-year-old Churchill was trying to prepare himself to do the
same. Like his mentor, he too wanted (as he would write of Cockran
thirty-five years later) to develop 'a complete scheme of political
thought which enabled him to present a sincere and effective front
in every direction according to changing circumstances.' The twenty-
two-year-old Churchill described for his mother how he was trying
to do so:

> The method I pursue with the *Annual Register* is [not] to read
> the debate until I have recorded *my own opinion* on paper of the
> subject – *having regard only to general principles*. After reading
> I reconsider and finally write. I hope by a persevering continuance
> of this practice to build up a scaffolding of logical and consistent
> views which will perhaps tend to the *creation of a logical and
> consistent mind*.[8] (emphasis added)

A week later, Churchill wrote another long letter to his mother
on political issues. The influence on the twenty-two-year-old Churchill
of the liberal Democrat Cockran as well as the Tory Democracy of
his own father is at once apparent as he strives, not always successfully, to bring the two major influences on his political life into
harmony – his father and Cockran. Speaking of the Conservative Party,
he wrote:

> There are no lengths to which I would not go in opposing [the
> Conservatives] were I in the House of Commons. I am a Liberal in
> all but name. My views excite the pious horror of the Mess. Were it
> not for Home Rule – to which I will never consent – I would enter
> Parliament as a Liberal. As it is – Tory Democracy will have to be
> the standard under which I shall range myself.[9]

On 21 April 1897, Winston wrote to his mother with a new bombshell,
akin to the one he had delivered in 1895 announcing that he was going to

Cuba. This time he grandly announced that he proposed to 'go to the front as a special correspondent' to cover the war recently declared by Turkey on Greece. There were two problems, and he expected his mother to solve them both.

First, he hadn't yet determined whether he would cover the war from the Greek side or the Turkish side, but he expected his mother to get him credentials from one side or the other. His second problem was finding a newspaper to retain him as a special correspondent. Again, he assumed his mother would take care of that as well.

Jennie took it all in stride. At this point in his life, his mother was as sophisticated in international affairs as Churchill, if not more so. In a letter written in late April to her son, Jack, who was in France studying for a year with a French tutor in Versailles, she wrote that 'I have had a long letter from Winston – who has, of course, a wild scheme to go as war correspondent with the Greeks – Luckily the war will be over by the time he gets home'.[10] Jennie's predictions were borne out. Churchill sailed from India on 8 May 1897, and three days later the war was over, long before he reached Brindisi.

Jennie's letter to Jack is significant for another reason. It confirms she and Cockran were still seeing each other because it was the third time in three months she had mentioned Bourke Cockran in a letter to Jack. Whether or not they were still romantically involved, they remained close friends. The letter in April told Jack that 'Bourke gave me an account of yr breakfast, etc.' Early in February, she had written to Jack telling him 'I believe Bourke is in Paris and has your address and means to ask you to go and see him'. In a letter on 26 February 1897, Jennie had written to Jack that 'I am very much afraid that it will be impossible for me to go to Paris with Bourke next week – as I had hoped – but I am really too hard up – and Winston has been overdrawing his account and I had to make a cheque for £50.' The possibility that Jennie would be seriously considering going 'to Paris with Bourke' and that Cockran would ask her to revisit the scene of their love affair is interesting and into which, for those romantically inclined, much can be read.

Cockran had spent the last month of 1895 and five of the first seven months of 1896 in Europe and England. A year later, he was doing much the same thing, spending most of the first six months of 1897 in Europe, from the latter part of January 1897 through most of June. Whether Jennie and Bourke remained lovers during this period is unknown.

BECOMING WINSTON CHURCHILL

Cockran's letters to Jennie do not survive and were probably destroyed by Jennie just as few of Jennie's letters to Cockran are found among the papers he donated to the New York Public Library. The inference can certainly be drawn that their affair was periodically resumed during Cockran's visits in 1896 and 1897 because neither Cockran nor Jennie were seeing others seriously during this time.

Cockran continued to be active in public affairs, notwithstanding he was no longer a member of Congress. On 28 November 1896, he gave a speech in New York sponsored by the Cuban League of the Ten Year War, in which he urged the United States to publicly announce its support for the Cuban rebellion. The meeting was chaired by Cockran's friend, Charles Dana, whose paper, the *New York Sun*, had long supported a free Cuba. John Dos Passos also spoke at the meeting.

Cockran was a prominent Catholic layman, and the Archbishop of New York, Michael August Corrigan, asked Cockran early in 1897 to be his personal representative to the Vatican to urge Pope Leo XIII to intervene and offer to mediate an end to hostilities in Cuba. Cockran spent three weeks in Paris before journeying on to Rome. He met with the Pope twice, and their conversations were conducted in Italian, in which Cockran was fluent. Cockran's trip was undertaken with the knowledge and support of the McKinley Administration, and President McKinley wrote to Cockran in June 1897 thanking him for his support.[11]

After leaving Rome, Cockran stopped in Paris to visit again with Jack Churchill and had breakfast with him before he returned to London and saw Jennie once more. Cockran stayed in London through the end of June 1897. While there, Cockran and Churchill dined together at Willis' Restaurant prior to Cockran's returning to America on 27 June 1897. Churchill's letter to Cockran on 10 June 1897 inviting him to dinner is the only surviving correspondence between them until 1899.

10 June 1897   35a Great Cumberland Place

My dear Bourke,

Will you come and dine with me tonight at Willis' Restaurant at 8:15. I beg you will not refuse unless compelled to – or I shall think you have not forgotten how badly I behaved last time you were to have dined with me. I am looking forward to seeing you and hearing some account of your rhetorical successes, so much that it makes me feel quite tired to wait.

Gratify therefore, my desire right away.

Yours very sincerely,
Winston S. Churchill

P.S. Telephone reply to Cumberland Place.[12]

When Churchill dined with Cockran, he had yet to give his first public speech. But Churchill had already written in his then-unpublished novel exactly how a great orator went about preparing a speech.

What was there to say? . . . His ideas began to take the form of words, to group themselves into sentences; he murmured to himself; the rhythm of his own language swayed him; instinctively he alliterated. Ideas succeeded one another, as a stream flows swiftly by and the light changes on its waters. He seized a piece of paper and began hurriedly to pencil notes. That was a point; could not tautology accentuate it? He scribbled down a rough sentence, scratched it out, polished it, and wrote it in again. The sound would please their ears, the sense improve and stimulate their minds. What a game it was! His brain contained the cards he had to play, the world the stakes he played for.[13]

What Churchill knew of preparing speeches at this point in his life, however, could only have been derived from his long conversations with Cockran, who had shared with him how he prepared a speech.

The speaking styles of Cockran and Churchill were similar, but it is likely that Churchill is describing in this passage Cockran's method for preparing a speech rather than his own. For much of his speaking career, Churchill would write his speeches verbatim before he gave them. Cockran, by contrast, made detailed notes for his speeches, but he otherwise spoke extemporaneously. In the quoted passage, Churchill's hero, Savrola, appears to be making detailed notes à la Cockran rather than drafting the speech verbatim à la Churchill.

Shortly after he dined with Cockran, Churchill gave his first public speech at a meeting in Bath of the Primrose League, a Tory Party association organized by his father in 1883. The speech was a good start, filled with humour, facts and attacks on the opposition as well as pleasing phases and well-received metaphors. Brief excerpts follow:

This measure is designed to protect workingmen in dangerous trades from poverty if they become injured in the service of their employers. [*hear, hear*] . . .

So far it is only applied to dangerous trades. Radicals, who are never satisfied with Liberals, always liberal with other people's money [*laughter*], ask why it is not applied to all. That is like a Radical – just the slap-dash, wholesale, harum-scarum policy of the Radical. It reminds me of the man who, on being told that ventilation is an excellent thing, went and smashed every window in his house, and died of rheumatic fever. [*laughter and cheers*][14]

The reviews on his speech were mixed. One paper wrote that he 'delighted his audience by the force and mental agility he displayed.'[15] Another paper was more restrained:

He seems to be a young man of some ability, anxious to take a part in public affairs. He is, however, in danger of being spoilt by flattery and public notice . . . Political talent is the least hereditary of any of our tendencies.[16]

Churchill, however, was soon to have much more than simply a famous political name. In a very real sense, it all began during the summer of 1897. Churchill had made the acquaintance of Sir Bindon Blood a year earlier and extracted a promise from him that he would take Churchill with him should he ever again command troops in action on the Indian Frontier. On 26 July 1897, a sudden uprising of Pathan tribesmen began on the Indian Frontier. As Churchill recounts in *My Early Life*, 'I read in the newspapers that a Field Force of three brigades have been formed, and at the head of it stood Sir Bindon Blood. Forthwith I telegraphed reminding him of his promise, and took the train for Brindisi.'[17] Churchill left England in haste, but it did him no good. Back in India nearly a month later, Churchill had still not heard from Blood. On 24 August 1897 he wrote to his mother, 'I am still disgusted at my not being taken. Sir Bindon Blood has never replied to any of my wires since Brindisi.'[18]

In the same letter, Churchill apologized for being late in writing 'because I have been writing my novel all day'. Later in the letter, he tells her about his novel *Affairs of State*:

> As to the Novel. I think you will be surprised when you get the MS. It is far and away the best thing that I have ever done. I have only written 80 MS pages – but I find a fertility of ideas that surprises me . . . I am quite enthusiastic about it. All my philosophy is put into the mouth of the hero. But you must see for yourself. It is full of adventure.[19]

This was the first of sixteen letters Winston wrote to his mother over the next seven months telling her of his progress on his novel on which he continued to work. While the novel has been criticized by many for its lack of literary merit, few of those are contemporary reviews. The fact that it was originally published in serial form in a magazine is proof that it was believed to be commercially popular at the time. By any modern account, the characters in *Savrola* (the eventual title of *An Affair of State*, a double entendre for the novel's love triangle) are as well realized as those in many popular thrillers of today.

Shortly after Churchill wrote this letter to his mother, he finally received a letter from Sir Bindon Blood, fulfilling his promise. So began his tenure with the Malakand Field Force. Churchill promptly set out to hook up with Blood, leaving it up to his mother, of course, to find a London newspaper which would engage him as a correspondent. Whether Churchill had achieved by this time the brother/sister relationship with his mother that he wrote of in *My Early Life* is doubtful, but no sister would want to receive from her brother, let alone a mother from her son, the letters Churchill sent Jennie before, during and after his adventures with the Malakand Field Force. A sampling:

> *[29 August 1897:]* [B]efore this letter reaches you I shall probably have had several experiences, some of which will contain the element of danger. I view every possibility with composure. It might not have been worth my while, who am really no soldier to risk so many fair chances on a war which can only help me directly in

a profession I mean to discard. But I have considered everything and I feel that the fact of having seen service with British troops while still a young man must give me more weight politically – must add to my claims to be listened to and may perhaps improve my prospect of gaining popularity with the country.[20]

[*5 September 1897:*] As to fighting – we march tomorrow, and before a week is out, there will be a battle – probably the biggest yet fought on the frontier this year. By the time this reaches you everything will be over so that I do not mind writing about it. I have faith in my star – that is that I am intended to do something in the world. If I am mistaken – what does it matter? My life has been a pleasant one and though I should regret to leave it – it would be a regret that perhaps I should never know.[21]

[*19 September 1897:*] When the retirement began I remained till the last and here I was perhaps very near my end. If you read between the lines of my letter you will see that this retirement was an awful rout in which the wounded were left to be cut up horribly by these wild beasts. I was close to both officers when they were hit almost simultaneously and fired my revolver at a man at 30 yards who tried to cut up poor Hughes' body. He dropped but came on again. A subaltern – Bethune by name and I carried a wounded Sepoy for some distance and might perhaps, had there been any gallery, have received some notice. My pants are still stained with the man's blood.[22]

[*2 October 1897:*] It is a war without quarter. They kill and mutilate everyone they catch and we do not hesitate to finish their wounded off. I have seen several things wh. have not been very pretty since I have been up here – . . . All this however you need not publish. If I get through alright – and I have faith in my luck – I shall try and come home next year for a couple of months. Meanwhile the game amuses me – dangerous though it is – and I shall stay as long as I can.[23]

What was a mother to do? Whatever Jennie felt inside, she kept up a positive front in her letters to Churchill, this one from 21 September 1897 being typical:

. . . There are so many things I want to talk to you about, but I am so in the dark as to yr whereabouts or knowledge as to when this is likely to reach you that I find it difficult. You see I do not know how you have managed to get to the front, in what capacity? How you managed to get round yr colonel is a mystery to me. Well! darling I can only hope for the best & pray that all will come out well. I believe in yr lucky star as I do in mine.[24]

In fact, Jennie had come through for Churchill as she invariably did, persuading the *Daily Telegraph* to publish his letters, albeit at only £5 a column rather than the £10 for which Churchill had hoped. Unfortunately, Churchill's published reports were unsigned. Jennie was responsible for this and tried to make the best of it in a 7 October 1897 letter to Winston:

> . . . I wrote to the Prince & told him to look out for yr letters. Also to lots of people. You will get plenty of kudos (can't spell it) I will see that you do darling boy . . .
> Don't be worried about yr letters, you will be able to use them again in a pamphlet form – "The Second Afghan Risings" etc.[25]

But Winston was having none of it. He was out for publicity and he chastised his mother for her decision to follow the advice of her friend Lord Minto, who had warned her that signed articles might get Churchill in trouble. On 25 October 1897, he wrote:

> I saw in the week's papers that arrived yesterday the first three of my letters to the *D.T.* I will not conceal my disappointment at their not being signed. I had written them with the design, a design which took form as the correspondence advanced, of bringing my personality before the electorate. I had hoped that some political advantage might have accrued. This hope encouraged me to take the very greatest pains with the style and composition and also to avoid alluding to any of my own experiences. I do not think that I have ever written anything better, or to which I would more willingly have signed my name . . . However I left the decision in your hands and you have decided – not for the first time – upon a negative course. I will only add that if I am to avoid doing "unusual" things it is difficult to see what chance I have of being more than an average person. I was proud of the letters and anxious to stake my reputation on them. They are I believe of some literary merit.[26]

By now, Churchill was back from the Frontier, spending all his time writing both his novel and what was to become his first published book, *The Story of the Malakand Field Force*. Of his novel, he wrote to his mother on 2 November 1897:

> . . . The novel is getting on excellently . . . The hero, the great democratic leader, is a fine character. A man full [of] romance, sentiment & nerves, who can talk to anyone on their own pet subject, can electrify a public meeting, and by his charm win any heart, male or female. In strong contrast is the president – a pure materialist. The ultra-crystallised military type. Practised to a degree. Matter of fact beyond patience, but able & doing. The struggle fought out in the book between the two is one between sentiment & materialism. The prize is not only political supremacy but as appears in the story "the most beautiful woman in Europe." . . . This occupation fills my mind and my time. I have read nothing since I reached India.[27]

Churchill also worked hard during this time on his book on the Malakand Field Force because he felt he was in a race with Lord Fincastle, who was writing his own book on the subject. On 22 December 1897, Churchill wrote Jennie of his progress on the book:

> A fortnight from today I shall, if the fates are propitious, send you *The Story of the Malakand Field Force* an Episode of Frontier War, by Winston S. Churchill. I hope you will like it. I am pleased with it chiefly because I have discovered a great power of application which I did not think I possessed. For two months I have worked not less than 5 hours a day and had I more time I should like to take another three or four months and produce something of value as well as of interest . . .
>
> Bullets – to a philosopher my dear Mamma – are not worth considering. Besides I am so conceited I do not believe the Gods would create so potent a being as myself for so prosaic an ending. Any way it does not matter.[28]

By the end of December, Churchill had finished the Malakand book and sent the typed manuscript off to his mother. He was clearly conscious that he was creating a career as a writer and wrote his mother on 26 January 1898:

The publication of the book will be certainly the most noteworthy act of my life. Up to date (of course). By its reception – I shall measure the chances of my possible success in the world. Although on a larger subject and with more time I am capable of a purer and more easy style and of more deeply considered views – yet it is a sample of my mental cast. If it goes down then all may be well.[29]

At this time, Churchill was also self-aware that he was creating the foundation for a life in politics. In this same letter, Churchill tells his mother what a kind of man he wants to be in politics. Cockran's influence on Churchill is readily apparent:

In Politics a man, I take it, gets on not so much by what he *does*, as by what he *is*. It is not so much a question of brains as of character & originality. It is for these reasons that I would not allow others to suggest ideas and that I am somewhat impatient of advice as to my beginning in politics. Introduction – connections – powerful friends – a name – good advice well followed – all these things count – but they lead only to a certain point. As it were they may ensure admission to the scales. Ultimately – every man has to be weighed – and if found wanting nothing can procure him the public confidence.

Nor would I desire it under such circumstances. If I am not good enough – others are welcome to take my place. I should never care to bolster up a sham reputation and hold my position by disguising my personality. Of course – as you have known for some time – I believe in myself. If I did not I might perhaps take other views.[30]

The Story of the Malakand Field Force had not been published, but Churchill was already looking ahead to the next adventure which he believed would be in Egypt and inevitably to be followed by his next book. From the beginning of January 1898, he continually advised his mother of his plans to somehow get to Egypt and he rarely missed an opportunity to ask for her help.

Churchill did not know it at the time but as 1898 dawned, he was on the cusp of a brilliant career and, in the next two years, he would be acclaimed throughout England as a writer, a politician and a military hero.

Illustrations

1. Lady Randolph Churchill, *c.*1885, during Lord Randolph's tenure as Chancellor of the Exchequer.

2. Lady Randolph Churchill with her sons Winston (right) and Jack (left), 1889.

3. Churchill as a Sandhurst cadet with two friends, Lord Dillon (centre) and Bertie Cook (right), 1893.

4. 'Champions in the Fray', by George Yost Coffin, published in the *Washington Post*, 13 August 1893. Editorial cartoon of Cockran during his leadership of the fight for repeal of the Sherman Silver Purchase Act.

5. William Bourke Cockran in 1895, the year he met Jennie Churchill and her son Winston.

6. Leonie Leslie, 1895. Jennie's younger sister in whom both Jennie and Cockran confided regarding their affair in Paris.

7. Lt. Winston Churchill in 1895, after his graduation from Sandhurst and before he met Cockran.

8. William Jennings Bryan accepting the Democratic presidential nomination in Madison Square Garden in 1896, where Cockran spoke a week later opposing Bryan's candidacy (and drawing a larger crowd).

9. Churchill in Bangalore, India, in 1897, inscribed by Churchill in 1899 to an American girl, Miss Christine Lewis, whom he took sightseeing in Cairo.

10. Churchill, Christine Lewis and George Sandys aboard SS Carthage, 1899. Sandys' son Duncan would marry Winston's daughter Diana in 1935.

11. Churchill aboard a ship at the Cowes Regatta, August 1899.

12. Telegram to Lady Randolph from Cockran, 29 November 1899, forwarding a cablegram message from the U.S. Consul in Pretoria after visiting Churchill in a Boer P.O.W. camp.

13. Churchill as a war correspondent in South Africa after his escape from a Boer P.O.W. camp, 1900.

14. Churchill in Boston in 1900 on his first North American lecture tour.

15. Churchill and his first cousin Sunny, the Duke of Marlborough, 1900.
Sunny married the American heiress Consuela Vanderbilt.

16. Portrait of Churchill by the artist Mortimer Menpes, 1901.

17. Family photograph of Churchill taken in the early 1900s.

18. Cockran in 1903 when he gave his speech 'The Essential Conditions of Natural Prosperity' at the Liberal Club in London.

19. Churchill in 1904, the year he left the Conservatives and joined the Liberals over the principle of Free Trade where he and Cockran had the same views.

20. Churchill at his writing desk in 1904.

21. Cockran in 1904 after his election to Congress, ending an eight year absence.

22. Formal portrait of Anne Ide, 1906.

23. Anne Ide in 1906, prior to her marriage to Cockran.

24. Clementine Hozier in 1908, the year she married Churchill, the fourth woman to whom Churchill proposed and the only one to accept.

25. Pamela Lytton, née Plowden, Churchill's first love, competing in a horse show in Calcutta in 1926. Churchill and Pamela remained close friends throughout their lives.

26. Cockran and his wife Anne on holiday in Ireland, c.1910.

27. Churchill's first cousin Sir Shane Leslie and his wife Marjorie, Anne Cockran's sister, in 1912, the year they were married at Cockran's Long Island estate, the Cedars. Both sisters had tattoos on their right arm from their childhood in American Samoa where their father Henry Ide was the governor.

28. Conservative Party leader Bonar Law, Ulster Leader Sir Edward Carson and Churchill's close friend F. E. Smith in an anti-Home Rule march in Northern Ireland, 1912.

29. Cockran at the Leslie family estate at Glaslough, Ireland, c.1912.

30. Cockran's wife Anne, Otala the Cockatoo, and Birdie Wilson in 1913.

31. Bust of Churchill by his first cousin, Clare Frewen Sheridan, daughter of Jennie's older sister Clara, c.1911–1914.

32. Family photograph of Cockran in early 1920s.

33. Cockran in 1920, after his sixth election to Congress.

Chapter 9
'How Little Time Remains'

New York City
29 November 1899

The cable had been waiting for Bourke Cockran when he returned to his law offices on 31 Nassau Street from a long day in court. It lay there in the middle of his desk, unopened, the late afternoon sun shining in the window. His secretary knew that he had been expecting it any day now – a cable from the State Department. It was personal, not business, which is why she had not opened it. Cockran sat down, picked up his onyx-handled letter opener and slit the envelope. He thought, but wasn't sure, that his hands trembled slightly as he pulled the flimsy paper out and read it, unaware that he was holding his breath while he did so.

Cockran exhaled slowly and felt the muscles in his face relax. Winston was safe and unharmed. 'Thank you Lord', Cockran whispered as he crossed himself.

It had been ten days since Cockran received Jennie's telegram telling him of Winston's capture by the Boers and asking him to check on her son's well-being. Cockran had immediately picked up the telephone and placed a call to Secretary of State John Hay, whom Cockran knew. Cockran was pleasantly surprised to be put directly through to Hay, especially since he had spoken out strongly against the McKinley Administration's imperialism during the past year – its annexation of the Philippines and the resulting guerrilla war that had cost the United States both treasure and the blood of its finest men.

Three years in politics is a lifetime, and Cockran knew he had long since used up any goodwill the Republicans felt towards him for his role in the 1896 election. Or the unsuccessful efforts he made – with the administration's blessings – to have the Vatican mediate between the United States and Spain prior to the war. It did not seem to matter to Hay that Cockran had once said of him in a speech that 'England's most valuable foreign possession is the American Secretary of State.'[1] Or, if it did, Hay didn't let on.

'Send your cable to our Consul General in Pretoria', he had said. 'His name is Macrum, Charles Macrum. Tell him what you want. I will send a cable as well and make sure he understands I want him to personally visit the camp and see young Churchill's condition for himself.'

Cockran had thanked Hay profusely, but he had waved it off as if it and their policy differences were nothing. Cockran's opinion of Hay, which was not especially high, went higher. Cockran had promptly sent the cable: 'Pray ascertain and cable if Churchill captured or killed at Chievely. Charge all expenses to me. Matter of deepest personal interest.'[2]

The extended family of the three Jerome sisters had become, in the past four years, almost a second family to Cockran. It had been a year since he had last seen Winston, who was off fighting wars and writing books, and his visits home to England rarely seemed to coincide with Cockran's own visits. To compensate, he had kept in touch with Winston's brother Jack and Leonie's two sons, Jackie and Seymour. It almost made up for having no children of his own, a point poignantly driven home to him last Christmas when he and Leonie together had taken Jackie all over London during the Christmas season – shopping, plays, musicals and restaurants, just as if they were an old married couple squiring their son around town.

Cockran and Jennie were still good friends, but he knew their romance was at last over, no matter how often since that Paris spring in 1895 they had renewed their friendship. That had occurred most recently last December where Cockran had been pleased and flattered by her soliciting his advice – and truth be told his money – for her new literary magazine.

According to Leonie, Jennie was now seeing a handsome, young army officer, George Cornwallis-West, who was barely Winston's age and Cockran knew he couldn't compete with that. More importantly, he knew he couldn't compete with Winston and his political career, to which his mother was firmly devoted. He had stood for Parliament in a by-election that summer and had narrowly lost before he headed off as a special correspondent to cover the war in South Africa.

Money always mattered very much to Jennie. Leonie had told him how proud Jennie was that the Morning Post *was paying Winston £250 a month as their South African correspondent. That coupled with Winston's earnings from his books meant the squabbles he and Jennie used to have over finances were a thing of the past. Now her focus on him could be exclusively with his career, and Cockran followed British politics closely enough so that he believed Winston would certainly succeed next time he stood for office.*

*Cockran rose from his desk and took the cable with him into the
reception area. 'Miss Wilson, kindly take a cable to Lady Randolph
Churchill at Witley Court, Worcester':*

*Following Cable just received . . . Churchill prisoner here in good
health and spirits uninjured sends best regards. Macrum*[3]

Publication of his first book, *The Malakand Field Force*, was the high-
light of Churchill's life in the first half of 1898, the first substantial public
evidence of the foundation on which he was to build his career. Still in
India, he thrived on press cuttings of the reviews and begged for more.

His greatest fear proved more or less well founded. When he sent
the completed manuscript of his book to his mother at the beginning
of 1898, he explained that, due to his desire to publish before his
competitor Lord Fincastle, he could not proofread the manuscript
himself because it would take too long to be sent to India and then
back again to England. Accordingly, he requested that his mother ask
his uncle, Moreton Frewen, to 'undertake the work of revising and
correcting' the manuscript. Frewen wrote to Cockran shortly thereafter
telling his friend that he was correcting the proofs of his nephew's book
and that 'he's a clever boy as you know & has got a future.'[4]

In the event, Fincastle's book came out before his and Churchill
learned a valuable lesson. When he received the revised proofs, he was
appalled. Churchill's 22 March 1898 letter to his mother recounts his
misery at being betrayed by his uncle.

> I add this letter to tell you that the "revised proofs" reached me
> yesterday and that I spent a very miserable afternoon in reading the
> gross & fearful blunders which I suppose have got into the finished
> copies . . .
>   I blame no one – but myself. I might have known that no one
> could or would take the pains that an author would bestow. The
> result, however, destroys all the pleasure I had hoped to get from the
> book and leaves only shame that such an impertinence should be
> presented to the public – a type of the careless slapdash spirit of the
> age and an example of what my father would have called my
> slovenly shiftless habits . . .[5]

In retrospect, Churchill need not have been so worried. His book was well received notwithstanding the many embarrassing typographical errors. Churchill was particularly taken with the review in the *Athenaeum*, about which he wrote to his mother:

> Here is one of those opinions to which I must bow. The vy great praise bestowed upon my style is more than ever in my most sanguine moments I had hoped for. The condemnation is less severe than that I should have myself pronounced.[6]

A few lines from the *Athenaeum*'s review will show why Churchill liked it so much. How could a young writer not appreciate being compared to Burke and Disraeli?

> Mr. Churchill may be only a reader of Burke and Disraeli, but in many passages these writers speak again, and the application of Burke's style in particular to the affairs of war yields here and there passages worthy of Napier's great history – the model of military literature.[7]

Churchill found the criticisms harsh but fair, and he knew he would never let such errors happen again. The review suggested that the book needs 'only a little correction of each page to make its second edition a military classic . . . Yet one word is printed for another, words are defaced by shameful blunders, and sentence after sentence ruined by the punctuation of an idiot or of a school-boy in the lowest form . . .'[8] Churchill lost no time in revising the book for a second edition and sent it back to the publisher in April 1898.

Notwithstanding his uncle Moreton's shortcomings as a proofreader and editor, Churchill drew considerable self-confidence from the publication of *The Malakand Field Force*. He had also nearly completed his novel, and it was with both these books in mind that he wrote to his mother on 25 April 1898:

> I have nearly finished my novel "Affairs of State". It is a wild and daring book tilting recklessly here and there and written with no purpose whatever, but to amuse. This I believe it will do. I have faith in my pen. I believe the thoughts I can put on paper

will interest & be popular with the public. The reception accorded to my first book, in spite of its gross and damning errors proves to me that my literary talents do not exist in my imagination alone . . .

This literary sphere of action may enable me in a few years to largely supplement my income. Indeed I look forward to becoming sooner or later independent. We shall see.[9]

Churchill finished his novel in May and sent the last seven chapters to his mother in June. Churchill had three months' leave coming to him as a consequence of having served in the Malakand Field Force. He wanted to go to Egypt, where Lord Kitchener was involved in a campaign against the Dervishes. When he was unsuccessful in being attached to a posting in Egypt, he left India in the latter part of June 1898, arriving in London early in July.

Once back in London, Churchill sent a manuscript of his novel to Pamela Plowden, clearly trusting her with his innermost thoughts as he did with his mother. He told her in a 23 July 1898 letter that the novel is 'in some respects a mirror of my mind. I do not know if you will care – even from a psychological point of view – to look into that mirror –; but if you do I am sure it will gain beauty by the reflection.' Later in the letter, Churchill wrote that 'I shall make no attempt to conceal the fact that you exercise a strange fascination over me.'[10]

Churchill's self-confidence as a public speaker was also growing. Shortly after his return to England in early July 1898, he gave a speech at Bradford, which was well received by the crowd. He wrote to his mother after the speech on 15 July 1898 telling her of the crowd's reaction:

Personally – I was intensely pleased with the event. The keenness of the audience stirred my blood – and altho I stuck to my notes rigidly – I certainly succeeded in rousing & in amusing them. They burst out of the hall & pressed all round the carriage to shake hands and cheered till we had driven quite away.

* * *

It may be perhaps the hand of Fate – which by a strange coincidence closed one line of advance and aspiration in the morning – and in the evening pointed out another with an encouraging gesture. At any rate – my decision to resign my commission is definite.[11]

Churchill's reference here to his decision to resign his commission was, in part, a reflection on his failure to be posted to Lord Kitchener's expedition against the Dervishes in Sudan. But this was soon to change when he was granted an audience with the Prime Minister Lord Salisbury. Churchill recounts in *My Early Life* that Salisbury was much taken with *The Malakand Field Force* and told Churchill:

> I have been keenly interested in your book. I have read it with the greatest pleasure and, if I may say so, with admiration not only for its matter but for its style . . . I myself have been able to form a truer picture of the kind of fighting that has been going on in these frontier valleys from your writings than from any other documents which it has been my duty to read.[12]

Lord Salisbury also told Churchill that if there was anything at any time he could do to be of assistance to Churchill, 'pray do not fail to let me know'. That was all the encouragement Churchill needed. He promptly wrote to Salisbury after their meeting asking his help to get him assigned to Egypt, helpfully volunteering to whom Salisbury should write and what to say. Salisbury kept his word and did so the next day. Within the week, Churchill had been attached to the 21st Lancers to replace a young officer who had died. He was soon on his way to Egypt.

Once in Egypt, Churchill wrote to his mother one of those cheerful letters which she must have dreaded receiving:

> . . . We are but 60 miles from Khartoum and on the 27th we march 21 miles putting us in front of the infantry and in full contact. Within the next ten days there will be a general action – perhaps a vy severe one. I may be killed. I do not think so.[13]

Less than two weeks later, on 4 September 1898, the day after the battle of Omdurman, Churchill wrote to his mother, who was undoubtedly relieved but horrified by what her son had gone through. As usual, Winston spared her little detail:

> . . . I was under fire all day and rode through the charge. You know my luck in these things. I was about the only officer whose clothes, saddlery, or horse were uninjured. I fired 10 shots with my pistol – all necessary – and just got to the end of it as we cleared the crush.

I never felt the slightest nervousness and felt as cool as I do now. I pulled up and reloaded within 30 yards of their mass and then trotted after my troop who were then about 100 yards away. I am sorry to say I shot 5 men for certain and two doubtful. The pistol was the best thing in the world.[14]

Churchill returned to England in early October 1898, where he stayed for the next two months. While in England, he took the occasion to give three more political speeches in October, all of which he believed were well received. He had also begun to write *The River War*, a two-volume effort depicting the campaign he had just completed. It took him fifteen months to finish compared with six weeks for *The Malakand Field Force*.

Bourke Cockran had been busy during 1898 as well but at no risk to life or limb. On 15 February 1898, the US Battleship *Maine* blew up in the harbour in Havana, Cuba. Cockran had long supported the Cuban insurrection but not necessarily a war with Spain. He believed Cuban freedom could be accomplished without it. That belief faded in the days following the destruction of the *Maine*, as war fever swept the country. With McKinley's approval, Cockran cabled his friend Archbishop Keene in Rome in late March, urging him to have the Pope intercede with the Spanish government to agree to President McKinley's proposal that Spain declare an armistice with the Cuban rebels until October, with negotiations carried on in the interim with a view to establishing peace between Spain and the Cuban insurgents. Cockran also wrote to Archbishop Martinelli, the Papal Delegate to the United States, suggesting that war with Spain could be averted if the Spanish government would immediately declare such an armistice 'employing substantially the very language of the President's proposal'.[15]

The Spanish government rejected both the Pope and the President, the Spanish prime minister calling McKinley 'a cheap politician who truckles to the masses'. On 25 April 1898, the United States declared war on Spain. Four days later, Cockran spoke publicly in favour of the war, even though he was to oppose, in its aftermath, the US occupation and administration of the Philippines.

Cockran did not travel to England that spring or summer. Leonie, for one, was disappointed. As Moreton Frewen wrote to Cockran on 17 June 1898:

Leonie wrote me a letter . . . to tell me to give you her best greetings & to say that you had neglected, I think even deserted, her.[16]

Cockran was active on the political front, and he stayed in America until after the fall elections in which he played a major role and was once more on the wrong side of Tammany Hall. To Cockran, the independence of the judiciary was at stake. To Tammany, patronage was more important.

Joseph Daly had been a highly regarded trial court judge for twenty-eight years. Unfortunately, he made the mistake of offending Boss Croker, and as a consequence, the New York County Democratic Judiciary Convention denied him a renomination.[17] The reason why was that Judge Daly had refused to appoint a court clerk recommended by Croker. As Croker told the *New York Tribune*: 'We had a right to expect proper consideration from Judge Daly, who owed his nomination and election to Tammany Hall. We didn't get it. That's why we turned him down.'[18]

The New York City Bar Association organized a non-partisan citizens committee to support the re-election of Judge Daly as an independent candidate. Cockran was its chief spokesman, and he assembled a broad coalition in favour of Daly and against Croker – Democrats, Republicans, Free Silverites and Socialists alike. Wisely or not, Cockran made Boss Croker the focus of his campaign and gave a speech in Carnegie Hall in September 1898 on the evils of bossism and the need for an independent judiciary. By all accounts, it was one of his better speeches. The *New York Tribune* was persuaded by Cockran's eloquence, but the voters were not. The *Tribune* wrote after Cockran's speech:

> Bourke Cockran has made many famous speeches before New York audiences but none more memorable than the speech he delivered last night in Carnegie Hall. With an eloquence worthy of Burke and a series of satirical thrusts that would have done credit to the pen of Swift, he depicted the appalling consequences of boss rule as revealed in Croker's latest attempt to control the judiciary.[19]

Cockran received the cheers, but Croker had the votes. Judge Daly was overwhelmingly defeated, but there was a silver lining for Cockran. The Democratic candidate for governor, Augustus Van Wyck, was defeated by the Republican candidate, Theodore Roosevelt. One prominent Democrat blamed the loss directly on Croker: 'When Croker turned down Judge Daly, he committed an act of treason against the Democratic party. Our great leader of Tammany Hall has given New York State a Republican governor.' The chairman of the Democratic State Committee said it was Cockran's Carnegie Hall speech which turned the tide, costing the Democrats 'not less than 25,000 votes' statewide where Roosevelt's margin of victory had been less than 17,000 votes.[20]

The election over, Cockran sailed for England, where he met with Churchill. Once Jennie heard he was in town, she promptly invited Cockran to lunch. Her eagerness in doing so is as interesting as her correctness in addressing him as 'My Dear Mr. Cockran', whereas he is always referred to simply as 'Bourke' in her letters to her son Jack.

My Dear Mr. Cockran,

I hear from Winnie that you have just arrived. Will you come and have lunch with me here today at 2 o'clock?

Hoping you can come,

yours sincerely
Jennie R. Churchill[21]

This is one of the few letters from Jennie in Cockran's papers, but Cockran undoubtedly accepted her invitation for lunch. It was no secret they still were seeing each other, and further evidence that they were doing so during this period comes in a letter from Cockran to Leonie, where he advises her that he sent word to Leonie's son Jackie 'by Lady Randolph's butler asking him to call at 3:30'. Among the subjects Bourke and Jennie discussed when they were together were her new literary magazine, then untitled but subsequently called *The Anglo-Saxon Review*. On 31 December 1898, Jennie wrote to Cockran:

December 31st, 1898   Blenheim Palace

My Dear Mr. Cockran,

I am too sorry to think that I shall not see you again before your departure for America – you were a "tower of strength" to me over my scheme and I regret that I can't pick your brains a little more – and get your advice on many points – I hope in a fortnight or so to get the financial statement I spoke to you about and before you leave I want to ask you – should the business part of the scheme meet with your approval – would you feel disposed to join the small syndicate I mean to form. As I told you fancy about £1500 will be required for the 1st year – and I want 6 contributors at £250.

Of course there must be a percentage and a bonus for Mr. Algernon Bowther who is here and who is a literary man, having written a very successful book, is very enthusiastic on the subject and has given me some valuable hints. He says the 1st no. ought to and probably will pay for the whole year and that I don't require a syndicate. – But I should feel safer if I have the money beforehand. Even if I repaid it after the publication of the 1st no. – Write and tell me what you think. I shall be at Chatsworth Chesterfield next week. Meanwhile I hope you enjoy yourself in Paris.

We are a gay party here – and high jinks ! going on all the time. Wishing you a very Happy New Year and all prosperity believe me,

yours sincerely
Jennie R. Churchill

I am so cold I can hardly hold my pen hence my peculiar caligraphy! – Don't forget about the Indiana Bonds ! when you get home and also try to find me a really clever pen – for my "American Notes". I have to get lots of American talents to write for me.

And Oh! Do find me a name for my magazine.[22]

Cockran did not return directly home to America but stopped in Ireland to see Leonie and atone for 'deserting' her that summer. Cockran wrote to Leonie on 16 December 1898 telling her 'I will leave here for Ireland instead of New York on the 7th and remain with you till the 9th'. He wrote it was possible he might stay with her another day beyond that but, 'this however is such a delightful prospect that I will not dwell upon it lest I might suffer too much if compelled to renounce it'.

December 16, 1898   The Berkeley, London

My Dear Mrs. Leslie,

Your note reached me this morning. I sent word to Jackie by Lady Randolph's butler asking him to call at 3:30 but he didn't turn up.

I waited till 4:20 P.M. for him and then I concluded he must have
been too much occupied. I wanted to get him something for Xmas
and to let him choose it but perhaps it is just as well that it should
reach him as a surprise. Will you do me the great favor to find out
what he wants *most* and let me know? You remember that
Christmastide when we last took him around London – to the plays,
the restaurants and the shops – well I always felt that although alone
in the world it was not a wholly desolate season just because I was
able to share in the happiness of a particular lovable little boy and
contribute to it in some slight degree. I cannot have his companionship this year but it is possible for me to take some part in his Xmas
merrymaking if you will help me and I am sure you will.

It was delightful to read your letter. It showed that my own
estimate of you was correct. I never thought your *friendship* open
to doubt though perhaps that manifestation of it varied somewhat.
I am not sure that vanities which seemed like caprices were not
necessary features of that character at once so complex and so
simple. – Complex if we consider the emotions which form it, simple
in its unvarying goodness. It is a keen disappointment that I cannot
see you under the conditions which now surround you. Although
I have many and urgent reasons for returning to America at once
I will make a desperate effort to run over to Glaslough for a day. But
this I cannot promise. Indeed it is doubtful if I will have enough
money left to pay my fare if the present rate of cabling is to continue.
I have just written that I will postpone sailing till the tenth and if
this announcement does not provoke a vehement cable message of
remonstrance and protest I will leave here for Ireland instead of
New York on the 7th and remain with you till the ninth. I suppose
I can get a steamer for Liverpool from some port near Glaslough
or perhaps I might be able to get railway communication with
Queenstown in which case I could remain another day. This however
is such a delightful prospect that I will not dwell upon it lest I might
suffer too much if I be compelled to renounce it. Meanwhile don't
forget to let me know what Jackie has his heart set on for Xmas. –
And pray be candid – otherwise I shall feel that I have been deceived
and I will see that Jackie knows he has been cheated.

Yours very sincerely,
W. Bourke Cockran[23]

Before leaving for India, Churchill wrote to Pamela on 28 November 1898 telling her of his progress in working on *The River War* and acknowledging the accuracy of some of her earlier criticisms, which do not survive as Churchill destroyed all of her letters to him.

> I will admit that you are quite right and that I make unnecessary enemies. The question is – Is it worth it? I confess I think so in many cases. It is an extravagance that is all . . . for all that I will try and take your advice. In any case believe that I am grateful for it. I remain persuaded rather than convinced.

Churchill closes the letter to Pamela with a sweet, if self-centred, profession of his love:

> One thing I take exception to in your letter. Why do you say I am incapable of affection. Perish the thought. I love one above all others. And I shall be constant. I am no fickle gallant capriciously following the fancy of the hour. My love is deep and strong. Nothing will ever change it. I might it is true divide it. But the greater part would remain true – will remain true till death. Who is this that I love? Listen – as the French say – over the page I will tell you.[24]

Churchill returned to India early in December 1898. Amateur athletes the world over will appreciate why he felt the need to do so for his sole purpose was to play in the annual Inter-Regimental Polo Tournament. On board ship, he worked on his manuscript for *The River War*, writing his mother on 11 December 1898:

> I have however made good progress with the book. Three vy long chapters are now almost entirely completed. The chapter describing the fall of Khartoum Gordon's death etc is I think quite the most lofty passage I have ever written.[25]

Churchill continued to be pleased with his progress on the book after he reached India. In another letter to his mother early in 1899, he told her that, while progress was slow, what he had written was 'really good'.[26]

On 9 February 1899, one week before the beginning of the
Inter-Regimental Polo Tournament, Churchill fell down some stairs,
spraining both ankles and dislocating his right shoulder. He wrote
his mother:

> I fear I shall not be able to play in the Tournament as my arm is
> weak and stiff & may come out again at any moment. It is one of
> the most unfortunate things that I have ever had happen to me and
> is a bitter disappointment. I had been playing well and my loss is
> a considerable blow to our chances of winning. I try to be philo-
> sophic but it is very hard. Of course it is better to have bad luck in
> the minor pleasures of life than in one's bigger undertakings. But I
> am very low & unhappy about it.[27]

In the event, Churchill played in the tournament, with his right arm
strapped to his side. He led his team to victory in the finals, where
Churchill, bound arm and all, scored three of his team's four goals, an
accomplishment to equal if not exceed his all-public schools' fencing
championship.

In early March, Churchill once more wrote to Pamela, this time with
an unmistakable declaration of love:

> I have lived all my life seeing the most beautiful women London
> produces . . . Never have I seen one for whom I would for an hour
> forego the business of life. Then I met you . . . Were I a dreamer of
> dreams, I would say . . . 'Marry me – and I will conquer the world
> and lay it at your feet.'

Possibly to encourage her to be equally forthcoming, he tells her at the
end of the long letter:

> Of course no human eye will read your letter. I destroy all paper
> records. My memory is my archives, and it will guard no document
> more carefully.[28]

Churchill left India in the latter part of March never to return. Christine
Lewis, a young American girl befriended by Churchill on the voyage

from India to Egypt (and whom he courted in Egypt and later in London), described Churchill's typically late arrival:

> The gangplank was about to be raised when down the wharf ran a freckled, red-haired young man in a rumpled suit carrying an immense tin cake box. Although he had nearly missed the boat, he seemed utterly unruffled and, seating himself by the rail – because there was not another spot left on deck – he carefully examined the other passengers.[29]

Lewis wrote of Churchill as a travel companion:

> At lunch, or *tiffan* as it was called then, we found ourselves sitting directly opposite Mr. Churchill. Hardly had he been seated when he bent across the table and said, "You are American, aren't you?" When we said he was right he explained, "I love Americans. My mother is an American." . . . Mr. Churchill at once took things in hand, ordering a small table for our party, himself and Captain Sandys. We found him a most amusing fellow traveler – full of fun, with a delightful sense of humor . . . . Every day he sat beside us on the deck, working intensely on his book. He paid no attention to the gay chatter of young people on the adjoining chairs as he wrote and rewrote in that peculiar small hand. His concentration was an example to all of us . . . We often played jokes on him, which he seemed to enjoy. Perhaps his one fault at this time was being a little too sure about everything, which the other young people did not always appreciate.[30]

Confident now of his ability to support himself, Churchill wrote to his grandmother in late March 1899, on his way home from Egypt, and explained his decision to leave the Army for a writing career:

> I can live cheaper & earn more as a writer, special correspondent or journalist; and this work is moreover more congenial and more likely to assist me in pursing the larger ends of life.[31]

To Churchill, 'the larger ends of life' meant his career in politics. Having finished his manuscript for *The River War*, he began to make plans. Churchill was courted by a number of Conservative constituencies who wanted him to stand as their candidate at the next general election.

One of them was Oldham, a working-class district where there were two members, one of whom, James Oswald, was in poor health. The other member, Robert Ascroft, asked Churchill to stand with him in Oswald's place at the next election. In the event, it was Ascroft who unexpectedly died on 19 June 1899 and Oswald resigned in turn, setting up a double by-election.

Churchill's Conservative Party running mate was a trade union leader named James Mawdsley, the General Secretary of the Lancashire branch of the Amalgamated Association of Cotton Spinners, for which Ascroft had long served as its lawyer. Matching the young Churchill with a union leader – 'The Scion and the Socialist' – was thought to be a good way to appeal to the working-class vote as their Liberal Party opponents were both wealthy men. It didn't work. As Churchill later wrote:

My poor Trade Unionist friend and I would have had very great difficulty in finding £500 between us, yet we were accused of representing the vested interest of society, while our opponents, who were certainly good for a quarter of a million, claimed to champion in generous fashion the causes of the poor and needy.[32]

Churchill spent most of the summer of 1899 in his first parliamentary election campaign, attempting, unsuccessfully, to persuade Pamela to join him. He wrote to her describing the campaign:

I shall never forget the succession of great halls packed with excited people until there was not room for one single person more – speech after speech, meeting after meeting – three even four in one night – intermittent flashes of Heat & Light & enthusiasm – with cold air and the rattle of a carriage in between: a great experience.

And I improve every time – I have hardly repeated myself at all. And at each meeting I am conscious of growing powers and facilities of speech, and it is in this that I shall find my consolation should the result be, as is probable, unfortunate.[33]

Churchill's prediction was accurate. He and his running mate, the trade union leader Mawdsley, lost the two Tory seats to the Liberals in the 6 July 1899 election. The results were close, however, and *The Manchester Courier* reported that Churchill 'might have been defeated but he was conscious that in this fight he had not been disgraced.'[34] His father's friend Arthur Balfour agreed, telling Churchill in a letter that 'this small reversal will have no permanent ill effect upon your political fortunes.'[35]

Churchill soon turned his attention to South Africa. Negotiations between the British and the Boers over the Boers' refusal to grant voting rights to the largely British immigrants ('Uitlanders') who had come to South Africa during the gold rush of the late nineteen century broke down in early September. War was imminent, and Churchill received an offer from *The Daily Mail* to serve as its war correspondent in South Africa on 18 September 1899, and Churchill used that offer as leverage to secure that same day a more rewarding position from *The Morning Post*, which agreed to pay all of his expenses and £250 a month. This was a far cry from the £5 a despatch he received in Cuba and India, more even than the £15 he received in his Sudan campaign.

The fall of 1899 began with Churchill the war correspondent travelling by ship to South Africa to report on the war between the Boers and Britain. The year ended with Churchill the escaped prisoner travelling by train surreptitiously out of South Africa into Portuguese East Africa. In between these two journeys, Churchill became famous throughout the world.

As a special correspondent for *The Morning Post*, Churchill sailed to South Africa on 14 October 1899, two days after hostilities began. It was not a pleasant voyage. Churchill called it 'a nasty, rough passage' and wrote his mother that he had been 'grievously sick'.[36] He arrived on 31 October 1899 at Cape Town and quickly made his way to Durban. Two weeks later he was a prisoner of the Boers.

Churchill accompanied an armoured train from Estcourt, which was ambushed by the Boers on its way to Ladysmith. While technically a non-combatant, Churchill was armed with his Mauser pistol and volunteered his services to the train's commander, Captain Aylmer Haldane, after the train came under fire. Several rail cars had been derailed by Boer artillery, preventing the engine from retreating to safety. Under constant machine gun and artillery fire from the Boers, Churchill directed the clearing of the line, helped load wounded onto the engine's tender and then accompanied the engine to safety at Frere Station. After doing so, Churchill returned on foot to the action to assist the remaining wounded and was captured. Captain Haldane, later wrote of Churchill's conduct:

> I would point out that while engaged on the work of saving the engine, for which he was mainly responsible, he was frequently

exposed to the full fire of the enemy. I cannot speak too highly of his gallant conduct.[37]

Gallant, but forgetful. Attention deficit disorder on the battlefield is not a virtue. In returning to help the wounded, Churchill had left his Mauser pistol on the engine so that he was unarmed when confronted by a Boer rifleman on a horse. His forgetfulness may have saved his life. Churchill described the moment of his capture in *My Early Life*:

> I thought there was absolutely no chance of escape, if he fired he would surely hit me, so I held up my hands and surrendered myself a prisoner of war. "When one is alone and unarmed," said the great Napoleon, in words which flowed into my mind in the poignant minutes that followed, "a surrender may be pardoned."[38]

Unfortunately for Churchill, his daring exploits in rescuing the train were widely reported in the press by his fellow correspondents who had accompanied the train. These news reports undermined Churchill's efforts to persuade the Boers to release him on the grounds that he was a non-combatant. Churchill claimed in a letter to the Boers' Secretary of State for War that he had taken 'no part in the defence of the armoured train' and was 'quite unarmed'. The Boers weren't fooled. They read the newspapers too. Contemporary correspondence from South African government officials gave Churchill complete credit for the train's escape:

> . . . but for [Churchill's] presence on the train, not a single Englishman or solider would have escaped. After the train was forced to a standstill the officers and men would definitely have fallen into enemy hands had he not directed proceedings in such a clever and thorough way, whilst walking alongside the engine, that the train together with its load escaped capture.[39]

While in prison, Churchill was visited by the American Consul-General in Pretoria as a result of a telegram from Bourke Cockran. Once Cockran learned from Jennie that Churchill was missing in action, Cockran sent a cable on 20 November 1899 to Charles F. Macrum, the US Consul in Pretoria:

> Pray ascertain and cable if Churchill captured or killed at Chievely. Charge all expenses to me. Matter of deepest personal interest.[40]

Cockran soon received Macrum's reply and was able to forward to Jennie the first eyewitness account of Winston's condition.

Following cable just received Pretoria Bourke Cockran NY . . .
Churchill prisoner here in good health and spirits uninjured sends
best regards. Macrum.[41]

Churchill was informed by the American diplomat of Cockran's telegram and wrote a long letter to his friend the same day, well aware that his Boer captors would read it first.

30 November 1899   Pretoria

My dear Bourke,

I was agreeably surprised to hear through the American Consul of your telegram, which I daresay was also the channel of my mother's enquiry. I am alive and have added another to the several vivid experiences which have crowded my last four years. I am also a prisoner, of which fact – as I am a correspondent and a non-combatant – I complain. But, that I am kept in it, is the only serious objection I have made to this place. I fear I shall be held until the end of the war, which I earnestly hope may come about March next. I want to come over to America afterwards and I rather contemplate some lectures. I wonder what view you will take of this war! I expect that you – like too many Americans, forgetful of the moral assistance we rendered your country no longer ago than the war with Spain, will disapprove of the British policy. But as you probably know, our existence as an Imperial power is staked on the issue and I do not believe that the nation will shrink from any sacrifice however great, however prolonged, to remove the causes of unrest from South Africa. However I must not write more of local politics or perhaps this letter will not reach you. Enough to say that this great country is reaping a bitter harvest which is sprung from the mistakes and follies of former years.

    You too have a big quarrel impending; and I take the vy greatest interest in the struggle against vast combinations of capital, which I am told will be the feature of the next Presidential election. I think we are on opposite sides in this matter. The economics of former days are on your side. But capitalism in the form of Trusts has reached a pitch of power which the old economists never contemplated and which excites my most lively terror. Merchant-princes are all very well, but if I have anything to say to it, their kingdom shall not be of this world. The new century will witness the great war for the existence of the Individual. Up to a certain point communication has brought us nothing but good: but we seem to have reached a period when it threatens nothing but evil. I do not want to see men buy cheaper food & better clothes at the price of their manhood. Poor but independent is worth something as a motto. "Then why" you will ask "with such views, do you not sympathize with the Boers?" It is a pertinent question, but though I should not shrink from answering it I cannot do so at length in this letter, even though time hangs heavy on my hands – and to answer it briefly were impossible. Perhaps I do sympathise with their love of freedom and pride of race: but self preservation seems to involve a bigger principle.

What about the Philippines? – Oh champion of the cause of Freedom! But I shall look forward to talking at length with you on all these things. I suppose you have never been in prison. It is a dull occupation – even under the mildest circumstances, perhaps all the duller because the circumstances are mild. I could nurse a savage anger in a dungeon. This is a damnable prosaic. My mind has become as stagnant as my body is penned up: and all the while great matters are being settled and history made – the history – mind you – I was to have recorded.

I have told my publishers to send you a copy of my new book *The River War* (two volumes), concerning which I shall be glad to have your favourable criticism and even submit to the reverse. Barnes is out here too – and was badly wounded in the leg fighting at the action of Elandslagte. He hopes to be well enough to come back to his duty and participate in the final actions of the war – which – rest assured in spite of all difficulties we shall carry through to the bloody bitter end: bloody that is to say as small wars go. I do not know whether his hope will be gratified for the main nerves of his leg, high up in the groin are shot through and the limb is at present paralysed.

I think more experience of war would make me religious. The powerlessness of the atom is terribly brought home to me, and from the highest human court of appeals we feel a great desire to apply to yet a higher authority. Philosophy cannot convince the bullet.

If you will write to me at my mother's house the letter will someday reach me and whenever it does you know I shall be delighted. If the war should drag out to six months or a year and this should come to you before it ends, anything that you can do to urge my release upon this government will make me still more in your debt. If nothing can be done, my detention – unwarranted, as I hold, and not fair war – will only make one tiny item in the long account that stands between Boer and Briton; which has been piling up for a century, but will be settled one way or the other before we meet. Once more thanking you for your kindness in telegraphing, and wishing you all good luck, Believe me.

Always your sincere friend
Winston Spencer Churchill

Nov 30th 1899 (I am 25 today – it is terrible to think how little time remains!)[42]

The last line is poignant and, in retrospect, ironic given Churchill's long life. But, as a young man, Winston believed that male Churchill life spans were short and that he might well die in his forties as had his father. It may, in part, explain his impatience at spending any more of that span in prison when, two weeks later, the opportunity to escape presented itself. Churchill was as impulsive – and reckless – here as he had been on the battlefields of India, Sudan and South Africa. But then he always believed in his star.

Chapter 10
'The Perfect Man'

New York City
14 December 1900

Winston Churchill looked expectantly out over the crowd. Impressive and a far cry from his first visit to America five years ago when no one knew him save his relatives and the people to whom he was introduced by Bourke Cockran.

In fact, it was a far cry from only a year ago when he had been the involuntary guest of the Boer Republic in a prisoner of war camp in Pretoria. They had detained him quite unfairly, of course, because he was a war correspondent and not a soldier. The distinction had been lost on the Boers, naturally, and the fact that Churchill had rallied the men on the train to withstand the Boer attack and help the train escape the ambush had much to do with it.

But he had shown them, hadn't he? Escaped and made his way over hundreds of miles of enemy territory and him not speaking a word of that vile Dutch-derived language, Afrikaans. As a consequence, Winston Churchill was a household name among the English-speaking peoples, and it had played no small part in his election to Parliament in Oldham in September, avenging the previous summer's loss.

Now he was rubbing salt in the wounds he had inflicted on the hide of the Boers. He had just completed a whirlwind speaking tour of Great Britain on the subject of his experiences in the South African War for £3,000 simply for doing what he did best – talking about himself. Now he was set to duplicate that in North America. First the East Coast of the United States, then up into Canada, followed by a swing back through the States.

Churchill was pleased. His boyhood dream of serving in Parliament had been achieved, but more than that he had become his own man. He had managed to accumulate in the last two years from his book royalties, speaking engagements and articles the sum of £10,000, which the financier, Sir Ernest Casell, a great friend of his father, was investing for him in the City. Not many young men his age with no inheritance could boast of having done the same. Not that Churchill would ever boast about money. Money was to be used, not talked about.

There was only one dark cloud on Churchill's horizon. Pamela Plowden. His beautiful Pamela, the only woman with whom he could ever happily spend the rest of his life. After his escape from the Boers and the fame which followed, Pamela wanted him to come home to her and start his political career.

Churchill had declined. He tried to explain to Pamela that it was a matter of honour to him. He could not return to England until, at the least, Great Britain had turned the corner in the South African War. But that was only partially true, and while she said nothing, he strongly suspected she knew it was his ambition which compelled him to stay and to risk his life as a soldier and correspondent in the relief of the siege of Ladysmith and then with General Sir Ian Hamilton on his fabled march. An ambition which matched, if not exceeded, his love for her.

It had been short-sighted of him to be as open and candid in his letters to Pamela about his involvement in battles as he was in his letters to his mother. Like Pamela, he knew Mamma worried about his safety. What mother wouldn't? But he had to write her letters every week, at least, and if he had been in battles or, heaven forbid, wounded and hadn't told her, she would never forgive him. Besides, she believed in Winston's star as much as her own. Pamela was different. She loved him, but she did not believe in destiny, at least not the same way he and his mother did. She worried too much, but in hindsight who could blame her?

By the time of the battle at Diamond Hill last April, Churchill already had acquired what he most valued: a reputation for personal courage. So, as a correspondent, he didn't have to take an active part in the British effort to capture the commanding heights of Diamond Hill. But he did. It was a calculated risk, to be sure, but not a heedless one. Because of what he had done, the British captured Diamond Hill and Ian Hamilton had recommended him for the Victoria Cross, England's highest military honour and something Churchill had long coveted. Prior to Diamond Hill, he never had the opportunity to so distinguish himself in such a valorous way.

Pamela had not been impressed. To her it was one more instance of Winston's risk-taking coming before her and their love for each other. Even with her father's refusal to consent to their marriage, Churchill had thought he could still bring her around. But it hadn't been a good sign when she declined to join him in Oldham last September for his election campaign. Why couldn't she see? He was safe now. He knew he could make money writing. Wasn't £10,000 proof enough? Not to mention another £5,000 he was aiming for with a biography of his father. And now Parliament. Surely she knew no one got shot writing or standing for election. There was still Canada. He would see her in Ottawa next month and attempt to redeem himself. Never give in, that was his motto. But he knew his chances were slim now whereas a year ago they weren't.

The loud applause of the crowd drew Churchill's attention away from his thoughts and back to his purpose for being here. A warm reception, he thought and then realized it wasn't for him. A man in a white linen suit, bushy white hair and a full white moustache was standing at the podium. Sam Clemens, better known to all as Mark Twain. Cockran had introduced them, and Churchill had fawned over the American writer. He had purchased all twenty-five volumes of Mark Twain's writings, and Cockran had persuaded the author not only to sign the volumes but to introduce Churchill tonight, the inaugural speech of his tour.

The audience had laughed again, and Churchill listened closely now as Twain's introduction concluded:

> *I shall presently have the pleasure of introducing to you an honoured friend of mine, Winston Churchill, member of Parliament, and although he and I do not agree as to the righteousness of the South African war, that's not of the least consequence, for people who are worth anything never do agree . . . I think that England sinned when she got herself into a war in South Africa which she could have avoided, just as we have sinned by getting into a similar war in the Philippines. Mr. Churchill by his father is an Englishman, by his mother he is an American, no doubt a blend that makes the perfect man. England and America; we are kin. And now that we are also kin in sin, there is nothing more to be desired. The harmony is perfect – like Mr. Churchill himself, whom I now have the honour to present to you.[1]*

Two weeks after his letter to Cockran, Churchill's confinement in Pretoria became too much to take. He had decided – correctly as it turned out – that the Boers weren't buying his excuse that he was only a correspondent and weren't about to release someone with such a well-known political name.

Having failed in his efforts to secure his release voluntarily, Churchill determined to escape. He joined a plot conceived by Captain Haldane and another British soldier who spoke both Afrikaans and a native language. The plan was to escape through the window of a latrine. Churchill was the first out the window and over the wall. He was also the only one to make it because the patrolling sentry made it impossible for the other two. After waiting an hour and a half and conversing with Haldane through the latrine window, Churchill determined to go it alone, and as he later described it, he got up 'without any attempt at concealment' and walked straight out at the gate into the streets of Pretoria.[2]

Churchill's escape made headlines around the world, and the Boers posted a £25 reward for him 'dead or alive'. Churchill walked through Pretoria unrecognized until he came to the railway leading to Portuguese East Africa and hopped aboard the train, concealing himself beneath empty coal bags. Churchill was lucky to make it as far as Witbank, 75 miles from Pretoria and still 200 miles from the frontier with Portuguese East Africa. He was luckier still to happen on the house of John Howard, the British manager of coal mines in Witbank, who hid Churchill in one of the mines and engaged the local storekeeper, Charles Burnham, to smuggle Churchill out of the country by train, concealed in a consignment of cotton bales Burnham was shipping to the port at Delagoa Bay in Portuguese East Africa. Churchill made it to Delagoa Bay on 21 December 1899 and by 23 December had returned safely to Durban, where he found that he had become world famous overnight, nowhere more so than in England, which hailed him as a hero.

Churchill spent Christmas Eve at the headquarters of General Redvers Buller, scarcely a few hundred yards from the location where he had been captured by the Boers thirty-six days earlier. In January 1900, General Buller gave Churchill a commission as a lieutenant in the South African Light Horse despite the fact that he continued to serve as a war correspondent for the *Morning Post*. The War Office had prohibited soldiers from holding a dual position, largely because of Churchill's dispatches during the Omdurman Campaign and his subsequent book. Buller indicated in a letter to a friend why he had been inclined to ignore the prohibition:

Winston Churchill turned up here yesterday escaped from Pretoria. He really is a fine fellow and I must say I admire him greatly. I wish he was leading irregular troops instead of writing for a rotten paper. We are very short of good men, as he appears to be, out here.[3]

Buller specified Churchill was to receive no pay from the Army while serving as a correspondent.

Churchill didn't care and was soon in the thick of fighting at the battle of Spion Kop, writing in late January to Pamela Plowden:

The scenes on Spion Kop were among the strangest and most terrible I have ever witnessed . . . I had five very dangerous days – continually under shell and rifle fire and once the feather on my hat was cut through by a bullet. But in the end I came serenely through.[4]

Pamela was not so serene and had been urging Churchill to come home as he had certainly achieved the notoriety and, indeed, public acclaim he was seeking. His escape had been the one bright spot for the British in their Black Week of the Boer War where, Churchill wrote, they had 'suffered staggering defeats, and casualties on a scale unknown to England since the Crimean War'. Churchill declined Pamela's entreaties, writing her that: 'I am quite certain that I will not leave Africa till the matter is settled. I should forfeit my self-respect for ever if I tried to shield myself like that behind an easily obtained reputation for courage. No possible advantage politically could compensate – besides believe me none would result . . . but I have a good belief that I am to be of some use and therefore to be spared.'[5]

He continued to be fatalistic in his letters to Pamela, however, even as he professed his love for her, telling her in a 10 February 1900 letter that 'I pray to God that I may have no thoughts for myself when the time comes – but for you my darling always.'[6] In late February, Churchill wrote her in the midst of combat: 'They have begun shelling us again which is a nuisance' but assures her that 'my nerves were never better and I think I care less for bullets every day.'[7]

On 22 March 1900, he wrote jealous and insensitive comments to her of a fellow soldier who had died whom they both knew:

[I]t was very sad his dying. Why were you so mysterious about him? I knew him fairly well at one time, but I thought him a shallow and unstable creature with a sanguine temperament. I wonder at his having influenced you. It is vy sad for you all your friends dying in the war. I trust I shall not fulfill the general rule.[8]

Churchill's mother, Lady Randolph, joined him in South Africa in late January along with his brother, Jack. Lady Randolph had organized and raised funds from Americans for sending a hospital ship, the *Maine*, to South Africa while Jack, with his brother's help, also had been named a lieutenant in the South African Light Horse. Despite his brother being wounded in a minor skirmish on 12 February 1900, Churchill persevered, through heavy fighting, and was with the first relief column on 28 February 1900 which lifted the siege of Ladysmith. Churchill stayed in Ladysmith for over a month, where he started work on his fourth book, *London to Ladysmith via Pretoria.*

His writing notwithstanding, Churchill was still very much engaged in the war against the Boers, heedlessly taking chances with his life on occasions where only his death would have afforded him any more publicity. On one occasion, in April 1900, Churchill, as a correspondent, joined a cavalry attempt to capture a small hill, racing a group of Boer horsemen to the summit. The Boers won, and Churchill and the others were in danger of being cut off. They had just dismounted when the Boers arrived and started firing. Churchill's horse was spooked and bolted, leaving him behind and on foot. Dodging bullets, he ran towards his own men and was saved by a trooper who picked him up but whose horse was killed in the process.

On another occasion in late May 1900, Winston risked being shot as a spy when, based on a report from a Frenchman he had just interviewed for an article, he rode a bicycle through the middle of Boer-occupied Johannesburg, dressed in civilian clothes, carrying a British military report from General Hamilton to Lord Roberts.

As a reward for his daring in Johannesburg, however, Lord Roberts let Churchill and his cousin, the Duke of Marlborough, ride at the head of the column which entered Pretoria a few days later. Churchill and his cousin made a beeline towards the prisoner of war camp he had escaped six months earlier, where, in poetic justice, he liberated the camp. As one of the freed prisoners wrote in his diary:

> . . . suddenly Winston Churchill came galloping over the hill and tore down the Boer flag, and hoisted ours amidst cheers and our people some of which had been in for 6 months or more were free and at once the Boer guards were put inside and our prisoners guard over *them*! It was roarable and splendid.[9]

On 11 June 1900, Churchill's initiative under fire enabled the British to win the decisive Battle of Diamond Hill. General Hamilton wrote in his memoirs:

> . . . Winston gave the embattled hosts at Diamond Hill an exhibition of conspicuous gallantry (the phrase often used in

recommendations for the V.C.) for which he has never received full credit .... The capture of Diamond Hill meant the winning of the battle, ending as it did with a general retirement by the Boers; also it meant that it was the turning point of the war. The capture of Pretoria had not been the true turning point but rather this battle of Diamond Hill which proved that, humanly speaking, Pretoria would not be retaken.[10]

Hamilton recommended Churchill for the Victoria Cross, but Roberts and Kitchener refused because Churchill had been only a press correspondent.

Two days before Diamond Hill, Churchill had written to his mother: '. . . I need not say how anxious I am to come back to England. Politics, Pamela, finances and books all need my attention . . .'[11] Such a ranking of Churchill's priorities – only days away from once more risking his life – probably explains as well as anything why Pamela did not defy her father and agree to marry Churchill. While now self-supporting, Churchill was by no means wealthy and the fact that he ignored her entreaties to return home to her after his escape and continued to write her letters describing the danger he was enduring could only reinforce for her the fact that she would always come second in Winston's life.

Churchill returned home on 20 July 1900 on the *Dunottar Castle*, the same ship on which he had arrived in South Africa eight months earlier. An election was in the offing, and Churchill set out once more for Oldham, where he was welcomed with enthusiasm. In a letter to his brother Jack, Churchill wrote:

Over 10,000 people turned out in the streets with flags and drums beating and shouted themselves hoarse for two hours, and although it was 12 o'clock before I left the Conservative Club, the streets were still crowded with people.[12]

Moreton Frewen proudly wrote Cockran about his nephew's return to England:

My wife is away, chiefly to meet and greet Winston who is back with all the honours of a successful war. Did dashing things; the race has produced no such soldier since John Duke. [Churchill's ancestor, the first Duke of Marlborough][13]

The 1900 campaign, the Khaki election, was fought largely on the issue of the Boer War. Parliament was not dissolved until the end of the summer, 17 September 1900, and the election was spread over a three-week period, with the Oldham constituency scheduled for an early vote on 1 October 1900. Two Liberal seats were up, and the Conservatives took both. It was close. The war hero Churchill was elected, placing second, sixteen votes behind the leading vote-getter, but only 222 votes ahead of the third-place finisher out of over 50,000 votes cast. But he had won. He was now in Parliament and that would make all the difference.

During 1900, Cockran was the leading spokesman in the United States against the Boer War, on which he gave well-received and highly publicized speeches in New York, Chicago and Boston. He spoke at Faneuil Hall in Boston on 26 March 1900 where he said that:

> This war on the Boers is a renewal of the old attempt by the governing class of England to undermine the institutions to which the English people have always been attached. In condemning this unholy war we are serving the highest interests of English men and women whose labor, intelligence and virtues have made England a mighty force in the civilization of the world. This is a war of the London smart set, the Stock Exchange gamblers and the street mobs. It has never been approved by the sober judgment of the English people; it is abhorrent to the conscience of the American people. It is a fashionable war on both sides of the Atlantic; it is a popular war on neither side.[14]

It was a popular view in America. Cockran's friend and client, Joseph Pulitzer, sent his lawyer a telegram of congratulations after the Boston speech:

> Your speech last night in Faneuil Hall was a noble plea for the little South African republic which is now being butchered to make a jingo holiday. You never spoke with more feeling or greater power in behalf of humanity and justice. You have earned the gratitude of every American who loves liberty and abhors tyranny.[15]

That summer, the Democrats once more nominated William Jennings Bryan, the man Cockran had opposed in 1896 over the issue of free silver.

Bryan still supported free silver as did the Democratic Party platform in 1900, but Cockran nonetheless supported Bryan and campaigned actively for him. Cockran hadn't changed his position on gold in 1900 just as he hadn't changed his position on free trade in 1896 when backing the protectionist McKinley. But free trade versus tariffs wasn't an issue in the 1896 campaign just as gold versus silver was not a vital issue in 1900. Cockran believed, incorrectly as it turned out, that American imperialism would be the issue that would defeat the Republicans.

Cockran was as vocal against the American war in the Philippines during the campaign as he had been against the British war in South Africa. Cockran spoke all over the country for Bryan, but especially on the East Coast his speeches drew bigger crowds and more enthusiastic receptions than did Bryan himself. Nevertheless, it was the booming American economy which carried McKinley and his new Vice President Theodore Roosevelt to victory.

Notwithstanding his vigorous campaign for Bryan, Cockran had been paying attention to British politics as well and, in particular, had been following closely his protégé Winston's electoral prospects. Upon hearing of Churchill's election victory, Cockran wrote him a letter inviting Churchill to once more visit him in America after the election. Cockran's letter does not survive, but Churchill's reply does. He clearly took pleasure in telling his mentor how much he was now in demand as a speaker 'engaged on a fighting tour of the kind you know':

Oct. 7, 1900   105 Mount Street W.
Private

My dear Bourke Cockran,

I was delighted to get your kind letter and shall look forward vy much to meeting you again.

I daresay you will have learned from the newspapers that I have been returned to Parliament as representative of almost the greatest constituency in England, containing 30,000 thriving working men electors; and this victory happening to come at the outset of the general contest, was of great use and value to the Conservative party, as it gave them a lead and started the movement. Moreover since to win involved turning over 1500 votes previously hostile – and recorded against me only a year before – it was something in the nature of an achievement. At any rate, I have suddenly become one of the two or three most popular speakers in this election, and am now engaged on a fighting tour, of the kind you know – great audiences (five and six thousand people) twice & even three times a day, bands, crowds and enthusiasm of all kinds.

Well – it will be vy pleasant to meet you again and to see something of the America quiet and seclusion after the clatter here.

Yours vy sincerely
Winston S. Churchill[16]

Money, or his lack of it, was very much on Churchill's mind in the fall after his election to Parliament. Thereafter, he toured the country during the remainder of the three-week polling period speaking on behalf of many Conservative candidates, including Arthur Balfour and Joseph Chamberlain. After the election concluded, he contemplated a proposed lecture tour in England and he wrote to his mother:

But you must remember how much money means to me and how much I need it for political expense and other purposes, and if I can make three thousand pounds by giving a score of lectures on the big towns throughout England on the purely military aspect of the war, it is very hard for me to refuse ...[17]

Churchill didn't refuse and ended up with over £3700 for twenty-nine speeches during a thirty-day period in November.

Churchill had even higher hopes for a lucrative pay day from a North America tour. As he wrote to his mother: 'I will not go to the Untied States unless guaranteed *at least* a thousand pounds a month for three months and I should expect a great deal more. Five thousand pounds is not too much for making oneself so cheap.'[18]

Once the details of his North American tour were shored up, Churchill wrote to Cockran. His American agent, Major Pond, had advised Churchill not to stay with Cockran for fear that his well-known pro-Boer, anti-British sympathies would diminish a pro-British turnout for Churchill's lectures. Money was at stake, and Churchill did not pretend to know more of American sentiment than his agent but he trusted Cockran's judgment. He wrote to him and frankly put forth his agent's concerns but left the final decision to Cockran.

25 Nov. 1900   105 Mount Street W.

My Dear Bourke,

I sail on the 1st Dec. & if all is well shall set foot on American soil on t[the] 6th or 7th. I sail in t[the] good ship "Lucania". I have been looking forward very much to coming to stay with you, where I know from experience I shall be entirely happy & comfortable. But Pond has written to me suggesting that if I come to stay with you it will be made use of by the newspapers to show that I have interfered in American politics. Of course I consider this all nonsense because in this country, as you know, we make it a rule & keep it to some extent never to bring politics into private life or private life into politics but I know not how bitter your struggles may be in t[the] States, and I put myself frankly in your hands. I have first of all to think of making my lecture tour a financial success & consequently as I shall be the butt for a good deal of idle comment I must be very guarded in my action. I do hope you will understand my position for you know that altho' I disagree very strongly from yours views – as you do from mine – on t[the] South African question I value your friendship & companionship very highly & have looked forward for a long time to some more pleasant talk & discussion in your house, 753, if I remember rightly, 5th Avenue.

Will you do me the kindness & see Major Pond & settle the matter from the point of view of my own interest for I pursue profit not pleasure in the States this time. If after talking it over with him you think his fears that my staying with you, might be misunderstood by, shd I call it, – the Pro-British section of the public – are all moonshine please allow me very heartily & with the greatest satisfaction to accept your kind invitation. If on the other hand you think it would perhaps do me harm & cause ill feeling among people on the other side of politics – our side to some extent, I fear now – then I think I had better go to a hotel, but I leave the matter to you knowing you are a good friend & will understand my position & decide what is best for me. I am looking forward very much to seeing you again although I feel no small trepidation at embarking upon the stormy ocean of American thought and discussion.

Yours vy sincerely
Winston S. Churchill[19]

In the event, Churchill stayed with Cockran in his Fifth Avenue apartment just as he had done in 1895. And his pro-Boer sympathies notwithstanding, Cockran did his best to make his young friend's tour a success, hosting a large dinner party at the Waldorf before Churchill's inaugural speech on the tour in New York. Through Cockran, Churchill met Samuel Clemens, whom he admired as a writer and who, as Mark Twain, introduced him to the New York audience. Churchill's American speaking tour was a financial disappointment, however, as he wrote to his mother on 21 December 1900 from Boston. He cleared only £1600 in a tour which started on 8 December and continued through 2 February 1901. He had an enjoyable time with Cockran, however, and asked her to write Cockran a letter of thanks:

> I stayed with Bourke Cockran in New York, who worked indefatigably to make the lecture a success and who gave a large dinner party at the Waldorf before it.
>
> I should like you to write him a line if you have any time because he has treated me in a most friendly way and that in spite of his strong Boer sympathies.[20]

Jennie undoubtedly did write Cockran, but her letter is not found in the Cockran papers. Moreton Frewen also wrote to Cockran thanking him for the hospitality he had shown his nephew:

> It was so good of you to take such care of Winston; he writes most grateful and sensible of your kindness which we all value, I need not tell you, very highly. He is a dear old boy & I think he will do well; he says that notwithstanding your strong Boer leanings, nothing could have been pleasanter than your relations! That is how it is when you & I get together; I disagree with all you say and think, but we never get to the point where we pull our guns![21]

Churchill's speech on the tour was illustrated with photographic slides projected by a kerosene lamp. Reviews were generally favourable. The *St. Paul Dispatch* wrote:

> Lieut. Churchill seems English only in one thing, and that is his accent. His sense of dry humour is peculiarly American. He is

open-hearted and perfectly fair in speaking of the good qualities of the Boers as fighters. What he does not admire about them he leaves unsaid.[22]

Churchill also visited Washington, staying with Republican Senator Chauncey Depew, who introduced Churchill to President McKinley, 'with whom I was considerably impressed' he later wrote to his mother.[23] Earlier, he had dined in Albany with Governor Theodore Roosevelt, the vice president elect. Given the friendship that would develop over the next ten years between Cockran and Roosevelt, personally and politically, it is mildly surprising that Roosevelt formed on this occasion an instant dislike for Churchill, which he maintained for the rest of his life. Given Cockran's high regard for both men, the answer once offered by Roosevelt's daughter, Alice Longworth, as to why her father disliked Churchill takes on added significance: 'Because they were so alike.'[24] Which indeed they were: well-known writers before they were politicians, impulsive risk takers, soldiers and accomplished speakers, one called a 'cowboy' by his detractors, the other a 'half-breed American'. Both eventually held their country's highest office and each were Nobel Prize winners, giants of their time. Winston apparently allowed Roosevelt to see all his faults on their first meeting, and Roosevelt had no occasion thereafter to discover Churchill's virtues.

Churchill spent Christmas in Ottawa as a guest of the Governor General Lord Minto, a contemporary and close friend of his parents. Pamela was also a guest. Their romance did not resume but not for want of affection on Winston's part. A New Year's Day letter to his mother makes evident that the wound of what was now their fading romance was still fresh and painful in Winston's mind:

Pamela was there – very pretty and apparently quite happy. We had no painful discussions, but there is no doubt in my mind that she is the only woman I could ever live happily with. I hope you will not write to me such things as in your last letter but one, when you say that "Perhaps Lady G. had sent P. to Canada so that the spectacle of Captain Graham being in love with me may clinch matters" or words to that effect. They are not at all kind & I do not think they are at all true either.[25]

In 1899, Pamela's father is reported to have refused Churchill his daughter's hand in marriage for monetary reasons.[26] Churchill later wrote in a letter to her that 'for marriage two conditions are necessary: money and consentment of both parties'.[27] If, indeed, money is the primary reason the two of them did not marry, Churchill was still stung by it because in that same New Year's Day 1901 letter to his mother where he wrote of Pamela that 'she is the only woman I could ever live happily with', he also wrote that, 'I am vy proud of the fact that there is not one person in a million who at my age could have earned £10,000 without any capital in less than two years.'[28]

After leaving Ottawa, he resumed his speaking tour, and on 20 January 1901, he wrote to Pamela upon the occasion of Queen Victoria's death, which caused the cancellation of his lecture tour. It was, he told her, a 'considerable inconvenience [which] complicates and clouds all my plans, disturbing not only nations but Winstons'. Acknowledging the change in the relationship, he told her: 'There is that between us, which if it should grow no stronger, will last forever. God bless you. Write [me] about ordinary things.'[29]

Pamela married Victor, the Second Earl of Lytton, a friend of Churchill's, in 1902, but Winston continued to write to her thereafter, his love for her still very much in evidence. Herewith a sampling:

[3 October 1906:] I often think of you & dwell with comfort & joy upon the profound associations of sympathy & friendship which unite us.[30]
[23 May 1907:] [H]ence no more to be called (since it prevents my coming to you) the "glorious first of June". The world is vry evil: & tonight my heart is sorrowful to think how little I see of you, & what gulfs & cliffs & dusty deserts separate true friends.[31]

Replying to a letter from her, Churchill wrote on 19 September 1907 that 'alas with my busy selfish life – I fear, as it is, I fail too often in the little offices which keep friendship sweet & warm. But you always understand.' He then told her that he found more pleasure in writing to her than being with other women – 'Those strange glittering beings with whom I have little or nothing in common' – cautioning her that this last comment was 'for the especial delectation of the demure kitten purring & prinking over what I trust will ever be to her the sweet & abundant milk of life.'[32] The pet phrase 'cat' or 'kitten' was to become a staple of

Churchill's endearing, lifelong correspondence with his wife Clementine, but she was not the first to be so labelled.

At age twenty-five, Churchill was now firmly in the middle of the novice phase's second period, 'entering the adult world' – establishing a first life structure as a politician and writer, no longer dependent financially on his mother. His progress on all four common tasks during this phase was remarkable: forming the dream, finding a mentor who supported it and forming two occupations which furthered it. The only setback he suffered was that the love he and Pamela felt for each other did not evolve, as he had hoped, into marriage. But he still had plenty of time. There were other beautiful women to woo (three, as it turned out), but it would take a good deal of time as he did not stop loving Pamela while he searched for another perfect woman. He would eventually find her because Churchill's astonishing good fortune in war served him in good stead in love as well. But as in war, it would be a close-run thing where, once more, Churchill would be his own worst enemy.

Chapter 11
'One More Sacrifice'

15 July 1903

*The tall, imposing figure of Bourke Cockran stood on the terrace of the
National Liberal Club of England, looking out over the Thames, alone,
with his thoughts in the moonlight. He had passed it off with a laugh last
month when his friend, T.P. O'Connor, a Liberal member of Parliament
(MP) from Ireland, had suggested that he stand for Parliament at the next
by-election in Ireland. He had treated it as a joke, although O'Connor
had protested he was serious. Ireland would always be in his blood, he
assured his friend, but he was an American now through and through.
The entreaty had been made in a London pub a few days earlier where
Cockran had been sipping tea and O'Connor, if he recalled correctly, had
been on his second if not third glass of whiskey.*

*But O'Connor had been quite serious. Cockran found out the next
day, 14 June 1903, when he was the guest of honour in the Members
Dining Room of the House of Commons at a banquet given by the
Irish Nationalist Party. Over a hundred Irish and Liberal MPs had been
present, the event presided over by John Redmond, the Irish Party Leader.
Like many Irishmen, Redmond had a smooth tongue, and his words of
praise foreshadowed the trap he was about to spring.*

*'So far as Ireland is concerned', Redmond had said of Cockran that
night, 'neither fame nor fortune, brilliant success nor the applause of men
has ever been able to turn him from a steadfast and self-sacrificing
devotion to Ireland's rights.'*

*Redmond then had invited him to make 'one more sacrifice' for the
land of his birth. 'In the name of the Irish Party, I invite him to join our
ranks and give us the aid of his unparalleled experience and matchless
eloquence in what we believe are the last stages of the struggle for Irish
Rights in the British Parliament.'[1]*

*All the Liberals and Irish Party members present had stood up and
cheered. But Cockran had politely declined with a gracious tribute
to Redmond's leadership. Redmond had not given up so easily. In the
weeks that followed, many other Liberals, even Cockran's schoolboy
classmate, Bishop Clancy of Elfin, had urged him to stand for
Parliament.*

Tonight had been different. Very much different. An entreaty from John Redmond was one thing, but when it came from the next prime minister of Great Britain, that was something else entirely.

Cockran had come to England in the spring as he had been doing nearly every year since his wife's death in 1895. He had received an invitation to address the National Liberal Club earlier this year on any subject he cared to address, and he had readily accepted. The Club had even offered to pay his steamship fare from America, but he had declined. He always paid his own expenses and never charged for a speech.

Cockran had been flattered, but he had an ulterior purpose in accepting the invitation. He followed British politics fairly closely and did so for two reasons. First, he was interested in freedom for the country of his birth, which meant to him, at a minimum, devolution or, more commonly, Home Rule. Any favour he could curry among Liberal MPs would guarantee him an audience to advance his views on Ireland should they come to power. The second reason was more personal and equally close to his heart: the political fortunes of Winston Churchill.

The protectionist forces arrayed behind the Tories' Joseph Chamberlain were set to fight the next general election, surely within two years or less, on the issue of protectionism versus free trade. Old Joe had gussied it up of course, calling it not protectionism – which it surely was – but rather 'Empire Free Trade', which effectively meant giving preferential treatment to imports from the Empire and tariffs for the rest of world. True free traders, like Winston, weren't fooled and spoke out strongly against it. But party discipline was taking its toll, and while the Tory Prime Minister Lord Salisbury was publicly taking a neutral position, Cockran knew from conversations with Winston and others that Salisbury was tilting towards Chamberlain, his colonial secretary.

To his credit, Chamberlain had been quite open about what he saw as the political merits of his new protectionist policy and had even urged Winston and some of his young free trade Conservative MPs to study tariffs. But, as Winston had once told Cockran, he didn't need to study tariffs. He had learned all he needed to know from his conversations with Cockran and the books he had read, many of them at Cockran's suggestion.

So while the election was probably a year or two away, Cockran had decided to focus his speech to the Liberal Club on the issue of free trade or, what he called, the essential conditions for national prosperity and, in so doing, give the Liberals ammunition for the campaign with the same kind of metaphors and anecdotes he used to entertain American audiences.

Judging from the reaction his speech had received tonight, his audience had certainly been entertained. What he hadn't expected was Sir Henry Campbell-Bannerman's offer of an open seat for Parliament in Ireland and the promise that Cockran would be one of their leading spokesmen on economic issues in the campaign. There wasn't exactly the offer of a cabinet post in a new Liberal government. That would have been too direct, too American. But the implication, the hint, was most certainly there.

As with young O'Connor, Cockran had initially declined Campbell-Bannerman's suggestion with a laugh. But the dour Scot had assured him that he was most serious. The Liberals had plenty of members to advance their cause on the hustings, he had said, but no one, not even their best speaker Lord George, had Cockran's knack for putting the case for free trade so plainly and persuasively. Campbell-Bannerman said Edward Grey had told him he 'would give anything' to hear Cockran debate Joe Chamberlain on the issue of tariffs. Cockran had laughed and said he wouldn't mind hearing that himself, but it simply wasn't going to happen on the floor of the House of Commons.

It was strange, Cockran thought, how opportunities presented themselves at inopportune times. Even after Campbell-Bannerman had made it clear he was serious, Cockran had still politely declined, once more expressing his appreciation for the offer. But there was a time, he thought, when he would not have declined so quickly. Had it been seven or eight years earlier, he would have thought long and hard before deciding. He believed he still would have declined, but it would not have been as easy a decision as now.

Now, Boss Croker was out at Tammany Hall and Cockran was back in. If Tammany's candidate for Mayor, George McClellan, was elected in the fall, then there would be a special election to fill McClellan's vacant seat in Congress. Tammany's new leader, Charles Murphy, had asked and he had decided to accept his invitation to stand for Congress. He believed the new Tammany leaders were relatively honest, certainly in comparison with Richard Croker, which was, he allowed, faint praise. But he had never been happier than his two terms in Congress during the Cleveland Administration in the 1890s. It wouldn't be the same, of course, because he no longer had Rhoda and he had not yet found someone to replace her in his heart.

Cockran turned back from the river and walked across the terrace. Well, actually, he had once found someone to replace Rhoda in his heart *and that is why he knew that seven or eight years ago he would have seriously considered an offer to stand for Parliament. Jennie had stolen his heart in a way he could not have possibly imagined. And, truth to tell, so had her sister Leonie, who, fortunately for Cockran, was quite safely married. Cockran and Jennie had never discussed marriage, but Cockran had once enquired, obliquely, whether she ever thought of returning to America now that her husband had passed. Jennie's answer had been firm and definitive. Her family – by which she meant her sons Winston and Jack and her two sisters – were all in England and there she would stay as well. Cockran had grown to love that family, and he had carried a torch for Jennie for a good three years until her remarriage effectively extinguished it.*

When Cockran next saw Winston, he would tell him of the conversation with Campbell-Bannerman and he would pass on – with a laugh for Winston's benefit – what he said to the Liberal Party Leader. He didn't want Winston to hear about it from someone else. But, in fact, he had been quite serious and Campbell-Bannerman knew it.

'There is a young man in the Tory Party, a good friend of mine actually, who's every bit as good as me when it comes to making the benefits of free trade easy for the common man to understand. You need to cultivate his friendship. If Chamberlain gets his way, I fear my young friend may be in the wrong party.'

An unaccustomed smile spread across Campbell-Bannerman's face. 'Oh, you mean Winston?'

Cockran had returned the smile with a nod of his head.

Queen Victoria died in January and Churchill sailed from New York to England on 2 February 1901, the day of her funeral. On the voyage, he began to prepare for his maiden speech in Parliament, which he was to give on 18 February 1901. The House of Commons was full that night, Lloyd George having spoken before him. Churchill's subject was the Boer War, and he defended the Army's conduct in prosecuting it:

From what I saw of the war – and I sometimes saw something of it – I believe that as compared with other wars, especially those in which a civil population took part, this war in South Africa has been on the whole carried on with unusual humanity and generosity.[2]

But Churchill criticized proposals to impose a military government over the defeated Boers, advocating instead a civil government administered by Sir Alfred Milner.

Churchill concluded his speech with a graceful reference to his late father:

> I cannot sit down without saying how very grateful I am for the kindness and patience with which the House has heard me, and which have been extended to me, I well know, not on my own account, but because of a certain splendid memory which many hon. Members still preserve.[3]

From the beginning, Churchill began to establish himself as a rising political star. One reason for this is that Churchill had spent many years in serious preparation for his new occupation. Not many young members of Parliament (MPs) would have already read twenty-seven volumes of the *Annual Register*, especially in the way Winston did by first recording on paper his 'own opinion . . . of the subject – having regard only to general principles'.[4]

Owing to this preparation, Churchill had achieved at a younger age than other first-time MPs an ability to think for himself when presented with new issues, relying on that 'scaffolding of logical and consistent views' he had built during his years in the field based on 'general principles'. As a consequence, he did not rely on party Whips to decide how to vote. And given that his mentor Cockran was himself an ardent Liberal, it is no surprise that Churchill's views were liberal as well, supporting free speech and due process in the military, while opposing conscription and excessive military spending, all issues where Cockran would have been firmly in his corner.

Churchill's liberal views were formed at an early age and not later, as some have suggested, under the influence of Lloyd George. As he had written to his mother in the spring of 1896:

> There are no lengths to which I would not go in opposing [the Conservatives] were I in the House of Commons. I am a Liberal in all but name. My views excite the pious horror of the Mess.[5]

Five years later, Churchill was as good as his word. But Churchill never opposed his party for the sake of opposition even if it sometimes seemed that way to his elders. Even where he supported his party, however, the manner in which he did so was not always appreciated. One such example occurred in March 1901 when he spoke in support of the government against an amendment seeking to appoint a commission to enquire into the Army's dismissal of Major-General Sir Henry Colville as Commander-in-Chief of Gibraltar. Colville had been dismissed when official enquiries into his conduct in South Africa disclosed that he had failed to attempt to relieve beleaguered British troops despite being in a position to do so. Colville refused to resign quietly, the War Office dismissed him, and Colville appealed to supporters in Parliament, claiming that he had not been criticized at the time in official dispatches.

The Tory government was in an awkward position. Opposing a commission could be perceived as a cover-up. The twenty-six-year-old Churchill came to its rescue, helpfully explaining to the House that 'those who have not themselves had any actual experience of war may have some difficulty in understanding' why Colville was not criticized in official dispatches at the time. The reason, Churchill candidly continued, was that the military in war time typically do not tell the truth:

> I say that I have noticed in the last three wars in which we have been engaged a tendency among military officers . . . to hush everything up, to make everything look as fair as possible, to tell what is called the official truth, to present a version of the truth which contains about seventy-five per cent of the actual article. So long as a force gets a victory somehow, all the ugly facts are smoothed and varnished over, rotten reputations are propped up, and officers known as incapable are allowed to hang on and linger in their commands in the hope that at the end of the war they may be shunted into private life without a scandal.[6]

Nevertheless, Churchill went on to tell the House, politicians must rarely, if ever, interfere with the War Department's promotion and dismissal of officers because that process is 'the only hope for increased efficiency in the army, it is the only way in which we can prevent the upper ranks from being clogged with incapable men.'[7]

Secretary of State for War, St. John Brodrick, expressed his gratitude in a note he passed to Churchill at the end of his speech: 'May I say you will never make a better speech than you made tonight . . . It was a great success and universally recognized.'[8]

Mr. Brodrick's comments on the next Churchill speech in the House on military matters were not so kind, expressing the hope that one day 'the hereditary qualities he possesses of eloquence and courage may be tempered also by discarding the hereditary desire to run Imperialism on the cheap.'[9] The occasion for these comments found its origin two days before Churchill had spoken in the Colville debate when Brodrick had finalized his plan for Army Reform, featuring the creation of three regular army corps. On 13 May, Churchill made a major speech in the House opposing 'Mr. Brodrick's Army'.

Churchill began his speech by making reference to his father's resignation fifteen years earlier as Chancellor of the Exchequer over excessive military spending. He then turned to Brodrick's main proposal and foreshadowed what the 20th century would become:

> I complain of the increase in Regular soldiers, and particularly of the provision of the three army corps which are to be kept ready for expeditionary purposes. I contend that they ought to be reduced by two army corps, on the ground that one is quite enough to fight savages, and three are not enough even to begin to fight Europeans. . . . A European war cannot be anything but a cruel, heartrending struggle, which, if we are ever to enjoy the bitter fruits of victory, must demand, perhaps for several years, the whole manhood of the nation, the entire suspension of peaceful industries, and the concentrating to one end of every vital energy in the community . . . a European war can only end in the ruin of the vanquished and the scarcely less fatal commercial dislocation and the exhaustion of the conquerors. Democracy is more vindictive than Cabinets. The wars of peoples will be more terrible than those of kings.[10]

During the winter of 1901, Churchill read and was much impressed by *Poverty, A Study of Town Life*, by Seebohm Rowntree. In December, Churchill wrote to a friend about the book:

> It is quite evident from the figures which he adduces that the American labourer is a stronger, larger, healthier, better fed, and consequently more efficient animal than a large proportion of our population, and this is surely a fact which our unbridled Imperialists, who have no thought but to pile up armaments,

taxation and territory, should not lose sight of. For my own part,
I see little glory in an Empire which can rule the waves and is unable
to flush its sewers.[11]

Throughout the winter, Churchill continued to give speeches on the war in
South Africa and Brodrick's three permanent army corps, whose original
proposal had included a call for conscription. After that proposal had been
dropped, Churchill told the Commons on 6 March 1902 that

[M]y right honourable friend has finally and thoroughly abandoned
the fatal and foolish theory of conscription, which no doubt would
be still of some use providing occupation for members in another
place [the House of Lords] who had not got too much to do . . .[12]

During his first full year in Parliament, Churchill had been critical of the
government, but in a manner consistent with his father's policies of Tory
Democracy. In 1902, Churchill began to write his father's biography. It
would be published, to great critical acclaim, in 1906. During this period,
Churchill also began to take more positions adverse to the government
and consistent with the Liberal opposition. One of the first was an issue
dear to Bourke Cockran's heart and on which he and Churchill had
conversed – free speech.

In April 1902, Churchill voted with the Liberal Party against the Tory
Government in support of a British journalist named Cartwright, who, after
serving a twelve-month sentence in South Africa for criminal libel over an
article critical of Kitchener, was denied the right to return to England. The
reason the Government offered was that 'it seemed inexpedient to increase
the number of persons in this country who disseminated anti-British
propaganda.' Speaking in the House, Churchill said:

What reason has the government to be afraid of Mr. Cartwright?
There are many people in this country who spread what is called
anti-British propaganda, but does that alter the opinion of the
British people? Has it in any way impaired the security of the British
Government? No Government has benefitted so much by the strong
support and opinions of the masses of the country as this Government. No Government has less right not to allow those masses
to receive any opinion within the law which may be properly
expressed to them. This is a great constitutional principle.[13]

Churchill and several other young Tory MPs who voted with the Liberals on that issue dined that evening with Joseph Chamberlain after the Liberal Party's motion had been defeated. Chamberlain criticized the young members of Parliament for their lack of support over Cartwright, saying: 'What is the use of supporting your own Government only when it is right? It is just when it is in this sort of pickle that you ought to have come to our aid.'[14]

Churchill records in *My Early Life* that at the conclusion of this dinner where Chamberlain had been 'most gay and captivating', he offered this parting advice:

> You young gentlemen have entertained me royally, and in return
> I shall give you a priceless secret. Tariffs! There are the politics of the
> future, and of the near future. Study them closely and make yourselves
> masters of them, and you will not regret your hospitality to me.[15]

Indeed, it was Chamberlain and the Conservative Party's support for tariffs and opposition to free trade which was to lead the young Churchill in less than two years out of his party and across the floor to join the Liberals.

Arson at the Royal Military College, Sandhurst, was the occasion for Churchill to once more publicly criticize the government. An inside job was suspected. Four fires had already been set and when a fifth fire broke out on 25 June 1902 in 'C' Company, the Army's Commander-In-Chief, Lord Roberts, ordered that all cadets in 'C' Company would be sent home without taking their examinations and all servants would be dismissed unless (a) they had an alibi and could prove they were not present when the fire was set or (b) those who set the fire confessed. No one came forward, and twenty-nine cadets were sent home and three servants dismissed when they could not furnish alibis.

Just as he had spoken out strongly for free speech in the Cartwright affair, Churchill did the same for due process in the military. In a letter published in *The Times* on 7 July 1902, Churchill wrote:

> I will not take occasion here to comment upon this travesty of
> justice further than to point out three cardinal principles of equity
> which it violates – that suspicion is not evidence; that accused
> persons should be heard in their own defence; and that it is for the
> accuser to prove his charge, not for the defendant to prove his

innocence. I therefore invite [the government] to answer three
questions: – What is the charge against these 29 cadets? What is
the evidence in support of it? When and before whom has it been
proved? These are short, plain questions, which not only involve the
interests of innocent and deserving people, but also raise various
ancient and valuable principles; and, if fair play is still honoured in
the British Army, they ought to be answered.[16]

Eventually, Lord Roberts reversed course and promised that each case
would be reviewed individually and investigated again. In the event,
all three servants were reinstated along with twenty-seven cadets.

Churchill was now making his own way in the world and did not need
his mother's assistance in making political contacts as much as he had in
the past. Still, Jennie remained a close friend of the King, and Winston
was not shy about making use of that connection. From Balmoral Castle,
where he was on holiday with the King in the fall of 1902, Churchill
wrote to his mother with helpful suggestions on how she should communicate to the King, when next they met, Churchill's feelings about his
own visit with the King: 'You will see the King on Weds when he comes
to Invercauld; mind you gush to him about my having written to you
saying how much etc etc I had enjoyed myself here.'[17]

During Churchill's first two years in Parliament, no correspondence
between Cockran and Churchill survives. Cockran visited England
annually during this period – the spring of 1901, 1902 and 1903. It was
Cockran's custom since 1895 to spend three to five months a year in
Europe, and it is likely that they met whenever they both were in London
at the same time. Frewen wrote in a letter to Cockran on 12 November
1901: 'Winston I saw last night & told him I was going to write to you;
he told me to send his love & greetings.'[18] Sir Horace Plunkett was
present in April 1902 for a conversation between Cockran and Churchill,
about which he later wrote to Cockran:

I cannot tell you how I enjoyed your visit brief as it was. I have
seldom heard a more brilliant conversation than that between you
and Winston Churchill.[19]

Among Churchill's other liberal views expressed during this period were
those on free trade and protectionist tariffs. They were to land Churchill

in hot water over the next few years, eventually including a vote of
no confidence by the Conservative Party Association in his Oldham
constituency. The leading Tory protectionist, Joseph Chamberlain, called
it Tariff Reform and Imperial Preference, but it was still protectionism
plain and simple. In the fall of 1902, Churchill wrote to a constituent,
elaborating upon his views on free trade:

> [I]t would seem to me a fantastic policy to endeavour to shut the
> British Empire up in a ringed fence. It is very large, and there are
> a good many things which can be produced in it, but the world is
> larger & produces some better things than can be found in the
> British Empire. Why should we deny ourselves the good and varied
> merchandise which the traffic of the world offers, more especially
> since the more we trade with others, the more they must trade with
> us; for it is quite clear that we give them something else back for
> everything they give to us. Our planet is not a very big one com-
> pared with the other celestial bodies, and I see no particular reason
> why we should endeavour to make inside our planet a smaller
> planet called the British Empire, cut off by impassable space from
> everything else.[20]

The correspondence between Churchill and Cockran resumed in 1903,
which was a critical and decisive year in Churchill's political career, the
year when the Tory Party split over the issue of free trade and Churchill
began to seriously contemplate joining the Liberal Party. Cockran himself
was invited to give a speech at the National Liberal Club in London
where he literally provided the Liberals with a keynote speech ('The
Essential Conditions of National Prosperity'), on which the Party would
campaign two years later, with Cockran's own protégé delivering the
most devastating attacks on the Tories.

The free trade battle was joined in earnest on 15 May 1903 when
the Colonial Secretary Joseph Chamberlain delivered a speech at
Birmingham advocating the imposition of preferential tariffs. Two weeks
later, Chamberlain spoke on the subject in the House. Foreshadowing his
eventual departure from the Tory party over this issue, Churchill rose
immediately in reply. Whenever he spoke of tariffs, Churchill would
frequently refer to the political corruption which would flourish in their

wake and cite the Republican Party in America as an example, showing he had absorbed his lessons from Cockran. He did so on this occasion:

> This move means a change, not only in historic English Parties, but in the conditions of our public life. The old Conservative Party, with its religious convictions and constitutional principles, will disappear, and a new Party will arise like perhaps the Republican Party of the United States of America – rich, materialist, and secular – whose opinions will turn on tariffs, and who will cause the lobbies to be crowded with the touts of protected industries. What is the cause of this change? Never was the wealth of the country greater, or the trade returns higher, or the loyalty of the colonies more pronounced. Is it that we are tired of these good days?[21]

To Cockran, free trade was a vital part of a foreign policy designed to achieve peace among nations. It was a constant theme in all his speeches on the subject. The young Churchill bought the argument in its entirety and, a week after Chamberlain's Birmingham speech, wrote on this topic in a letter to Moore Bagley, a Tory free trader from Birmingham. 'I do not want a self-contained Empire,' Churchill wrote.

> It is very much better that the great nations of the world should be interdependent one upon the other than that they should be independent of each other. That makes powerfully for peace and it is chiefly through the cause of the great traffic of one great nation with another during the last twenty-five years, that the peace of Europe has been preserved through so many crises.[22]

A few days later, Churchill underscored just how important free trade was to him when he wrote to the Prime Minister A.E. Balfour and informed him that he would cease his long and vigorous opposition to the government's plan to increase the size of the army if Balfour would continue to support free trade:

> I feel perhaps that I may have sometimes been the cause of embarrassment to the government. It is difficult to write about such things because of obvious rejoinders, but I should like to tell you

that an attempt on your part to preserve the Free Trade policy &
character of the Tory party would command my absolute loyalty.
I would even swallow six army corps – if it would make any
difference & sink all minor differences. But if on the other hand
you have made up your mind & there is no going back, I must
reconsider my position in politics.[23]

In America, Cockran was beginning to resurrect his political career after
a rapprochement with Tammany. Boss Croker had been forced out as
Tammany's leader in early 1902. The new leader, Charles Murphy, made
an overture to Cockran, who responded positively. Cockran wrote to
Moreton Frewen on 26 September 1902 of this development:

What all this may portend I don't undertake to say, but I have never
for a moment been shaken in my firm belief that while the decadence
of politics seems to make the ground under one's feet somewhat
uncertain, the progress of the race will continue and all things are
ordained to promote it.[24]

Murphy's overture was to lead to Cockran's return to Congress when
Tammany's candidate, the popular New York Congressman George
McClellan Jr., son of the Civil War general, was elected Mayor in
November 1903 with Cockran's active support. At a special election held
in February 1904, Cockran was elected to serve out the remainder of
McClellan's term.

Cockran was in Europe during the summer of 1903 and delivered
a speech in Paris at the annual Fourth of July celebration sponsored by the
American Chamber of Commerce. The month before, on 14 June 1903,
Cockran was in London and had been given a banquet in his honour by
the Irish Nationalist Party in the Members Dining Room of the House of
Commons. The affair was attended by more than a hundred Irish and
Liberal Party members of Parliament. The Irish party leader John
Redmond praised Cockran in extravagant terms and appealed to him to
return home and stand for election to Parliament:

In the name of the Irish Party, I invite him to join our ranks and give
us the aid of his unparalleled experience and matchless eloquence in
what we believe are the last stages of the struggle for Irish Rights in
the British Parliament.[25]

Cockran declined, but that was not the end of it. The Liberal Party leader and future Prime Minister Henry Campbell-Bannerman also urged Cockran to become a candidate. During this same time, Edward Grey, the future foreign secretary during World War I, told a group of Liberal MPs in the House of Commons smoking room that he 'would give anything' to hear Cockran and Chamberlain in a debate over tariffs.[26]

Grey's comment was undoubtedly prompted by having heard Cockran speak on 15 July 1903 at the National Liberal Club in London on 'The Essential Conditions of National Prosperity'. The speech was well received, and the *London Times* quoted extensive excerpts of the speech the next day with 'laughter', 'cheers' and 'hear, hear' interspersed throughout.[27] Even protectionists were impressed by the speech. The London correspondent of the *New York Tribune* wrote:

> Let it not be supposed that I have any intention of treating Mr. Cockran with unfairness or prejudice. His services in the cause of monetary reform and public morality ought to secure for him immunity from unfriendly criticism even when he comes abroad and assails what convinced Protectionists like myself are accustomed to regard as the foundations of American prosperity. . . . Some English took a patriotic pride in the brilliant performance of a natural orator who came over from America to teach the English Free Traders how to argue their case and to revive their enthusiasm in a lost cause. Mr. Cockran's speech both in manner and in matter was a revelation to his liberal auditors who rose in a body in ecstasy of applause and admiration and delight like a swarm of gushing school girls.[28]

Churchill was not present for the speech, possibly because his attendance at a Liberal Party dinner could have been misinterpreted, as his decision to switch parties was still months away. Churchill was in London on 14 July 1903, however, and on 15 July 1903 wrote a letter to *The Times*, published the next day, where he criticized the prime minister for attempting to silence Tory free traders in the House of Commons.

Cockran's speech is worth a close study because it contains his most comprehensive views on political economy in general and free trade in particular. More importantly, for our purposes, the themes in Cockran's speech would be repeatedly echoed by Churchill over the next two and a half years, giving Grey the next best thing to a debate between Cockran and Joseph Chamberlain.

Cockran began by defining 'prosperity':

> Prosperity I should define as an abundance of commodities fairly
> distributed among those who produce them. . . . If this definition
> of prosperity be correct, then the merit of any policy or system can
> be tested by its effect on the volume of commodities available for
> the use of the people. What would tend to increase it everyone
> should support; what would tend to diminish it every honest man
> will oppose.[29]

Cockran then moved on to how prosperity – in the form of possessions –
could be achieved:

> Now it must be obvious, as I have often said elsewhere, that there
> are but two ways by which property of any kind can be secured –
> one is by production and the other by plunder.
>   If a man wants anything, he must either make it or he must take it.
> It must be produced in the sweat of his own brow, or he must take
> it from someone who has produced it. There is no other way. . . .
> Everything a man produces by industry must be taken from the
> soil, and therefore constitutes an addition to the general wealth.
> Everything he obtains by plunder – whether perpetrated by fraud or
> violence – must be taken from his neighbor, and cannot, therefore,
> add anything to the total possessions of the community.[30]

Cockran then gave the Liberals one of those allegories for which he was
so well known:

> An "invasion of cheap goods" means that some foreign producer
> will sell me a suit of clothes for £5 which, under other circum-
> stances, would cost me £7. Instead of taking money from me, this
> invader would be seeking to give me £2.
>   Now, if any man invades my pocket to take something from it,
> I will resist him as long as I can. But if he invades my pocket to fill it
> with sovereigns, he is welcome. I certainly won't try to stop him.
> My only motion would be to urge him to continue if he manifested
> any signs of fatigue. Yet it is by conjuring up such spectres as this
> that men ordinarily sane have been persuaded to aid in their own
> spoliation.[31]

Cockran warned that government could play no helpful role in the wealth creation process:

> A Government can create nothing. It cannot by any exercise of its powers, by legislative enactment, or judicial decree, or executive command, cause two blades of grass to grow where one grew before. It cannot make a withered tree blossom or a barren field fruitful. It cannot summon stones from their bed in the earth and make them form walls to enclose a building. It cannot command a tree to fall in the forest, and divide itself into planks and boards, from which chairs and tables may be made. All these results can be accomplished only by the labor of human hands.
>
> Since Government of itself can create nothing, it can have nothing of its own to bestow on anybody. It cannot, then, be both just and generous at the same time, for if it be generous to some it must be oppressive to others. If it undertakes to enrich one man, the thing which it gives him it must take from some other man. If it have a favourite, it must have a victim; and that Government only is good, that Government only is great, that Government only is just, which has neither favourites nor victims.[32]

In a speech at Birmingham on 11 November 1903 (and before Cockran had sent him a copy of his Liberal Club speech), Churchill echoed Cockran's phrase 'a Government can create nothing', showing how closely attuned were their thoughts on political economy:

> The finished product of one trade is the raw material of another. By placing taxes on any of these commodities to raise their price you may indeed for a time help this trade or that trade, but it will only be at the expense of this or that other trade and to the impoverishment of the general consumer . . . . You may, by the arbitrary and sterile act of Government – for, remember, Governments create nothing and have nothing to give but what they have first taken away – you may put money in the pocket of one set of Englishmen, but it will be money taken from the pockets of another set of Englishmen, and the greater part will be spilled on the way. Every vote given for Protection is a vote to give Governments the right of robbing Peter to pay Paul, and charging the public a handsome commission on the job.[33]

Churchill also repeated at Birmingham Cockran's argument that free
trade led to peace among nations:

> Now, Free-traders declare that both the selling and the buying of
> these things were profitable to us; that what we sold, we sold at
> a good profit, for a natural and sufficient return; that what we
> bought, we bought because we thought it worth our while to buy,
> and thought we could turn it to advantage. And in this way
> commerce is utterly different from war, so that the ideas and the
> phraseology of the one should never be applied to the other; for in
> war both sides lose whoever wins the victory, but the transactions of
> trade, like the quality of mercy, are twice blessed, and confer
> a benefit on both parties. Furthermore, the fact that this great trade
> exists between nations binds them together in spite of themselves,
> and has in the last thirty years done more to preserve the peace of
> the world than all the Ambassadors, Prime Ministers, and Foreign
> Secretaries and Colonial Secretaries put together.[34]

Both Cockran at the Liberal Club and Churchill in Birmingham stressed
in similar terms that free trade had made England great.

> *Cockran*: Your Free Trade system makes the whole industrial life of
> the World one vast scheme of cooperation for your benefit. At this
> moment, in every corner of the globe, forces are at work to supply
> your necessities and improve your condition. As I speak, men are
> tending flocks on Australian fields, and shearing wool which will
> clothe you during the coming winter. On Western fields men are
> reaping grain to supply your daily bread. In mines, deep under-
> ground, men are swinging pick-axes and shovels to wrest from the
> bosom of the earth the ores essential to the efficiency of your industry.
> Under tropical skies dusky hands are gathering from bending boughs
> luscious fruit which, in a few days, will be offered for your consump-
> tion in the streets of London. Over shining rails locomotives are
> drawing trains; on heaving surges sailors are piloting barks; through
> the arid desert Arabs are guiding caravans all charged with the fruits
> of industry to be placed here freely at your feet.[35]

> *Churchill*: Again our Free Trade plan is quite simple. We say
> that every Englishman shall have the right to buy whatever he

wants, wherever he chooses, at his own good pleasure, without restriction or discouragement from the State. That is our plan; we have followed it for sixty years, and, whatever they say, we are not quite ruined yet. In pursuance of this simple plan there came last year into England, from every land and people under the sun, five hundred and twenty-eight millions worth of merchandise, so marvelously varied in its character that a whole volume could scarcely describe it.[36]

While Churchill had not finally determined to leave the Tory Party to join the Liberal Party over the issue of free trade versus protectionism, he was drawing very close. In October 1903, Prime Minister Balfour gave a speech in which he declared himself in favour of retaliatory tariffs. An insight into Churchill's reaction to this and into his thinking at that time can be found in a contemporary letter he wrote – but did not send – to his close friend, Lord Hugh Cecil:

> I am an English Liberal. I hate the Tory party, their men, their words & their methods. I feel no sort of sympathy with them . . . It is therefore my intention that before Parliament meets, my separation from the Tory party and the Government shall be complete & irrevocable; & during the next session I propose to act consistently with the Liberal party. This will no doubt necessitate re-election which I shall not hesitate to face with all its chances.[37]

A month after the unsent letter to Cecil, Churchill received a long letter from Cockran in which he enclosed a copy of his speech at the Liberal Club.

November 27, [1903]

My dear Winston:

I read in this mornings papers that the members of Hugh Cecil's party in his own constituency, have decided to refuse him their support at the next election. If this is true, I regret it exceedingly. I never met a man who impressed me more profoundly with admiration for his ability and sincerity or whose disappearance, even temporarily, from the public life of the world I should regret more deeply. At the same time, I should not regard this action of his constituency as proof that Englishmen generally are inclined to look with favor upon the proposal to abandon their civilized policy of Free Trade, but rather as an indication of the skill with which the party machinery has been managed by adherents of Mr. Chamberlain in the interest of their leader. If this outcome of the contest is to be judged by the volume of noise made by either party, there can be little doubt of Mr. Chamberlain's success, according to the reports that reach us here, but noise is always misleading in politics. A proposal to make people rich at the expense of others is sure to awaken the enthusiasm of those who hope to be its beneficiaries, and who, just as they doubt its morality, always seek to distrust their consciences by vehemence of words and violence of bearing. But the beneficiaries of plunder must always be in a minority, and this important fact is certain to become conspicuous through discussion. I have been through similar campaigns here and I never yet knew the side which provoked the greater volume of noise to succeed in polling the greater number of votes. At any time during our Presidential campaign of 1896, if the result were to be estimated by the tumult and demonstrations on one side and the other, Bryan would have been considered absolutely sure of election by an overwhelming majority. And as the shouts of the street corners have never, in my experience, actually expressed the sober judgement of this country, I am reluctant to accept them as reliable indications of public opinion in England.

It seems to me that Mr. Chamberlain's proposal of plunder never had but one chance to success and that laid in pressing it to a vote of the constituencies while it was still a novelty and before people had time to inquire who under its operations would be the plunderers and who would be plundered. Delay gives time for reflection and nothing is so fatal to an extravagant suggestion as discussion and examination. However deafening or distracting the cries of a mob may be for the moment, time always fights on the side of sense and justice. For this reason I am confident that if the life of the present Parliament continue for two years more, or even for one year, the common sense and common honesty of the common people will realize the exact nature of the economic and moral question involved, and this will suffice to insure a crushing defeat for the scheme which is as immoral in its essence as it would inevitably be disastrous in operation.

These conclusions are the result of my own cogitations. The newspaper reports which I have seen tend rather to obscure than make clear the progress of events. It is impossible for instance, to make out just what position Sir Michael Hicks Beach has finally assumed. At one time we read of him as assisting at a meeting where Mr. Chamberlain's proposals are denounced, and at another time we are told that he has given his unqualified adhesion to Mr. Balfour. This is but one specimen of the contradictory statements on which we are fed. I need hardly say that apart from the profound interest which no man can withhold from the campaign itself, I am deeply concerned about your own fortunes, and therefore, I would take it as a great favor if you send me your views of the situation, especially as it affects yourself.

If you followed our late municipal election in this city, you must have seen that I made the tariff the prominent issue of the canvass, and that people of New York answered my appeal for a condemnation of this inquisitious system by a very decisive majority. I think there is little doubt that the next Presidential campaign will turn upon the same question, and if the Democrats succeed in finding a candidate who can satisfy public opinion that he will be at once efficient in protecting all property, which is the fruit of industry, and vigilant in preventing every one from acquiring any profit by plunder, I have no doubt that he will be elected.

Your election, according to present indications, will not be held till a year after ours, and it might be worth your while to spend a month or two in this country next autumn watching the Presidential campaign. If you decide to come over, pray remember that my house must be your headquarters, and in the meantime believe me to be,

Yours very sincerely,
W. Bourke Cockran

P.S. My speech at the Liberal Club delivered in July last has been published in pamphlet form – I send you a copy lest you may not have seen it.[38]

Churchill promptly replied to Cockran early in December, where he referred to himself as a 'permanent politician'.

Dec. 12. 1903   105 Mount Street
Private   W.

My dear Bourke,

I was glad to get your letter and also to read in the "Democratic
Campaign Guide of Massachusetts" your excellent Free Trade
speech.

  We are fighting very hard here, but I think on the whole, the
outlook is encouraging. I believe that Chamberlain will be defeated
at the General Election by an overwhelming majority. What will
happen to the Free Trade Unionists by whose exertions this result
will have been largely attained is quite another matter for I regret to
say that the Liberal party think a great deal more of winning a seat
here and there by destroying a Unionist Free Trader than for the
principles for which we are fighting in common.

  I do not think people like Lord Hugh Cecil and myself will be
shut out of Parliament. The freedom which we possess here of
standing in any constituency enables those who are well known and
looked upon as permanent politicians to find another road back in
the House of Commons when one particular constituency rejects
them. But I fear the rank and file of our small party will suffer
terribly – many of them being altogether extinguished and ending
their public life once and for all.

  I can quite understand your being perplexed by the attitude of
Sir Michael Hicks-Beach, but he is an old Tory, has lived all his life
high in the councils of that party, and although he is a staunch Free
Trader, he cannot bear the idea of severing himself in his old age
from all those other causes for which he has fought. Consequently
he tries to run with the hare and hunt with the hounds in perfect
good faith though not I fear without some loss of public credit.

  I think when the Address comes on, there will be a very bitter and
protracted Debate culminating in a decisive decision. Those
Unionists who fought against the Government will move steadily
forward and endeavour to obtain Liberal support, those whose
courage fails them will probably be engulfed in the Chamberlain
abyss.

  It is more and more plain that there is no real collusion between
Mr. Balfour's government and Mr. Chamberlain, but their weak

position is untenable. Nobody trusts them, nobody wants to fight them; and now that the Duke of Devonshire, who is moving with more determination every day, has taken the decisive step of advising Unionist Free Trade to vote against Protectionist candidates irrespective of party considerations, I would not be at all surprised if the Government, to save their lives, are not obliged to throw themselves into Mr. Chamberlain's arms. Once they do this, the line between the parties will be very sharply drawn. Feeling is getting much more bitter on both sides than when you were here last and I think there are very stormy times ahead. The accession of the Duke is a matter of enormous importance to us, not only because he commands immense weight in the country, but he has so much social influence that leaving the Conservative party with him does not mean going out in the wilderness as it would have done a year or two ago. That perhaps is a small consideration compared to the great issues with which we are dealing; but it is a small consideration which counts for a good deal with many people. I have had all sorts of rows and troubles in my own constituency and I am thinking of trying my luck in pastures new. After all, Oldham will most certainly return a Liberal and Labor member at the next election, both staunch Free Traders, so that I do not feel that I shall be losing a counter in the game if I looked elsewhere.

I have never received a copy of your speech at the Liberal Club. I wish I had been able to get hold of it. It would be very useful. I should not be surprised if the General Election took place between Easter & Whitsuntide but I think the Government have bargained successfully for the Irish support so that they will not go out unless they want to.

I am sorry you are not going to run Bryan for the Democratic presidency. He has made a very good impression over here and his oratory was considered very remarkable. Surely it cannot be true that Mr. Hearst of the New York Journal will be the democratic nominee.

I wish you would send me some good Free Trade speeches that have been made in America, and some facts about corruption, lobbying, and so forth.

If all is quiet in this country, I shall certainly come over to see the Presidential Election next autumn and very likely Lord Hugh Cecil will come with me. It is rather an inspiring election to think that so many of us on both sides of the Atlantic are fighting in a common cause – you to attack protection, we to defend Free Trade. I think what the double victory would mean for the wealth and welfare of the world.

Yours vy sincerely
Winston S. Churchill

P.S. Moreton is stumping the country for Chamberlain. What fools these Bimetallists are![39]

The 'P.S.' reference to 'Moreton . . . stumping the country for Chamberlain' is to Churchill's uncle, Moreton Frewen, who had so badly edited the first edition of *The Malakand Field Force*. Frewen was one of Cockran's closest friends and the one who arranged his introduction to his wife Clara and her sisters Jennie and Leonie. Their correspondence from the 1890s through the early 1920s is the most extensive contained in the Cockran papers.

Notwithstanding their close friendship, the two men agreed on little politically and argued their positions whenever they were together. Shane Leslie, Leonie's son, Frewen's nephew and eventually Cockran's brother-in-law, described discussions he had witnessed between the two men at Cockran's Long Island estate, The Cedars:

[T]hey differed on all subjects, and they could relentlessly debate the Silver Question, the Irish Question, the Tariff Question together, and when each was fought to exasperation they would laugh and turn to another. Often was I deafened between their rival torrentades.

Afterwards Moreton would confide to me: "Poor Bourke! Such a windbag, but a good fellow!" and Bourke would mutter: "Was ever so much intelligence so sublimely misdirected?"[40]

Chapter 12
'An English Liberal'

London
31 May 1904

Winston Churchill was at peace with himself. The evening was crisp and clear, and he had decided a brisk walk home from that night's sitting of the House of Commons was just what he needed to top off what he believed to be the most important day in his life, more important than when he escaped from the Boer prison or even his first election to Parliament. The battles would continue. He did not mind them. Indeed, he rather enjoyed them. Too much so at times. But now his enemies in the Tory Party would have to face him head-on across the floor of Parliament. No more sniping away from behind his back.

Churchill wondered whether his father would have approved of what he had done today. He thought so. His father had never switched parties as Winston had just done, but he had certainly formed his own party in a way – the Fourth Party – and had tried, unsuccessfully, to recast the Conservatives around his own ideas of Tory Democracy. His son had fared no better.

Churchill paused beneath a street lamp to light a fresh cigar and then resumed his late-night stroll, his walking stick rhythmically tapping the pavement as he did so. Churchill knew he had been an English Liberal at heart for almost ten years now. He simply hadn't told anyone except his mother. If others had known, it might well have lent ammunition to his opponents and the charges of opportunism being bandied about. Churchill dismissed them. What did they know? What was it Bourke Cockran had said to that blackguard Republican who accused him of inconsistency for having supported McKinley in 1896 and switched back to Bryan in 1900? Something like, 'Once in my life I was forced to change candidates to avoid changing principles. Gentlemen on the other side have always cheerfully changed principles to avoid changing candidates.'[1]

Churchill thought it a good phrase and one he could put to good use as he frequently did with Cockran's phrases. It ought to be something like 'once in my life I was forced to change Parties to avoid changing principles. Gentlemen on the other side have always cheerfully changed principles to avoid changing Parties.' Churchill smiled again. Yes, he would have that retort ready the first time the Conservatives attacked him for switching parties.

Besides, he was his father's son. He had every right to attempt to bring the Conservatives over to the principles of Tory Democracy and succeed where his father had failed. He had attacked his own government's conduct of the war in South Africa without attacking the war itself, as did the Liberals, and he had certainly kept Brodrick on the defensive. But retrenchment at home, a strong navy, no large standing army and a foreign policy designed to keep England out of Europe's quarrels were not enough if they were accompanied by protectionist tariffs.

Free trade was, to Churchill, the crown jewel of England's remarkable prosperity. If the Conservatives were going to follow Joe Chamberlain down the protectionist path in the hope of seeking electoral success, he wasn't signing on to that forced march to oblivion. He was in a hurry and time was running out.

Plainly put, Churchill was changing parties based on principles he had first heard from the man who, his Aunt Leonie once hinted, had for a time enjoyed a romance with his mother. That hadn't surprised Churchill at all and neither had the fact that Bourke Cockran seemed as concerned over his health, well-being and political welfare as he was certain his own father would have been. He had held off until now replying to Cockran's last message delivered by his Uncle Moreton. Cockran had expressed anxiety at the episode in the House of Commons last month where Churchill had been speaking in favour of restoring to trade unions the right to strike and had been about to conclude his speech when his mind went blank. Utterly blank. And his notes were of no help. He always made detailed notes for his speeches – almost verbatim – and largely memorized them beforehand. The conclusion had seemed so obvious to him when making his notes that he hadn't bothered to write it down. Embarrassing, but what could he do? So, he simply thanked the House for their attention and sat down.

Except, of course, he was Randolph Churchill's son and, in the late stages of his father's illness, similar episodes had characterized his father's speeches. There was no comparison in Churchill's mind, but that didn't stop others from making the connection, usually behind his back.

Cockran was different. He was genuinely concerned that it was a manifestation of Churchill working too hard and not paying proper attention to his health. Churchill shook his head. Cockran sounded just like his mother and his Aunt Leonie. But it was kindly meant, and

Churchill wanted to assure his old mentor that it was a momentary thing; that he was fine and well rested; and that it had never happened again. Which, in fact, it hadn't. And it wouldn't. Churchill had vowed never again to speak on the House floor without comprehensive notes readily at hand.

When he received Cockran's enquiry, however, Churchill had known that tonight was coming, and he had waited until now to write to Cockran. He specifically – and symbolically – wanted to do so on the same day he had emulated his great friend and, with the whole country watching, placed principle over party. Because, after tonight, he was going to continue to emulate Cockran. Just as Cockran had set out on a nationwide speaking tour on the issue of sound money in 1896, Churchill intended to do the same for free trade. He would speak on free trade on any platform the Liberal Party and their allies provided, and he would continue doing so wherever he was wanted, right up to the general election, which would surely come some time in the next year and a half. Then, he would have his revenge on the party that had ostracized him and abandoned his father.

Churchill let his mind wander ahead to the summer and Cockran's invitation to attend the Democratic Convention. He would very much like to see that spectacle. He had sent a cable earlier that day to Cockran accepting the invitation and now he would write a letter to accompany it.

Churchill's letter to Cockran in December 1903 made clear that he believed Chamberlain's policy on tariffs and Imperial preference would lead to an overwhelming defeat at the polls for the Conservatives. He also made clear that he expected to be standing for re-election somewhere other than Oldham, where he 'had all sorts of rows and troubles'.

On 8 January 1904, the troubles continued when the Oldham Conservative Association nearly unanimously passed a resolution of no confidence in Churchill because of his outspoken views on free trade. The vote of censure did not deter Churchill, as he continued to speak on free trade, now armed with his mentor's 1903 Liberal Club speech.

In February 1904, Churchill made a speech at the Free Trade Hall in Manchester which *The Times* of London described as 'one of the most powerful and brilliant he has made'. In it, Churchill said,

> It is the theory of the Protectionist that imports are an evil. He thinks that if you shut out the foreign imported manufactured

goods you will make these goods yourselves, in addition to the
goods which you make now, including those goods which we make
to exchange for the foreign goods that come in. If a man can believe
that, he can believe anything. [*laughter*] We Free-traders say it is not
true. To think you can make a man richer by putting on a tax is like
a man thinking that he can stand in a bucket and lift himself up by
the handle. [*laughter and cheers*]²

Already ostracized by the Oldham Conservative Association for his
support of free trade, the parliamentary wing of the Tories added insult to
injury on 29 March 1904 when Churchill rose to speak in the Commons
and Prime Minister Balfour conspicuously exited the Chamber, followed
by all the front-bench ministers and most of the back benchers as well.
Churchill was isolated, and the only Tories left in the House were a few
Unionist free traders like Churchill.

On 22 April 1904, Churchill addressed the House on a trade disputes
bill, arguing that the rights of trade unions to engage in peaceful strikes
should not be left in an uncertain state. The subject on which Churchill was
speaking is one more example of Cockran's influence. Since the 1870s,
unions in England could not be sued for damages as a result of strikes.
The law had changed with the Taff-Vale case of 1901, and Churchill had
spoken in favour of a private members' bill to reverse that decision.
Unfortunately, Churchill faltered at the end of his speech, losing the thread
of his argument, and abruptly sat down, saying 'I thank honourable
members for having listened to me.'

Churchill was clearly affected by this memory lapse because, as
always, he had memorized his speech beforehand. Unfortunately, he
had been speaking for forty-five minutes and that is a long time even for
someone with Churchill's prodigious memory. Both Churchill's brother
Jack and his cousin Shane Leslie visited Churchill the next day at his
home on Mount Street to sympathize. Moreton Frewen wrote to
Cockran on 27 April 1904 advising him of the memory lapse and
expressing his concern:

Winston has overworked himself & ought to get a long holiday.
He has shown lots of fight & lots of ability; but he has attracted
an amount of personal & social hostility that I had gladly seen
avoided.³

Cockran promptly replied to Frewen and extended an invitation to Churchill to visit him in America for a long rest. But the next sentence in Frewen's letter to Cockran shows that Winston had things other than politics to entertain him: 'Pretty Ethel Barrymore arrives tomorrow.'[4]

Cockran had been back in Congress since his special election on 23 February 1904 where he ran unopposed. Not having been in Congress for ten years, Cockran was nominally a freshman. Yet such was his reputation from years earlier that the Democrats kept a position open for him on the prestigious House Ways and Means Committee, then and for most of the twentieth century, the most powerful committee in Congress and on which he had served in the 1890s.

Cockran hit the ground running, attacking the Roosevelt Administration, whose Secretary of the Interior had provided pension increases for Civil War Veterans without the authority of Congress. Cockran did not disagree in principle with the increase in pensions. Rather, it was a separation of powers issue. The Constitution gave the House – not the Senate or the Executive Branch – the power to originate revenue bills. Cockran believed that the Executive Branch could not spend revenue without legislative authorization.

Cockran's enforced, involuntary absence from the House had not dimmed his powers of persuasion. Cockran's resolution was to instruct the House Judiciary Committee to enquire into the authority for what the Secretary of the Interior had done. The Republicans were in the majority yet, on a vote to table his resolution, a surprising number of Republicans flocked to Cockran's side. His resolution was only tabled by the narrow margin of three votes, a near vote of no confidence by the House on the popular Roosevelt Administration.[5]

Cockran prided himself on maintaining cordial relations with members on both sides of the aisle. Cockran, therefore, was taken aback during a speech opposing ship subsidies by an *ad hominem* attack on him by Republican representative John Dalzell of Pennsylvania, a strong protectionist and also a member of Ways and Means, who accused Cockran of having accepted money from the Republicans in 1896 to campaign for McKinley.

Cockran appeared to let his Irish temper take over at what may have been the first occasion where someone ever accused him face-to-face of a lack of integrity. But he never lost his cool and gave better than he got:

> Mr. Speaker, that is a statement which has been made whenever there has been found a mouth foul enough to utter words behind which there was no conscience .... It has been my fortune at various times to support different political parties. I have never yet, thank Heaven, gone through a campaign where someone did not want to throw a stone at me, as the gentleman does now.[6]

Cockran went on to say that he had always paid his own expenses for his speeches, political and non-political alike. He concluded by saying:

> [T]hat the gentleman attributes to me what he knows and must know to be the universal custom among Republican politicians, who thereby illustrate the utter demoralization worked by this system of organized corruption as the basis of government, which makes all industry depend not upon the excellence of the product, but upon skill in corruption.[7]

Dalzell came back two days later and accused Cockran of political inconsistency, but Cockran's reply left Dalzell bleeding and speechless on the House floor. The New York papers left no doubt as to who prevailed, the *Evening Post* being the most colourful. Dalzell, it wrote,

> [m]ade a pathetic exhibition of himself in his encounter with Bourke Cockran. The joints of Mr. Cockran's armor are not open to any shafts from such pygmies as Dalzell .... It was, therefore, to be expected that Dalzell would come out of the contest like a whipped cur.[8]

The duel with Dalzell made news across the Atlantic as well, and Cockran received letters of congratulation from Lord Charles Beresford; John Redmond, John Dillon; T.P. O'Connor; Moreton Frewen; Sir Horace Plunkett; Lord Grey, Governor-General of Canada; Henry Adams; James C. Carter; Joseph Pulitzer; Henry Watterson; Finley Peter Dunne; Richard Harding Davis, Charles Dana Gibson and, of course, Winston Churchill.[9] Cockran was clearly pleased with his performance against Dalzell because he sent copies of the Congressional Record to

Churchill, who wrote to Cockran that 'you appear to have crushed him altogether and I need not say how much I sympathise with you in resisting the blackguardly personal attack of which you were the subject.'[10]

Churchill was twenty-nine in May 1904 when he joined the Liberal Party and left his father's Conservative Party. He was now in his 'age thirty transition', that time in a man's life where he works on the flaws in his initial life structure and creates the basis for a more satisfactory structure in the future.

Entering Parliament as a Conservative in 1900 had not been a flaw at the time, but it clearly had become one by the end of 1903 as Chamberlain and the protectionists completed their hijacking of the Tory Party much as Bryan and the Populists had done with the Democratic Party in 1896. By 1904, Churchill knew he had to make a change in his life's structure if he were to have a future in politics. His options were stark in their simplicity: change his principles or change his party. He had to do one or the other if he were ever to achieve his dream of government office and following in his father's footsteps.

Doing nothing and isolating himself as a maverick, out of step with the Tory Party's new protectionist policy was not an option. Changing principles to support protectionist tariffs even though he knew they were wrong – as Chamberlain would have him do – would have betrayed the foundation he had erected with Cockran's guidance during his years of self-education in India. In retrospect, given all that Churchill had done in creating a life structure since 1896, leaving the Conservatives and staying true to the principles he had developed during the past eight years was his only option. Anything else and the foundation upon which he had built his career would have begun to crumble because, in his heart of hearts, he would have known he had placed party and power over principle and gravely disappointed the one man besides his father he most looked up to, a man who freely walked away from power on more than one occasion rather than abandon his principles. Churchill chose to emulate his mentor.

31 May 1904, therefore, was the most important moment in Churchill's young political career – the day he formally left the Tory Party and joined the Liberals. That same day, he wrote a long letter to Cockran, tentatively accepting an invitation to travel to America for the 1904 Democratic Convention and offering his assurances that his memory lapse was no matter for concern.

May 31, 1904   105 Mount Street
Private   W.

My dear Bourke,

I have to thank you very sincerely for the kind message conveyed
to me through Moreton. I am much taken with the plan. It would
interest me enormously to see, the Democratic Convention and
I should learn from contact with politicians on your side an
immense amount of argument which will be of the greatest value
to me in my Manchester campaign. I should also be the better for
a rest and a break. The end of the Session here is always hot and dull
and I have had a good deal of work lately. You need not be worried
by my losing my thread in a speech some weeks ago. The slip was
purely mechanical, and was due to my style of preparation, which
as you know, is very elaborate. I had reached the very last sentence
in my speech, and as the concluding phrases were not in the nature
of argument but of rhetoric, when my memory failed me, I could
not bring the reasoning faculty to bear, and as I had nothing more
to say – having finished my remarks – and no clue on my notes for
the concluding sentence, I had no choice but to sit down. I am
actually in very good health at present – in much better health in
fact than when I was in America four years ago – But all the same,
I think a change would devote the month of July and August to that
purpose.

    I have therefore cabled to you to-day saying that if the
Democratic Convention is not earlier than the 11th July, I will
accept your invitation to attend and I would start from England on
the 2nd July.

    I shall look forward immensely to having some long talks with
you. You are in some measure responsible for the mould in which
my political thought has been largely cast, and for the course which
I have adopted on these great questions of Free Trade. It is in
different spheres we are fighting in a common cause, and there can
be no doubt that a democratic victory in America resulting in the
reductions of the tariffs through the deliberate convictions of the
American people, would utterly smash once and for all the
Protectionist movement here. Whether American competition
would not become much more formidable if industries were erected

on a natural basis, and whether as an ultimate consequence we should be the losers by the change, I do not now examine.

Now I have also to thank you for the two copies of the Congressional Record together with a pamphlet you have been good enough to forward me. I have read the speeches with great interest and I shall make free use of the arguments contained in them – many of them will be most useful to me –

You appear to me to be permitted a very much wider range of invective than prevails here and I am bound to say you seem to me to have taken full advantage of your liberty in your encounter with Mr. Dalzell. Certainly you appear to have crushed him altogether and I need not say how much I sympathise with you in resisting the blackguardly personal attack of which you were the subject.

I cannot resist subscribing so far to the principles of reciprocity, as to send you in return for what you have sent me, an article and an utterance of my own with which I am sure you will sympathise.

Yours most sincerely,
Winston S. Churchill[11]

Having left the Tory Party to join the Liberals, Churchill quickly became their most effective speaker on the subject of free trade.[12] Some have claimed that Herbert Asquith was more effective because he answered Chamberlain with a relentless combination of 'statistical memory and command over the rules of logic.'[13] Perhaps. But metaphor and poking fun, rather than statistics and logics, are what people remember. Speaking on 15 June 1904 in Manchester, Churchill exposed and held up to ridicule Prime Minister Balfour's claim that retaliation against foreign tariffs would lead to more free trade:

> [I]f retaliation is unproductive in theory, let us see how it would work in practice. We are often told the Retaliator is an active Free-trader. [Prime Minister] Balfour said, 'We are prepared to fight for Free Trade.' I wonder what would happen to Free Trade if it had been left alone in a dark lane with such a champion as that. [laughter][14]

A few days after the Manchester speech, Churchill wrote to Cockran retracting his earlier acceptance of an invitation to visit America. His new party needed him.

19 June [1904]   Blenheim Palace

My dear Bourke,

I am vy sorry indeed to have been forced to abandon my projected
visit to St. Louis. It would have been an experience valuable &
interesting: & I should have profited much from your views
and thoughts. But I find too much uncertainty rose to enable me
to disentangle myself. Chamberlain & his Merrie Men are stirring again, and the government are shaking with subterranean
disturbances. This year is such a critical one, & my task in
Manchester is so important that it would be foolish & even
improper to neglect anything that may conduce to success. So I
have had to telegraph you that I cannot come. I do hope that my
hesitation has not caused you inconvenience. It was a kindly
thought on your part to suggest my coming to Moreton: & the
prospect charmed me – tho as you know I greatly fear the ocean.
    The decisive trial of strength here cannot I think be delayed beyond
next March, & may be precipitated in October. Free Trade is safe
for this time – but of the future no man can pronounce – & we are
confronted with the gravest difficulties. All democratic parties lack
cohesion – & their enthusiasts are nearly always importunistic.
    Send me some more of your speeches. They are rowdy & short.

                                        Yours most sincerely,
                                        Winston S. Churchill[15]

Cockran was disappointed that Churchill could not come for the
convention but urged him to come anyway once Parliament had
adjourned. He suggested that, for reasons of health, 'a rest is highly
desirable' and that America was the 'place above all others' where he
could be 'amused and interested without being fatigued.'

July 1, 1904   31 Nassau Street
                                                    New York

My dear Winston:

Before leaving for St. Louis I want to tell you how deeply I regret the
change of plans which prevents you from being my guest at the

Convention, and for the remainder of the summer at this quiet retreat.

Your explanation of the incident in the House of Commons is very reassuring, not only to me but to a great many others who, though they are not acquainted with you personally, take a deep interest in your career.

While it is clear that the newspaper accounts were greatly exaggerated it is equally clear that the hard work of the last year must have told on you to some extent, and therefore it seems to me a rest is highly desirable, if not absolutely necessary now, as a precaution against graver trouble hereafter. The difficulty about rest is not in finding a place where one can take it if he will but a place where he must take it. It is very difficult for an active mind to put itself entirely out of operation or activity and I think it would be quite impossible for you to stop thinking or working for any sensible period of time. What you can get is not a cessation but a change of employment – a substitute of occupations which amuse the mind without affecting the nerve for those labors which wear both mind and nerves.

I cannot help thinking that this country is the place above all others where for the next four months you could be amused and interested without being fatigued for here you could watch a mighty struggle in the result of which you could have no personal concern.

Of course, the most interesting feature of the contest will be the convention to which I am about going, but since it is impossible for you to assist at the selection of a candidate or the adoption of a platform, the next best thing would be to see the electoral battle itself in progress. This you can do any time up to the eighth of November and I most earnestly hope you will come over and stay with me for as long as you can spare.

A chance to observe at close quarters a fight affecting the conditions under which a population of eighty millions must live for four years and in which all its male members are engaged should be well worth embracing, to a mind like yours. Moreover closer intercourse between all the great nations of the world is certain to be a feature of the new century and you would undoubtedly find it a great advantage to form acquaintance with men active in the political life of this country, and who are very likely to affect its course during the next generation. While you would be likely to

meet in my establishment just now only the moving spirits in the
Democratic party, matters could easily be arranged so that you
would also come in contact with the leading Republicans, and thus
see for yourself how both sides of the campaign are managed.

Think over this and let me have a line saying that I may expect
you immediately after the adjournment of Parliament.

I am very curious to learn all about the conditions and prospects
of the Free Trade fight in England. So far as we on this side can
judge events on the other side of the Atlantic it would seem as if
Chamberlain's plan has wholly failed, while on the other hand the
opposition is so divided and incoherent that the Government is
likely to escape the defeat it so richly deserves for recklessly
countenancing and encouraging proposals which if adopted would
have imperilled the foundations of your own prosperity and
beclouded the whole prospects of civilized progress.

Pray give my cordial regards to your mother and believe me to be,

Yours very sincerely,
W. Bourke Cockran[16]

Churchill's reply to his mentor was kind and flattering, but he declined
the invitation. If Churchill was tempted – and he likely was not because,
between speeches, he was also hard at work on his father's biography –
he still resisted his mentor's entreaties while noting, not for the last time
in his life, that 'I consider myself a Democrat so far as American politics
are concerned.'

July 16 1904   105 Mount Street
Private   W.

My dear Bourke,

I am delighted to get your kind letter and I most sincerely wish
I could accept your invitation. It is very friendly of you to extend it
to me after I fear I may have somewhat unsettled your plans by my
changes of mind. I quite recognise what you say about the
importance of a rest. No doubt when one is absorbed in politics,
and watching day by day the development of a great political

situation, it is very hard to abstract oneself and to find new interests, which, by exercising other muscles of the mind, relieve the general strain. But the reasons which prevented me from coming to the States to see the Convention still operate in full force. I must be here in England on the spot and I must endeavour to get what rest, and change I can without going far away. My plans for two months in the country are now practically complete and I have most reluctantly had to relinquish all idea of visiting America this autumn. I much regret this from every point of view. American politics interest me immensely and they have a real and sympathetic bearing upon the course of our political struggle over here. Now that the Tariff Question is prominent there could not be a more profitable experience to politicians than a tour in the United States. I should like to meet very much your leading Democratic politicians. I consider myself a Democrat so far as American politics are concerned, and I earnestly hope for the sake of America and for the sake of the world, that the great campaign in which you are now engaged, may terminate extremists. But yet I am very hopeful that when the Election comes, it will result in a sweeping and unmistakable verdict in favour of Free Trade, and I cannot help thinking if this country should ratify the decision of 1846 after sixty years of practical experience, that would be a great fact in the history of the world and will influence the nations besides our own.

I beg you to send me as much of your political literature as you can – particularly your own speeches. As I have told you before you have powerfully influenced me in the political conceptions I have formed and I like to think that under different skies and different lands we are fighting in one long line of battle for a common cause.

Yours always most sincerely,
Winston S. Churchill[17]

Churchill continued to speak out during the fall of 1904 against the government of his old party on free trade and other issues in a series of speeches in Wales and Scotland. Speaking at the Grand Theatre in Llandudno, Wales, on 19 October 1904, Churchill attacked the growing expense of government with rhetorical questions still being used by politicians today:

In a period of little more than five years, the cost of governing Great
Britain has increased half as much again. Is the government half as
good again? In the same period we have practically doubled our
expenditure in its most unproductive branch – the expenditure
upon armaments. We have doubled our armaments; have we
doubled our security?[18]

On 28 November 1904, he poked fun at his likely Tory opponent in the
next general election, Joynson Hicks, who had taken a public position
supporting protectionism and imperial preference in principle but had
agreed with Prime Minister Balfour that 'the time was not ripe for the
taxation of food.' Churchill called his position 'nonsense', saying,

He [Mr. Joynson Hicks] said that he agreed with Mr. Balfour, and
that the time was not ripe for the taxation of food. [*laughter*] But
if Mr. Joynson Hicks believes that Mr. Chamberlain's object is
desirable and his method right what nonsense it is to say that the
time is not ripe . . . What would have been said of the Manchester
Regiment or the Lancashire Fusiliers if when they were ordered to
make an attack upon a position they replied, "We have unabated
sympathy with the object but we think that the time is not ripe."
[*loud laughter*][19]

A day later, speaking at the Free Trade Hall in Manchester, Churchill had
them rolling in the aisles as he made fun of the Conservatives' recent loss
of several by-elections:

I noticed last week that a Minister, speaking somewhere – I forget his
name – [*laughter*] – I have to make a great many speeches, and I really
should never get through my work if I filled my mind with a lot of
trivial and insignificant details. – [*renewed and loud laughter*] But he
was a most important Minister – [*laughter*], – and I noticed that he said
in his most important speech – [*laughter*] – that by-elections were an
unsatisfactory and inaccurate test of public opinion. I can quite
understand that he finds them an unsatisfactory test. – [*laughter*] ...[20]

As the run-up to the anticipated general election in 1905 continued,
however, Churchill's attacks would become more cutting and personal,
drawing rebukes from friends and foes alike. It was not something he

learned from Cockran. Rather, his father's posthumous influence should not be overlooked. Lord Randolph's words could wound, and Churchill had read all his father's speeches. Moreover, during this time, Churchill's work on Lord Randolph's biography had him reliving what he believed to have been his father's betrayal by the Tories. A letter to Cockran from Moreton Frewen on 23 October 1904 betrays both an uncle's pride and his concern:

> Winston is collecting a considerable following in the country. His speeches are far too violent for my taste; personal and vindictive; yet he will go far should he not engender too much personal dislike.[21]

Chapter 13
'Confound the Hostile and Surprise the Indifferent'

On Board the Scharnhorst
12 June 1905

It was the longest sea voyage Bourke Cockran had ever taken. While he was looking forward to it, six weeks was a long time compared to a week crossing the Atlantic, voyages of which there had been so many he had by now lost track. Moreover, he had never gone abroad as an agent of the president, his Long Island neighbour Theodore Roosevelt.

He had sailed from Naples late last night, and he had been pleasantly surprised at his accommodations in the captain's cabin. It was just behind the bridge and had a large sitting room, a good-sized bedroom and a spacious bathroom with, blessed be, its own shower. He would certainly not want for creature comforts for the next six weeks as he had brought with him a goodly supply of both books and excellent tea.

Cockran paused and took a sip of tea from the table beside the large easy chair in his sitting room, watching the waters of the Mediterranean pass by. The tea really was excellent and had been made for him by the attractive young widow from Java, whose acquaintance he had made at dinner on their first day at sea. She was a true Eurasian beauty whose father was Dutch and her mother a native of Java. In her late twenties, she had married a wealthy Dutch planter, older even than the fifty-year-old Cockran. Her married name, however, was as unpronounceable as her maiden name, so Cockran found it much easier to think of her simply as 'the Java girl'.

Married at twenty, the Java girl's husband had died of a massive heart attack five years ago and left her distraught because, even though the marriage had been arranged, as was the custom in the East, she had grown to love her husband very much.

Cockran sympathized, offered his condolences, and the two soon found themselves exchanging memories of their departed spouses, Cockran's Rhoda and the Java girl's Dutch Burgher. When Cockran volunteered that he had brought his own supply of tea with him on the voyage out of an abundance of concern that tea served on a German ship might be of a quality comparable to the food which was, to put it mildly, questionable, the Java girl's eyes lit up. She enquired as to the nature of the teas he had brought with him. He had named several varieties packed in tins purchased at Fortnum & Mason's in London, and the Java girl had laughed with delight. She would make tea for him every day, she promised, using the same methods she had learned as a girl on her father's tea plantation.

Cockran's weakness for strong drink and beautiful women had not abated after he celebrated the fiftieth anniversary of his birth. The former was still under control, but he saw no reason to do likewise with the latter. The most fair of the Lord's creations were put on earth for a purpose, and if one of them wanted to make him tea twice a day and join him in his cabin, the door always propped open for propriety's sake, and sit there in companionable silence as they sipped their tea, who was he, a mere mortal, to interfere with God's plan? But if Cockran were to truly enjoy this ocean voyage and any shipboard romance which might ensue with the Java girl, he had to get something off his chest. Until he did, he would not only be unable to focus on the charm and beauty of the Java girl, but also be unable to focus on the purpose of his voyage – a diplomatic mission for the president as well as serving on a fact-finding mission to the Philippines led by the Secretary of War, William Howard Taft.

Cockran and Theodore Roosevelt were friends and neighbours, both having rambling estates on Long Island, Cockran at Sands Point and TR at Oyster Bay. Cockran was one of the token Democrats on the Commission as well as the token anti-Imperialist. Further, the president had made Cockran his personal envoy to the Vatican to negotiate a resolution of the dispute which had arisen over the sale of Church-owned property in the Philippines to the United States for $7 million. The Pope had agreed to return the money to the Philippines to rehabilitate the former Church property, but so far the money hadn't been transferred. That was why Cockran was sailing on a German ship out of Naples, having spent the previous week in Rome meeting with Vatican diplomats. Cockran had ideas on how to expedite this problem. But, first things first.

Cockran picked up the issue of the Pall Mall Gazette *and stared once more at the political cartoon which had caught his attention. The cartoon showed a horse-drawn coach in which resided the Liberal Party leader Sir Henry Campbell-Bannerman. Campbell-Bannerman's hand was swatting at a flying insect disturbing his repose, possibly a wasp or a fly but one that unmistakably wore the face of his young protégé, Winston Churchill.*

The paragraph beneath the cartoon helpfully noted that Churchill was not to be given a cabinet position in the next Liberal government, thus explaining why the Winston wasp was buzzing the Campbell-Bannerman coach. It wasn't especially funny, but the message it conveyed about Winston was not pleasant. Winston had changed parties, the cartoon's message conveyed, only in the hopes of achieving office. If he didn't get it, he was going to cause his new party trouble.

Cockran knew all about the slings and arrows of political opponents keen on portraying the opposition in the most mendacious manner they could muster. Cockran had certainly seen his share of that from the 1896 campaign when the Bryanites had whispered and newspapers had published rumours that Cockran was being paid off to campaign for McKinley. Cockran had ignored them for the insects they were. No man could ever buy his allegiance. Perhaps he had been wrong, however, in not denouncing the lies for what they were the moment they were made. If he had, perhaps that unpleasantness with John Dalzell last year on the House floor would never have occurred.

It was his experience with Dalzell which weighed heavily on his mind. If he had spoken up at the time in the same manner and ferocity he had displayed in his duel with Dalzell, there would have been no duel because Dalzell would have had no ammunition.

The same thing was true with Winston. Cockran had admired Winston for changing parties over a matter of principle and he had told him so, but his enemies did not believe it was principle or, if they believed it, wouldn't say it. Opportunism was their conclusion. It was inescapable to Cockran that the judgement which unbiased men formed now of his young protégé would follow him throughout life. Did Winston change parties for principle or for power? Cockran knew the answer, but he wanted others to look on Winston as he did.

For that to happen, Cockran was convinced that Winston would have to, temporarily at least, forego office, an act which would totally undercut the Tory's subterranean campaign against him. Confound the hostile and surprise the indifferent was his prescription. If Winston did so, it would be absolutely unique and unprecedented in English public life – a young man furnishing to a political party his most powerful support and yet declining to accept office under it – giving it success and yet refusing to profit by the triumph to which he would surely have made a large contribution. If Winston did that, Cockran believed, his word in the House would acquire such weight that no other man could possibly possess.

So Cockran had written Winston a letter last night. A very long letter. The longest he had ever written to him in the ten years they had known each other. Still, Cockran was concerned. It was a sensible suggestion but a radical one. He had agonized over even making it. Perhaps it wasn't his place to do so. He knew Winston had his heart set on office. What young politician wouldn't?

Perhaps he had come on too strong in the letter. Perhaps he could make his point more clearly. Cockran placed the teacup down, walked over and sat at the writing desk in his cabin, reopened the letter and began to write:

P.S. I have opened this long screed to add another word – I am not sure that I have made clear the extent to which I think the renunciation suggested should be carried . . .

Churchill continued in 1905 the speaking campaign he had embarked upon the previous summer attacking the government in a series of colourful attacks on protectionists which echoed Bourke Cockran's 1903 Liberal Club speech.

[28 December 1904, Malmesbury:] Mr. Chamberlain's changes constitute a world's record. They are more like some unusual acrobatic feat than an ordinary political transformation.[1]
[17 January 1905, Manchester:] [M]y father used to say that when he heard people going about saying, "Something must be done, something must be done," he always noticed that something very stupid was usually done.[2]
[19 January 1905, London:] Lord Selborne is engaged in "thinking imperially." That must be a very restful occupation, because while engaged in it he does not require to use ordinary purposes of thought in the ordinary manner at all.[3]
[26 January 1905, Northwest Manchester:] And I would at the same time offer a piece of advice to the Prime Minister. It is very presumptuous on my part, no doubt, but, after all, these great men, dealing so much with complicated matters, are apt to forget some of the little simple truths.[4]
[6 February 1905, Gainsborough:] Protection is the art of doing business at a loss. The more we carry out the principle of Protection the greater and the deeper will be the loss.[5]
[3 March 1905, Bradford:] [N]onentities . . . fill the great offices of State, and . . . owe their position in the public eye only to the favour of a harassed Prime Minister clutching at the trailing skirts of power;

and on top of all this, the last straw, or perhaps I should say the last cartload of bricks, that breaks the camel's back has come this great and alarming Protectionist agitation.[6]

Cockran had been re-elected to congress in 1904. An isolationist as well as an avowed anti-imperialist, Cockran opposed a bill for the expansion of the Navy urged upon Congress in February 1905, by President Roosevelt. It was an expenditure, Cockran argued, that had tripled if not quadrupled in the wake of the Spanish – American War and Philippine insurrection. National greatness, Cockran said, came from the peaceful pursuit of commerce, not military or naval strength.[7]

Notwithstanding his opposition to increased expenditures for the Navy, Roosevelt invited Cockran to join a special delegation to investigate conditions in the Philippines led by Secretary of War William Howard Taft, who had previously served as the Civil Governor of the Philippines. It was a high-powered delegation which included Secretary of State Elihu Root and Speaker of the House Joseph Cannon.[8]

Roosevelt had also asked Cockran to join the official party because he had a diplomatic assignment which he wished Cockran to undertake. The United States had purchased 400,000 acres of farmland for over $7 million in the Philippines, owned by several orders of Catholic friars who were considered by native Filipinos to be symbols of Spanish oppression. In turn, the United States had resold the land to Filipino farmers and the Vatican had agreed to send the $7 million back to the Philippines to restore run-down Church property. The Vatican, however, had been dragging its feet. If the funds had not been returned as promised by the time the US delegation returned to America in October, Roosevelt wanted Cockran to proceed directly to Rome and register directly with the Vatican a protest of the US government. Roosevelt had chosen Cockran because of his high standing with the Vatican stemming from the role he had played to have the Pope mediate between the United States and Spain in the days leading up to the Spanish – American War.[9]

The US delegation travelled to Manila via San Francisco, but Cockran did not join them. Instead, as was his usual habit, he travelled to Europe in the spring and met with Churchill, his Aunt Leonie and other friends before travelling on to Italy and meeting with Vatican officials prior to departing for the Philippines from Naples early in June.

Cockran had a wide range of friends and acquaintances from both parties in England. The dust had settled from Churchill's defection a year earlier from the Tories, and while in England, Cockran would inevitably have heard both good and bad opinions about Churchill's motives and his ambition. He also would have had long conversations with Churchill about his prospects. Cockran was clearly troubled by what he heard. He thought long and hard about the best course of action for his young friend to follow, but uncharacteristically, Cockran held his tongue and did not share his advice directly with his young friend. Perhaps it had not been fully formed before he left for the Orient.

In any event, Cockran's concern resulted in an extraordinary letter from him to Churchill, the longest letter in their correspondence. Cockran offered, possibly for the last time, advice on Churchill's career, specifically that he announce that he would not accept office in the Liberal government, which was sure to be on offer following the next election.

Cockran was always careful and restrained in offering Churchill his advice, always reminding Winston that his advice might not be appropriate.[10] As he said in his second letter to Winston on 27 April 1896: 'Do not My Dear Winston feel that I am troubling you with this long letter merely to air my views . . . I give it to you for what it is worth, firmly convinced that your own judgement may be trusted to utilize it if it be of any value or to reject it if inapplicable to your plans or your surroundings'. This letter in 1905, three times as long as that long letter in 1896, shows all of the same sensitivity and restraint.

Cockran was an orator, but he also was an experienced trial lawyer who knew how to marshal his arguments to a jury. In this letter, however, Cockran the trial lawyer marshalled his arguments to persuade an audience of one.

June 12/05   DAMPFER "SCHARNHORST"
Private and
Confidential

My Dear Winston

I assume that Leonie has explained how I found the North German office closed when I went there in search of a time-table on Saturday week. She promised she would make it clear to you and what she undertakes to do I have learned, from long experience to consider as good as done. At any rate I have at last been able to secure one and I send it herewith – When I boarded the boat at Naples late at night there seemed to me no one who could tell me where anything was to be found – not until the afternoon when we are drawing close to Port Said was I able to get my hands on this copy. I have underlined the dates at which this boat will touch the various ports on the present voyage. A cable addressed to me Scharnhorst Nordlloyd will reach me at any of them till July 16th when I get to Yokohama where my address will be care of the American Minister. After July 26th if you want to communicate with me you had better send the message to the care of Maj. Gen. Corbin in Army Headquarters Manila P. I. I don't believe any telegraphing will be necessary but if occasion should arise for using the wire you will know how to make it effective – though you should not find any such urgent necessity for communication as would justify cabling. I hope none the less you will write to me care of Gen. Corbin a brief synopsis of the situation political more especially as it affects yourself – so that I will get the letter when I reach Manila about August 5th or at any rate before I leave the Philippines some three weeks later.

I am very comfortably situated on this craft. The food is to put it mildly questionable though doubtless according to German notions it is excellent. But I have been able to secure the Captain's Cabin a fine apartment just abaft the bridge and on the same elevation comprising a large sitting room a good bed-room and a spacious bath-room with a shower. I have provided myself with excellent tea and I am the happy possessor of a tea-basket which contains everything necessary for a brew. Moreover there is a Lady aboard who lives in Java – I believe she is half Dutch and half native – whose acquaintance I have just made and who promises to make tea for me hereafter in the method peculiar to tea-growing countries – thus equipped I look forward to the six weeks which must elapse before I reach Yokohama with quiet composure if not with wild enthusiasm.

There is one idea in my head which will not down and which I fear will rob me of all rest unless it be given expression. Here then it is. It concerns you and I beg for it just such attention as you may deem it deserves after weighing it more or less carefully.

It arose from a paragraph in one of the newspapers which prompted a cartoon in the *Pall Mall Gazette* on Saturday last. This latter I saw on my way to Folkestone. It represented you as a

mosquito or a fly or a wasp or some variety of winged irritant
perched on the coach of Sir Henry Campbell-Bannerman whose
repose you have evidently disturbed and are plainly striving to ruin.
Under it is the paragraph to which I have referred and which states
in substance that Mr. Winston Churchill will not be given a place in
the Liberal Cabinet if one should be formed after the next election.
The cartoon was not particularly clever or funny but the idea
conveyed by the paragraph has become a subject of extensive
reflection with me.

To begin with it shows two things. First that your opponents
believe you expect a seat in the Cabinet if a Liberal Government is
to be formed and second that if you be not gratified in this
expectation they count on your making trouble for the party which
you have recently joined. Now this conception of your attitude
presents you in rather a sordid character. It assumes that your sole
object in politics is place and that to attain your ambition party
success or party prospects would be sacrificed without scruple or
hesitation. Of course we must realise that where a man has changed
sides, however lofty the motives which actually govern him, he is
very likely to be accused by those whom he has left of being actuated
by the very basest desires and ambitions. And the public – the vast
masses of them – absorbed in busy occupations have little time to
sift and examine the evidence on which these personal assaults are
supported. They can only see facts that are patent & so conspicuous
that they cannot be overlooked. They know that you have changed
sides. – They vaguely feel that you have explained why you crossed
the floor of the House and that your former associates have refused
to accept the explanation, but have assigned motives for your
conduct [other] than you yourself would avow or admit. The public
mind on this question in my judgement is not yet formed. Your
career has been brilliant enough to arouse their interest, and so they
have followed your movements as far as they are unmistakable. But
when it comes to judging your motives I believe the majority of men
who are not bigoted partisans are as yet of open minds – not at all
convinced that the insinuations of your hostile critics are justified
nor yet wholly satisfied that they are entirely baseless. The majority
are waiting further developments before reaching their final
conclusions. This then is very probably the crisis of your career. The
judgement which men fairly unbiased will form of you now is very

likely the one that will follow you through life. For my part I don't
think you could possibly desire a more favourable opportunity for
confounding decisively and irretrievably your enemies and
vindicating your career to the full satisfaction of the friends who
hold you dear. You have a chance now to take a position which will
make it impossible for any one to question your motives for it will
be so conspicuously unselfish that everyone must notice it and be
impressed by it.

Every one has made up his mind that you are eagerly bent on
being admitted to the Cabinet – Under ordinary conditions this
would be an ambition so natural that it would be praiseworthy –
Indeed to acknowledge yourself without it would be to confess
yourself unfitted for public life – But your circumstances now are
not normal. They are unusual. Your course then it seems to me
should not be governed by usual principles of conduct. The thing
above all others for you to do now is exactly the opposite of that
which your enemies expect and which your lukewarm associates
rather anticipate – All these are agreed that you will insist on
entering the Cabinet or fight. Why not confound the hostile and
surprise the indifferent by declaring now that you won't seek or
even accept membership in a Liberal government if one is formed
with the new parliament? Such a declaration would be in the nature
of a bomb whose explosion would resound throughout the whole
Empire but whose fragments would damage none but your critics. It
would stamp as absolutely unselfish you whom all the Tory leaders
and organs have combined to brand as self-seeking, self-centred,
and self-conscious. It would not leave one rag left of the garment
which they have been laboriously trying to fit on your shoulders for
the last two years and all the world would realize how baseless this
conspiracy of slander has been.

What now would you sacrifice by such a declaration made at this
moment?

First you will say that of course it involves renunciation of high
office. That may be, but the renunciation would not be final. Indeed
at the very worst it would be merely a brief adjournment. The man
who has made your position in the House and in the Country can't
keep out of office. If he refuses to seek it then the office must in the
nature of things seek him. Moreover the moment you cease to be
a competitor for all the men now watching you suspiciously on your

own side of the House will all at once turn their jealousies in other directions – and you, no longer an object of their distrust, will very likely acquire their friendship. And if this be the result, as I believe it must be, then you would be the only man prominent in your party without personal animosity or rancour. Think what such a position would mean. Conceive to what it must inevitably lead. Beyond any doubt it must result in your becoming the unquestioned leader before the lapse of ten years.

It would be an attitude absolutely unique and so far as I know unprecedented in English public life – this of a young man furnishing to a political party its most powerful support and yet declining to accept office under it – giving it success and yet refusing to profit by the triumph to which he has largely if not decisively contributed. Mind I don't mean that you should remain aloof from both parties as Gladstone did after the fall of Peel for some ten years I believe – on the contrary I think you should be the most active and devoted partisan of the Liberal side – but a wholly unselfish one. Your word in the House would thus acquire a weight that no other could possibly possess. You would be the chief support of your party but not its beneficiary. If Gladstone's isolation led to the Premiership merely because it freed him from personal contentious concern [think] what the result must be of a course which would keep you free from jealousies and competitions while at the same time placing a whole party under steadily growing burden of obligation to you.

I beg you to weigh all this in the same spirit which inspires me to write it. I have spoken with absolute frankness all that has come into my mind through reflection on that paragraph reprinted in the *Pall Mall Gazette* and whether you adopt these views or reject them I am sure you will realize that they are fruits of much solicitude for your future – I count on your reaching the highest place in your country – and this letter is sent in the hope that it may serve to throw a ray of light, however faint, on your pathway.

Yours very sincerely
W. Bourke Cockran[11]

In a way, Cockran was right that 'this then is very probably the crisis of your career. The judgement which men fairly unbiased will form of you now is very likely the one that will follow you through life.' Churchill detractors to this day cite his switching parties as evidence of ambition, not principle.

Cockran anguished over the letter. This was bold and specific advice which, if taken, would have far more impact on Churchill than his general advice ten years earlier ('I hope you will allow me to assume the privilege of my years and advise you strongly to take upon the study of sociology and political economy.'). Cockran was sufficiently concerned about his advice that he added a long P.S. in which he tried to temper his earlier message. Now that Churchill was a member of the Liberal Party, Cockran wrote it was 'incumbent on you to accept office if pressed upon you,' even though he preferred that Churchill not do so.

P.S. I have opened this long screed to add another word – I am not sure that I have made clear the extent to which I think the renunciation suggested should be carried. I don't mean that it should be permanent or absolute. The fact that you are now a member of the Liberal party – not merely an independent acting with it on one question but opposed to it on practically all others – makes it incumbent on you to accept office if pressed upon you. All that I think you should do now is to announce that you won't accept office during the *next* parliament nor until you have earned it by service to the Country *through* the Liberal party. If after such an announcement there was an imperative demand that you take a place in the government or such cabinet then a new situation would arise. It would present an entirely new question – whether you would *accept* office at the demand of your party differs widely from getting office under a threat or possibility that if refused you might make trouble.

Personally I should prefer that you kept out of office altogether for the present. A man who could support all party measures effectively and yet keep free from the differences and jealousies inherent in the most homogeneous cabinets would establish such a position, – in my judgement, that very soon he must be invited to join the govt on his own terms – even though these embraced the Premiership. Indeed I am not at all sure that the first place would not be forced on him for the simple reason that he would probably be the only means through whom all factions could unite for effective co-operation. In time my suggestion is to renounce the small merely to make sure of the great, to be slow about looking for a minor post in order to increase the chances of having the greatest placed at your feet. And this great result I would have to reach not by conduct that the most envious or hostile could criticise but by a course that the most scrupulous must praise. I have found through long experience that there is but one path to durable success and that is the straight & narrow one. To this I have never known an exception.[12]

Cockran did not return to the United States from the Philippines until October and did not visit England again until 1906 after Churchill had accepted his first government office, albeit not at the Cabinet level. It is not known whether the two corresponded in the interim, but Cockran's June 1905 letter clearly anticipated correspondence between them as he specifically told Churchill how to reach him in the Philippines. The next letter in the correspondence, Cockran's 18 May 1906 letter to Churchill, suggested that an exchange of letters occurred between the men during this period ('much has happened since last we exchanged letters'). If there were, they do not survive.

Cockran's diplomatic mission for the president was unsuccessful for reasons beyond Cockran's control, and he did not visit the Vatican. Subsequently, the Vatican reneged on its pledge, and instead sent the $7 million to Spain to build up religious orders in that country, adding insult to injury and confirming the hostility which the United States had found among Philippine natives towards the land-owning friars.[13]

Cockran's professional disappointment, however, was more than offset by the impact the journey had on his personal life. The twice-widowed Cockran met and fell in love with his future and third wife Anne Ide. Miss Ide was the beautiful twenty-seven-year-old daughter of Judge Henry Clay Ide of Vermont – the acting Governor of the Philippines and previously the American Land Commissioner in Samoa. Anne was serving as her father's hostess at the Malacañan, the official residence of the Governor-General, and Cockran was designated as her dinner partner.

Cockran was late in arriving – a trait he shared with Churchill – and his first words to the striking young woman are not enshrined in the annals of the most memorable pick up lines: 'You are a lawyer's daughter and understand the law of salvage.'[14] More interestingly, Anne's birthday coincided with Christmas and as a young girl in Samoa where her father had been the Governor, the author Robert Lewis Stevenson declared he had no more use for his birthday and signed a formal document conveying his November birthday to her, something she celebrated thereafter for the rest of her life.[15]

Cockran's official biographer James McGurrin, who was selected by Anne Cockran and given unrestricted access to all of Cockran's papers, wrote of the couple's first meeting, where his only source could be Anne Cockran herself. They were each interested in politics and, despite their party differences (her father was a Republican), agreed on 'all the important public issues of the day'. It was literally love at first sight. Cockran moved quickly and

> told her that he should like to make her interest his for the rest of his life. Although he was her senior by twenty-five years (he being fifty-two and she only twenty-seven) his ardor and determination won an immediate acceptance of his rather sudden and unique proposal.[16]

Shane Leslie's brother Seymour wrote of the Cockran's marriage:

> To hear Bourke and Anne together, "beauty and the beast" as they said, his teasing Irish, her quiet retorts, with her Vermont wit, was to know a happy if childless marriage. They were at every party when they were not entertaining themselves, with the inevitably English butler sweating with three times the work (at four times the pay), he had done in England. It was here that I met with "cocktails" – and the driest martinis at that – for the first time.[17]

Shortly after Cockran's death in 1923, a grieving Anne discussed their age difference, telling a close childhood friend, the stepdaughter of Robert Louis Stevenson: 'Bourke was not old. To the end he remained a boy – an Irish boy – and I loved him.'[18]

On 30 November 1905, Churchill was thirty-one and, echoing his letter to Cockran six years earlier, wrote to his mother that 'Thirty-one is very old.' Four days later, the Conservative government resigned, and ten days after his birthday, Churchill became a junior minister. After first turning down an offer of a more senior position at the Treasury which would have led more quickly to a cabinet office,[19] Churchill asked for and received the post of Under-Secretary of State at the Colonial Office where he could conduct all the department's business in the House of

Commons because the head of the Colonial Office, Lord Elgin, sat in the House of Lords.

On the surface, it would appear that Churchill ignored Cockran's advice. But Cockran's letter initially referenced only Cabinet-level offices, and his postscript allowed that there were circumstances under which Cockran thought it would be perfectly proper to accept office and indeed it would be ungracious not to do so ([t]he fact that you are now a member of the Liberal party . . . makes it incumbent on you to accept office if pressed upon you'). Whether office was 'pressed upon' Churchill or not, the Liberals were well aware of how valuable he had been in the year-and-a-half run-up to the election. The fact that Churchill had initially been offered the most senior of all the junior minister posts is proof of that. Under the circumstances, Cockran might not have thought his advice was being ignored and wouldn't have taken offence even if he had.

On 3 January 1906, Churchill travelled to Manchester to begin his first election campaign as a member of the Liberal Party. While Manchester was solidly Conservative, it was also the centre of free trade fervour in England, the home of Cobden and Bright, and free trade was to be the issue on which the election campaign was to be fought. With a turnout of 80 percent of eligible voters, Churchill was elected on 13 January 1906 with 56 percent of the vote in Manchester where Conservatives lost all eight seats they had previously held. Across the country, Chamberlain and the protectionist Conservatives were crushed. Liberals won an absolute majority of 377 seats, Conservatives only 157, while Redmond's Irish Party had 83 and the Labour Party 53.

Breaking with a decade long practice, it would appear that Cockran did not travel to Europe in the spring of 1906 for he and Churchill exchanged letters in May and June which indicate that the two had not talked since the National Election in January.

May 18, 1906

My dear Winston:

Much has happened since last we exchanged letters. The election in England seems to have made one reputation, and to have unmade several. Looking at it from this distance, its productive results appear to be embodied and exhausted in yourself, its destructive efficiency in the ruin of the Tory Party, and the complete collapse of

Balfour, Chamberlain, and the men who have been its leaders for fifteen years. Your position seems to be the only one made distinctly powerful by the campaign itself. On the other side, there does not appear to be anything visible more than some wreckage, with here and there a few survivors clinging to it in rather forlorn shape.

I have been following with great interest the proceedings of this Parliament. The task which confronts the new ministry appears to be the most serious ever undertaken by a British administration. If, as is generally assumed on this side, the labor men, though their representatives constitute but a small minority in the House of Commons, are nevertheless the active, dominant influence in the liberal party, and if their policy be as socialistic in its tendencies as some correspondents of American newspapers seem to believe, it will require abilities of the very highest order on the part of men charged with legislation to withstand revolutionary and extravagant proposals without provoking revolts that may defeat the government, and even disrupt the party.

The same questions which confront you have also arisen to perplex us. A number of very active men, well organized and plentifully supplied with money, who while they do not acknowledge the name of socialists yet are held together solely by discontent with present social conditions and determination to subvert them, (however skillfully contrived to veil its real significance may be the language of their platform,) are making a determined effort to capture the democratic party. Against such calamity I am striving with all my might. The greatest difficulty with us, as I assume it will be with you, is to dispel the delusions caused by misapplication of terms, sometimes deliberately adroit, and sometimes unconsciously misleading.

I have recently undertaken to define the limits within which the authority of government can be exercised over the industrial field, and beyond which it cannot be extended without impairing that principle of industrial initiative which is an essential feature of Christian civilization. Some weeks ago, I succeeded in persuading the New York State Democracy assembled at Tammany Hall to ratify unanimously a platform which I had framed dealing with the subject. I send you a copy of it, together with a speech previously delivered in support of a bill pending in the New York State Senate to establish a Board charged with full power to regulate the operation of public utilities in the City of New York, where the same principle is elaborated. I think I sent you a copy of my first speech in the House of Representatives, supporting the Hepburn bill to regulate railway rates. Since this measure reached the Senate, its opponents no longer hoping to defeat it, have sought to emasculate it by proposing to make every proceeding of the railway commission subject to review by the Courts. Although the bill was no longer before us, I took occasion while discussing the rules of the House to express my views on how far the authority of the Judiciary could be extended with safety to its own efficiency and to the public welfare over the question of finding reasonable railway rates. I send you a copy of this speech also. I should like your opinion about all these matters as they affect you in England.

While I was ill in California last winter, a letter arrived from Montague White, which is enclosed. You will remember that he was formerly diplomatic agent of the South African Republic in England. While he was in this country I became acquainted with him, and I learned to appreciate and like him very much. I think he was absolutely sincere, moderate in expression, and well disposed to your country, though he always remained strictly loyal to the cause which he espoused. The fate which has overtaken him seems to be particularly hard. His letter describes his condition well, that I hope you will find time to read it. If something were done to relieve his distress I think it would be highly creditable to your government, and to your country.

Our little friend Miss Daly will be at Claridge's with her mother, in the month of June. I hope you will bring her down to the House of Commons, so that she can see it and you in operation. I may go over myself after the adjournment of Congress for a few weeks. Is there any chance of your coming to this country during the autumn? There will be very interesting elections in November, including a new House of Representatives and a governor in New York State. This struggle is almost certain to develop the issues on which the next Presidential election will be fought, and it is more than likely that its result will foreshadow the candidates on both sides. If you come, needless to say I shall insist upon the pleasure of taking charge of you.

Yours very sincerely,
[no signature line][20]

Churchill promptly replied:

June 5, 1906.   Blenheim Palace
Dictated Confidential

My dear Bourke,

I need scarcely say how delighted I am to hear from you again. Much has happened since we breakfasted at Claridge Hotel, and I am glad that viewing events as you do from a position absolutely detached from party politics of the country, you feel able to write to me in a congratulatory strain. Thinking it all over, I am prepared to claim the Manchester election as a great event. Manchester was the home of Free Trade, Free Trade was assailed. I left my party and went to Manchester to contest its great commercial division, and the division which contains the historic Free Trade Hall. When I went, Manchester and Salford were represented by nine Conservative members – all with more or less pronounced Protectionists views – including the Prime Minister. The result of the Poll dispossessed all these nine gentlemen from seats which many of them had held for twenty years, and installed in their place – by immense majorities – nine Liberal or Labour members all definitely pledged to Free Trade. The results of this electoral turn over, which, so far as I know, is unexampled in English political history, were undoubtedly effective throughout Lancashire. In that great industrial county which plays a part in English political life, disproportionate even to its wealth and population, we have actually won nearly thirty five seats counting seventy upon a division and in itself enough to have destroyed, or almost destroyed, the whole majority with which the late Government went to the country. Could anything be a plainer tribute to the wisdom of an instructed democracy than this emphatic asseveration of the economic doctrine of Mr. Bright and Mr. Cobden, after the successful practice and matured consideration of fifty years. I think it will be a long time before Protection is ever raised in the same form in England.

I am indebted to you for your kindness in sending me copies of the speeches you have made. I will read them with great care and will let you know how they strike me when I have finished. But I did not want to delay my answer to you until I had digested your material. I should think we would probably find ourselves again in agreement upon this large group of questions. It is quite evident that a rigid application of Collectivist doctrines would be no more compatible with human existence than an equally rigid application of Individualism. Man is an individualist for some purposes, a collectivist for others, and it is in the harmonious combination of the opposite philosophies that future statecraft is comprised. Whatever people may say, society is practically agreed upon an infinite number of varying compromises and these will multiply and refine with every additional complication which science and civilisation add to your life. But no one seems to have yet discovered the principle or code of principles by which these compromises should be governed and limited; and in the absence of any such code, all minds are vexed by inconsistencies and apparent insincerities which render them very unequal in combating the clear-cut arguements of doctrinaire extremists on either hand. If the politics of the past consisted in discovering the true principles, the politics of the future will consist in discovering the principles upon which these principles are to be interblended. As I gather from your letter that your speeches on the Hepburn Bill attempt this task – in reference at any rate to one sphere of modern activity, I shall read them with the utmost interest.

I have sent Ms. Montagu White's letter to you to the Colonial Office in order that I might make definite enquiries about the position, but I remember quite clearly seeing a telegram from Lord Selborne only a month ago in which he asked permission immediately to pay Ms. Montagu White some considerable sum of money – I think £1,500 – I presume in commutation of any claims which he may have had against the late Boer Government, and I remember that I myself sanctioned the payment and that Lord Elgin did not reverse my decision. However, I will have this more precisely ascertained. I am very glad to hear Miss Daly is coming over to Claridge's Hotel and I should be glad if you would let me know when she will be here. But I am still more glad to hear that there is a prospect of your return to England. I have now got a nice house – No. 12 Bolton St. – where I can entertain at dinner, and it would give me the greatest pleasure to talk over men and things.

The Irish party are very friendly to the Government. We do not pretend that we are going to give them all they want and they do not pretend to expect it, but some very considerable readjustments on Sir Anthony MacDonnell's lines, will, no doubt, be submitted to Parliament next year, and may very likely carry us a long way in the direction of Irish self-government. Meanwhile, we have introduced a Labourers Bill which enables a further four millions to be borrowed upon the same terms as the Irish Land Act for dealing with the conditions of the labouring population in Ireland, who have not benefited directly from the measure which affected tenant farmers. This, I understand, has given much satisfaction. Nothing can exceed the skill and judgement with which J Redmond manages the Parliamentary party and his position in the House of Commons is certainly superior to that of any man on the Speaker's left.

The Labour members look more formidable than they are. None of them could have been returned in the face of Liberal opposition. But on the other hand, in the absence of a second ballot, it would have been in their power to split many Liberal votes. The reason that they have exerted a greater apparent influence upon the course of policy pursued this Session, has been that in nearly every case the demands which they have made have been well within the limits of the general pledges given by the mass of the Liberal party at the election. I am bound to say I find their demands in nearly every case very moderate and reasonable. They are a stable force in the House of Commons and add a great deal to the sincerity and reality of our Debates. To me at the Colonial Office they are far less embarrassing than some of the more hysterical Radicals below the gangway. The English labour leader is not a logician. He has nothing in him of the French "Red". He is essentially bourgeois at heart, and the Trade Unionists whose funds and organisation sustain the whole of the Labour party, are the most respectable and the most responsible working class element in the country. So far as the rank and file of the Liberal party is concerned, we have got at least three hundred absolutely faithful supporters of the Government, so that I do not think there is any danger of our being defeated even if we had to take a course to which the entire Labour party was opposed. Altogether I do not find in the immediate future of English politics any cause for serious anxiety. The sterility and mediocrity of democracy – as exemplified in its leaders – is the most depressing circumstance which I can discover.

I should indeed like to be able to come over to the States in the autumn: but that would be to make adventurous plans. I daresay

you or that side are fated to show the world the solution of some of
the economic and sociological questions by which we are puzzled. If
there is an American revolution of property, I hope that by sitting
quietly here, we shall contrive to adopt all its solid advantages as
we did those of the French Revolution without suffering from its
excesses! This is a sentence so completely complacent that I hasten
with best wishes to subscribe myself.

Yours most sincerely,
Winston S. Churchill[21]

By now, Cockran was officially engaged to Anne Ide, and their wedding
was scheduled for November 1906 after the fall elections. Cockran,
meanwhile, had gained new prominence at Tammany Hall. Earlier in the
year, he had been elected 'Grand Sachem', largely an honorary title which
essentially signalled that he was first among equals with the other Sachems
who were leaders at Tammany Hall. Charles Murphy, however, was still
the chairman of the Tammany General Committee and effectively the boss
of Tammany Hall. In addition to being named the Grand Sachem, however,
Cockran had a more substantive position as Chairman of the Platform
Committee. That is what Cockran was referring to in his letter when he
wrote to Churchill that 'I have recently undertaken to define the limits
within which the authority of government can be exercised over the
industrial field'. It was the platform on which William Randolph Hearst
ran for governor in New York as the Democratic candidate.

The Republicans controlled the governorship and the state legislature
in 1906. There had been scandals for the past two years in the insurance
and banking departments, and in an interesting (and eventually familial)
sidelight, Cockran had criticized William Jerome, the crusading New
York District Attorney, for failing to prosecute criminals in the insurance
scandals. Jerome was Lady Randolph Churchill's first cousin, the nephew
of her father Leonard Jerome. All Jerome had done, Cockran charged,
was deal with those individuals who came forward and confessed. He did
nothing to investigate those who did not come forward.[22]

Churchill made reference to this in a letter to his mother on
29 September 1906 while he was on holiday in Siena. The Democratic
Convention had concluded on September 24, and it is apparent that
Cockran wrote Churchill a letter advising him of all that happened
because Churchill seems remarkably well informed on New York politics

and specifically makes reference to William Jerome's attacks on Hearst and his supporters like Cockran. Churchill clearly sides with Cockran and the Democrats, not the Republicans and his Jerome relative:

> The situation in New York is most interesting. B. Cockran is working for Hearst, & Jerome denounces him and all his backers as 'a gang of disreputable crooks'. The papers willfully misrepresent the situation in the interests of the Republican Party. I don't pretend to know; but I have a sort of feeling that the Democrats will sweep the board in spite of everything & that Hearst will be Governor. This is a piece of quite gratuitous prophesying, & vy likely you will be able to rebuke me for it when the result is known.[23]

Hearst narrowly lost the election, but Cockran was re-elected to Congress in November 1906. Cockran and Anne Ide were married on 15 November 1906 at the St. Regis Hotel in New York. Cockran and Anne then set off on their honeymoon, an extended tour of Europe, which included a stop in England and a visit with Churchill after Cockran and his wife had met Jennie in Monte Carlo. Cockran wrote Churchill from Paris:

> April 17/07   Hotel Bristol
> Paris
>
> My dear Winston
>
> Your Mother whom I met at Monte Carlo said you would be at Biarritz near the end of last week – which explains my telegram.
>   Since I received your answer I have been busy making arrangements to spend a day or two in London before our return to America.
>   We had intended sailing on the 3rd from Cherbourg but now we propose to defer our departure for a few days and take the train from Liverpool on the 8th – crossing over on the 5th.
>   This will afford me a chance to see you and compare notes on the very interesting conditions political now prevailing in both England and America.
>   Events have been moving rather rapidly of late though nothing has transpired as yet which I have not foreseen for some time and which I have not foretold in many speeches during the last five years.

I won't weary you now with any discussion of perplexing problems further than to repeat I am still an optimist. There is nothing among all the evils which men are condemning as vehemently in both hemispheres that does not show conclusively the inexorable faces of progress, moral and material, steadily at work and moving inevitably to success.

But of all this we have much to say at the meeting to which I look forward with eagerness.

We will stop at Claridge's. Drop a line if you have a chance and believe me always your friend.

W. Bourke Cockran[24]

Chapter 14
'Sins of the Father'

London
5 October 1913

Winston Churchill, the thirty-eight-year-old First Lord of the British
Admiralty, was displeased. More than any other single person, the safety
and security, nay the future, of the British Empire lay in his hands. For, as
he had been saying for the past thirteen years, it was the British Navy
which had gained England its pre-eminent position in the world,
protecting its vast commercial empire from predators, whether they be
pirates marauding in the South China Sea or the Kaiser and the German
High Seas Fleet prowling the North Atlantic. That was where all of his
focus and attention should be directed, not diverted as it now was
towards the problems of Ireland.

Churchill walked over to a window of his office in the Admiralty and
looked out over Whitehall. Clouds were gathering and rain would soon
come. He hoped war would not, whether it be civil war in Ireland or
a European war on the continent. With judicious diplomacy and a navy
twice as strong as any other power, England might well avoid the latter. But
unless the Ulster leader Sir Edward Carson and the Tory Party's leader
Bonar Law agreed to compromise and ceased what Churchill believed to
be their treason and sedition, he saw no way to avoid the former.

And so, the sins of the father are visited upon the son, thought
Churchill, because if it were treason for Carson and Law to threaten
to resist with force the Home Rule for Ireland Act which the Liberal
government proposed to pass, then the same could and should be said
of Lord Randolph Churchill. For it was his father who went to Belfast
in 1886 when another Liberal government had been on the verge of
enacting Home Rule for that troubled island and later coined the
memorable phrase 'Ulster will fight; Ulster will be right'. That had been
the tipping point, the beginning of Lord Randolph's meteoric rise to
power and twenty years of Tory rule broken only by the Liberals after his
son had joined their ranks. Churchill knew that his father had passed it
off as a prediction, and indeed Churchill had done so himself in his
father's biography. But sitting now on the other side of the table faced
with the stark reality of such a 'prediction', Churchill took it now as

*what it most certainly had been – a threat. His father had been wrong,
he saw that now. Violence was not how you resolved political differences
in a democracy. Violence and democracy were incompatible. The
Protestants were in the majority now in Ulster, but if they could use
violence, or even the threat of violence as Carson and Law were doing
now, to achieve political ends, what would keep the Catholics in the
South from doing the same? Their majority was even greater. What was
sauce for the goose, after all. And Churchill well knew there was a long
tradition among some Irish Nationalists of using physical force, the
Fenians and John Devoy in America among them.*

*Churchill wondered when he had begun to change his views on Ireland
and what role Bourke Cockran had played. It wasn't at first, that was
certain. He had to admit, however, that the speech which Cockran had
sent him on Ireland nearly twenty years ago had made him think twice.
He hadn't changed his mind then, of course, because he believed the evils
of British rule in Ireland soon would be cured by honest British
administration. But it had never happened even though there had been
eighty-three Irish National members of Parliament (MPs) sitting in the
House of Commons representing their island's interests.*

*Not for the first time did Churchill wish that Cockran had agreed to
stand for Parliament back in 1903 when Campbell-Bannerman, John
Redmond and T.P. O'Connor had asked him. He admired Redmond and
O'Connor and respected them as honourable men, but they weren't
Bourke Cockran. By now, Cockran would have been the leader of the
Irish Nationalist Party, and even if he weren't, his presence in the House
of Commons alone would have given Ireland a voice that people would
have listened to.*

*Churchill walked back to his desk, lit a fresh cigar and sat down to
once more read Cockran's letter and his advice on how to handle what
Churchill saw as the coming civil war in Ulster. Did Cockran really have
the solution? Churchill certainly hoped so for if he didn't, it would take
something like a war with Germany to distract the Irish from their
internecine quarrels and to focus them on a common enemy.*

*Churchill had to admit there was an elegant simplicity to Cockran's
suggestion. Cut off Ulster from the outside world. No rail traffic, no
ships, no cables, no commerce and, Cockran believed, no bloodshed.
It could work in theory, but would it work in practice? Cockran's
experience, alas, was only in legislative matters. He had never established
policy nor faced the often messy detail of carrying it out. England could*

surely strangle Ulster to death economically simply by using its army and navy to seal the borders, but as Ulster slowly starved, would Catholics be safe in Protestant areas? Would Protestants be safe in Fermanagh and Tyrone? Churchill didn't think so.

There was another thing on which he disagreed with his old mentor. The sincerity of Edward Carson. He had every reason to doubt Carson. Bourke was like that, always looking for and finding the best in every man but too often overlooking the bad. That was a luxury Churchill couldn't afford, not in his position. To Churchill, the sincerity of Carson was akin to that of the Kaiser, and accordingly, he would trust neither. Hope for the best. Plan for the worst. Mentors could be helpful at the start, but the rest was up to him.

The years 1907 through 1912 once more saw Cockran at odds with Tammany Hall, out of Congress and again opposing the Democratic candidate for president. Cockran returned from his honeymoon at the end of April to find America in the midst of the Panic of 1907 and an American president once more seeking his advice and counsel. This time, however, the president who had summoned him to the White House to discuss economic affairs was a Republican, his Long Island neighbour and friend, Theodore Roosevelt.

In the fall of 1907, the Knickerbocker Bank in New York City failed, and this was quickly followed by runs on other banks which led to their failure as well. This rapidly spread to the rest of the country even though the Secretary of the Treasury attempted to increase liquidity by depositing $35 million in national banks. President Roosevelt consulted with Cockran during the panic and told his friend Finley Peter Dunne that he derived 'infinite comfort' from his talks with Cockran who 'always open[ed] up new avenues of thought for me'.[1] At Roosevelt's request, Cockran prepared a long thirteen-page memorandum which reflected Cockran's classical liberal view of the causes of and remedies for panics.

Runs on banks didn't just 'happen', Cockran wrote, and certainly weren't caused by excessive demand for money. Rather, some banks were fraudulently overextended and depositors rightly suspected that their money was at risk. Allowing the panic to run its natural course would wipe out the bad investments these banks had made. Cockran's suggestion was simple: Open the books on all banks and expose the weak sisters. After that, punish malfeasance. Banks who concealed their speculation, misrepresented their reserves or otherwise defrauded their investors should pay the price. Send them to jail. An informed market would make rational decisions and industry would begin to revive within thirty days if they thought banks could be trusted and the government would punish those who couldn't be.[2]

While Cockran never sought publicity for his talks with the president or the advice he gave, he had clearly come under TR's spell. On the floor of Congress on 3 February 1908, Cockran said that he would like to see Roosevelt nominated for president by both the Republicans and the Democrats. He described Roosevelt as a man 'who would cheerfully face political disaster rather than compromise a principle . . . a shining ornament of popular government, a loyal exponent of truth and an intrepid champion of justice'.[3]

In the event, Roosevelt chose not to run. The Republicans nominated Secretary of War William Howard Taft, who defeated William Jennings Bryan, the only major party candidate to be defeated three times for the presidency. Cockran did not run for re-election in 1908 and took no part in the presidential campaign as he was once again cast into the wilderness by Tammany Hall. Cockran's closeness with Roosevelt had not stood him in good stead with Tammany Boss Charles Murphy. What eventually did Cockran in, however, was fallout over the panic of 1907, specifically the Knickerbocker Trust Company which triggered it.

Murphy believed that appointing a receiver for the Knickerbocker was a simple matter of patronage, but Cockran disagreed. Murphy intended to appoint a Wall Street insider, a lawyer for the National Bank of North America. The appointment would be made by State Attorney General William Jackson, a Democrat who was not in Tammany's pocket. Cockran contacted Jackson and offered his opinion that certainly no one identified with Wall Street, and only an individual of the highest character, should be appointed. Unfortunately for Cockran, and without his knowledge, Jackson appointed as a receiver Henry Clay Ide, who was not only a Republican but Cockran's father-in-law as well. Murphy was livid, and Cockran was soon out of Congress.

Murphy, of course, claimed that the Knickerbocker receiver appointment had nothing to do with denying Cockran the renomination and said that Cockran was dropped because he was not a Democrat. The former boss Richard Croker, licking his wounds in Ireland, was delighted to hear that his old enemy had once more been expelled from Tammany and sent Murphy a cablegram: 'I told you so'.[4] Asked to comment on Croker's cable to Murphy, Cockran said:

> Mr. Croker never said anything worth commenting upon, except when I used to write what he had to say, and then it was commented upon all over the country.[5]

An editorial in the *Washington Post* at the time summed up popular Washington opinion on Bourke Cockran:

> What nonsense! If Tammany is Democratic, Bourke Cockran is a Democrat. This gifted public man suffers, as other public men have suffered, from the disparaging envy of lesser men and the obtuseness of those who stand too close to him to appreciate his true measure. Bourke Cockran is the peer of the great of other lands. He is fit to stand in the English Parliament and command the admiration and respect of the British nation. He could cross the channel to France and address the Chamber of Deputies in its own tongue, without loss of power or eloquence. He is broad enough to give credit to the opposition when it accomplishes a worthy task, and able enough to furnish and frame the ideas that save his own party from extinction. In the House of Representatives he stands today without a peer. In the social life of Washington he is admired and esteemed for his intellectual brilliance, charming manners and unrivalled conversational powers. Since he really does not belong in Tammany let us hope that another district in New York State will lay claim to his service and great ability.[6]

There was extensive correspondence between Theodore Roosevelt and Cockran from 1910 through the presidential election of 1912 as Cockran became one of TR's chief economic advisers. Roosevelt tried but failed to secure the Republican nomination for president in 1912, but there can be little question that Cockran would have supported him regardless of which party's nomination he received. After being denied the Republican nomination, Roosevelt was named by the Progressive Party and Cockran campaigned throughout the eastern half of the country on his behalf but to no avail. In the event, the Southern born Democrat Woodrow Wilson was elected by 41 percent of the popular vote, the lowest total for an American president in the twentieth century.

In England, Churchill stayed at the Colonial Office through early 1908. In March, Herbert Asquith, who was soon to become prime minister, offered Churchill his first Cabinet position, the Local Government Board, which he declined because there was 'no place in the Government more laborious, more anxious, more thankless, more choked with petty & even squalid detail, more full of hopeless and insoluble difficulties.'[7] In April 1908, with Asquith now as prime minister, Churchill was appointed to his first Cabinet post, President of the Board of Trade, where he served until 1909.

The novice phase in Churchill's life was rapidly coming to a conclusion. The change he effected in his life's structure in 1904 was now firmly in place, and at the tender age of thirty-three, he had his first Cabinet position. All the common tasks of that phase were now complete save one – romance and marriage. No one had replaced Pamela as the love in his life and she had married another in 1902. Subsequently, he had romanced and proposed, albeit unsuccessfully, to Muriel Wilson and the American actress Ethel Barrymore. Churchill's spectacular luck, however, was to hold, and in September 1908, Churchill married the beautiful twenty-three-year-old Clementine Hozier.

On the first two occasions Churchill was in Clementine's company, however, he did not make a good impression. The first time was in 1904 where Churchill lived up to Pamela Plowden's description about seeing all his faults upon first meeting him. Clementine later described the occasion to their son. It was at a dance and Clementine was nineteen years old. Churchill noticed Clementine and asked his mother Jennie to introduce them. Jennie professed not to know the girl but said she would find out and was surprised to discover she was the daughter of a close friend of Jennie, Blanche Hozier, who had an even more promiscuous reputation in the Victorian Era than Churchill's mother. Jennie then introduced Winston to the daughter of her well-travelled friend. Clementine politely responded and recounted to her son years later how his father had behaved.

> Winston just stared. He never uttered one word and was very gauche – he never asked me for a dance, he never asked me to have supper with him. I had of course heard a great deal about him – nothing but ill. I had been told he was stuck-up, objectionable et cetera. And on this occasion he just stood and stared.[8]

Winston did not meet Clementine again until a dinner party in March 1908 in his last days at the Colonial Office. The dinner party was given by Clementine's great-aunt who, while ostensibly asking her to attend at the last minute because there was only thirteen for dinner, was obviously intent on matchmaking. Churchill was late, as usual, and was seated between Clementine and the guest of honour, who thought herself an authority on Colonial matters and had a low opinion of Churchill. Not surprisingly, Churchill ignored the guest of honour and devoted all his attention to the strikingly attractive Miss Hozier. During the course of their conversation, Winston enquired whether she had read Churchill's biography of his father. Clementine answered honestly that she had not, and Churchill asked 'if I send you the book tomorrow, will you read it?' Clementine agreed. Whether Churchill was still suffering from the attention deficit disorder which had plagued him as a child and a young man (and most likely he still was) or was simply determined to prove Pamela once more correct in her assessment of initially putting his worst foot forward, Churchill never sent her the book. 'That made a bad impression on me' Clementine later told their son.[9]

That Churchill fell in love with a girl as beautiful and brilliant as Clementine is no surprise. That he was able to win her love after not one but two inauspicious debuts is a testament to the accuracy of Pamela's observation. The couple was engaged in August, and Churchill wrote this endearing note to Pamela the same day he proposed to Clemmie:

> I am to marry Clementine & I say to you as you said to me when you married Victor – you must always be our best friend.[10]

Pamela undoubtedly replied, but as with all of her other letters, Churchill apparently destroyed it. Churchill managed to stay on good terms with other old flames for he notified both Molly Hacket and Muriel Wilson of his engagement and both women wrote back in warm and affectionate terms.[11]

Churchill wrote an interesting letter to Pamela a few weeks later on 30 August 1908 where he asked her if she had been 'thinking about me a little sometimes recently' before confessing his concern about his forthcoming marriage – 'the vast domain of possibility is closed down to one single definite solution.' He concluded by telling her there was 'stress as well as hope in my heart; with much reverence & resolve; & even the tenderest feelings cast their shadows upon the strange soul of your friend'.[12]

Churchill continued to write to Pamela and she to him after his marriage. A small sampling:

> [*17 October 1910:*] I should *so* like to talk to you. Ages of time & rivers of wrath have divided us – and the clumsy world creaks along on wobbling axles – but I suppose you have still got a little tiny place in your heart for/Winston.[13]
> [*March 1922:*] It stirs me much – yr going back to those Indian scenes where my eyes were first lighted by the radiance of Miss Pamela Plowden. Remember what I said to you yesterday & always count on me.[14]

When Victor was appointed Governor of Bengal and Pamela returned to India, Churchill wrote on 12 September 1922 of the 'shining scenes where we first met so many years ago . . . I wish events could have taken another turn'.[15]

Victor died in 1947 and Pamela wrote to Churchill in October 1950 reminding him that he had proposed to her fifty years ago. Churchill wrote back:

> I have had (as you may guess) an awful time lately – exciting, exhausting, absorbing – and it is not till now that I can tell you how much I cherish yr signal across the years, from the days when I was a freak – always that – but much hated & ruled out – but there was one who saw some qualities, & it is to you that I am most deeply grateful . . . Fifty years! – how stunning but after all it is better than a hundred. Then there would not be memory.[16]

Cockran and his wife Anne travelled to Europe in the spring of 1909, less than a year after Churchill's marriage. Churchill wrote to Clementine on 30 May 1909 asking her to come dine with Cockran and his wife:

> Bourke Cockran – a great friend of mine – has just arrived in England from USA. He is a remarkable fellow – perhaps the finest orator in America, with a gigantic C.J. Fox head – & a mind that has influenced my thought in more than one important direction. I have asked him to lunch on Friday at H of C & shall go

to London that day to get my Money Resolution on the Trade
Boards Bill.

But what do you say to coming up too & giving us both (& his
pretty young wife) lunch at Eccleston? We could settle up lots of
things & see each other. Reynolds would 'hand over' etc. Do think
about this; & let me know whether it is feasible.[17]

Churchill became Home Secretary in 1910 and began to become more
actively involved in policy regarding Ireland. In 1911, he was appointed
First Lord of the Admiralty and continued his interest in Irish matters,
which was to lead to the last long letter extant between Cockran and
Churchill.

Cockran and Leonie Leslie's oldest child, Jackie (Jack and later Shane),
carried on an extensive correspondence between 1901 and 1922. Shane
entered King's College in Cambridge in 1908 and a year later moved to the
slums of the East End of London with other Cambridge Catholics and told
his astonished parents that he intended to convert to Catholicism and
become a priest.[18] Inasmuch as the Leslies were a pillar of the Protestant
Anglo-Irish ascendancy, this was devastating news. Shortly thereafter,
Shane renounced his inheritance to the family estate as well.

In the event, Shane became a Catholic but not a priest. In 1911, he
was in America for a lecture tour and, naturally, stayed with his friend
Cockran. While there he met and fell in love with Anne Cockran's
beautiful sister, Marjorie. Like her sister Anne, Marjorie had also acted
as hostess for her father and was self-assured, outgoing and had her pick
of men to marry, reportedly turning down over one hundred marriage
proposals. Both Marjorie and Anne had tattoos on their shoulder from
their days in the Pacific with their father, Anne with a lizard and Marjorie
a snake curled around a dagger.[19] The couple were married in an outdoor
ceremony at the Cedars in June 1912.

With Shane's marriage to Marjorie Ide, Churchill was now beset on all
sides by relatives who were ardent Irish Nationalists. To his first cousin
Shane was now added, by marriage, his own mentor Bourke Cockran. To
that had been added earlier, in December 1910, his own uncle Moreton
Frewen, whose mother was Irish. Moreton was elected in December 1910
as a member for West Cork as an independent Nationalist MP. The only
difference between Frewen on the one hand and Shane and Cockran on the
other was that he was more willing to seek an accommodation with Ulster
in order to secure Irish Home Rule in the South.

Churchill first publicly supported Home Rule in 1908. After the two elections of 1910, however, the Liberal government, including Churchill, began working in earnest to pass a Home Rule bill. The supremacy of Parliament was not to be impacted in the least, i.e., war, defense, treaties, and taxes. The Liberal bill was supported by Cockran's friend, John Redmond and the Irish Nationalist Party. It allowed counties in Ulster to temporarily opt out of Irish Home Rule until there had been two general elections. Even with this concession, Ulster remained opposed, violently opposed and led by the Ulster leader, Sir Edward Carson who was supported by the Conservative Party leader, Bonar Law.

Churchill had always supported some form of self-government for Ireland in a way Ulster Unionists and their Conservative allies never did. Indeed, the April, 1896 exchange of letters between Churchill and Cockran on the issue of self-government led his mentor to observe that "I do not think you and I are very far apart in our convictions. We differ more in phrases than in principle." His father, Lord Randolph, also had shown surprising sympathy toward Irish grievances during his career but he always stopped short of supporting Home Rule. When he joined the Liberal Party, Churchill did not object to its policy of Home Rule for Ireland so long as it was "subject to the supremacy of the Imperial Parliament."[20] To Churchill, that phrase meant that the minority rights of Ulster would always be protected by the Imperial Parliament in Westminster.

Lord Randolph might not have differed with his son's attitude in this regard as there is much historical evidence to the effect that Lord Randolph's opposition in 1886 to Gladstone's Home Rule proposal was more political than principled, a not uncommon criticism of the father. Churchill strongly disagreed with such an assessment in his father's biography. Regardless, Lord Randolph played the "Orange Card" in 1886 to his party's political advantage and was condemned by the Liberal government for treason and encouraging insurrection in Ulster.

Ironically, his son would make the same accusations of treason and insurrection in 1912 and 1913 against Sir Edward Carson and Bonar Law because they too were playing the "Orange Card" just as Churchill's father had done. Churchill believed democracy and violence were incompatible. In the fall of 1912, Bonar Law threatened that if Home Rule were "forced" upon Ulster and there were "bloodshed", the guilt, should such a tragedy take place as a consequence, would fall upon the

Liberal government. Equally combative, Churchill replied that Ministers who 'talk of revolution ought to be prepared for the guillotine'.[21]

A year later, in August 1913, the Home Rule bill had nearly passed through Parliament, twice being approved by Commons and twice being rejected by the House of Lords, which could not prevent the bill from becoming law after its third reading. In the interim, Carson had threatened to set up a provisional government in Ulster, independent of the British Empire, much as Ian Smith was to do in Southern Rhodesia (now Zimbabwe) later in the twentieth century.

As they did every year since their marriage, Cockran and his wife Anne once more travelled to Europe and were in London in October 1913. Cockran and Churchill met and discussed the dilemma facing the Liberal government in Ireland. Having completed a 180-degree change in his position on Ireland from his 1896 letter to his mentor, Churchill sought Cockran's views on Ireland and encouraged him to elaborate upon them in a letter which Cockran did on 4 October 1913 while he and his wife were still in London.

Oct 4/13   Ritz Hotel
                                                                 Piccadilly London, W.

My Dear Winston

Ever since we met I have been on a continuous rush engaging passage on one steamer after another only to surrender each one as circumstances entirely unforeseen arose to embarrass my departure – that is now fixed for the fifteenth aboard the Olympic and here I am redeeming in rather belated fashion my promise made at the Admiralty to send you a few notes on the present situation in Ireland as I see it.

While the temper which has called what is known as the Ulster movement into life is a matter of great concern to all sensible men and while there is no reason to doubt the perfect sincerity of Sir Edward Carson or those who follow him it is nonetheless a fact that the specific proposals embodied in the declarations which have been published and in the speeches which have been made during the last few weeks are wholly impracticable not to say preposterous.

For what is it that these men propose to do according to their own definition of their purpose?

They propose to establish a provisional government in the event of a certain bill being enacted by the British Imperial Parliament to resist the British government and this provisional government is to be in "Trust for the British Empire". I am quoting from memory but I am quite confident that these quotations are accurate.

Now consider for a moment the significance of such a proposal! Consider (if you can) such an anomaly as a government held in Trust – who is to enforce the Trust if the trustor or the trustees should prove faithless, inefficient or corrupt? Surely never before in the whole experience of mankind has excited fancy betrayed men through exaggerated rhetoric to conclusions so extravagant and absurd. I think it was John Bright who drew attention in a memorable debate to the grave consequences of allowing attorneyship to usurp the place of statesmanship. Here we have men who have proved themselves most capable attorneys or lawyers deliberately proposing to entrust the legal device of Uses and Trusts to government itself. – If absurdity has ever gone further in political affairs history fails to reveal the instance.

But it may be said that the principle professed in the organization with establishment of a government is a mere matter of abstract declamation and that so long as the govt. has power to enforce its decrees and provide for its maintenance the declaration put forth on its behalf are of no practical consequence.

Granting all this (and I do not think it can be denied) the so called provisional government of Ulster in the very nature of things could neither maintain itself nor enforce its decrees.

Conceding that the people of Ulster were unanimous in supporting this separatist movement (which they are not) or assuming that they are in the majority and that the minority would submit to their domination (which is exceedingly improbable) how could such a government subsist even for a week?

It could not enter into a Postal Union. It could not make treaties with other Countries. The Judgement or decrees of the Courts it might establish would have no weight or validity in other Jurisdictions.

Of course if the British govt or the new Irish Government were to invade the province with armed forces the path of the leaders would be plain. It would be perilous – desperate – but at least it would lead to constitutions with which men of desperate purpose could deal.

But suppose Ulster be left separately alone in the isolation it had chosen for itself. How could the population support itself for six days or even for three?

It is hardly conceivable that the British govt whose authority would have been flouted, its enactments resisted by armed forces – could continue to serve the conveniences or necessities of men actually in rebellion against it.

Of course every govt is bound by the very conditions of civilized society to enforce its authority against subjects who defy it. But the method of enforcement must always depend upon the peculiar conditions under which the necessity for it may have arisen. Here all the British govt need do to bring the seceding Ulsterites back to their allegiance is simply to leave them alone.

Excluded from the mails not a business house in Belfast or any other city in the seceded territory could keep its doors open for a day. Nor could the supply of food necessary to support existence be secured. I can realize the extent to which all great commercial communities live from hand to mouth and what a delicate and complex machinery is constantly in operation to meet the daily necessities of such a population. Dislocation – abrupt and complete – of the system by which an industrial community exchanges the products of its labor for the commodities essential to its subsistence would entail disasters so appalling that the men whose leadership had produced such bitter fruits would – be either hiding from the vengeance of the people they had misled or else suffering from it.

It is doubtful if a single bank could remain in operation – even the branches of concerns with headquarters elsewhere would be driven to close their doors.

Not a ship could clear from an Ulster City for a foreign port.

If a resident of Ulster died leaving a large estate – portions of it – perhaps the largest – would – be deducted in other countries. No probate of a will by an alleged Ulster Court would be recognized in a foreign jurisdiction. And therefore his executors would be without power to collect debts or give release from them or dispose of property left by the deceased.

In a word the conditions of Civilized Society would be suspended and the vast populations which civilization be called into existence deprived of subsistence would soon be clamoring for readmission to the Empire from which in moments of ill-judged passion they had withdrawn.

This view of the matter answers completely the criticism in the press for failing to take punitive measures against Carson and his confreres.

The govt will be employing the most effective means of repression when it does nothing. A government that is defied is not found to consult its rebellious subjects as to the means by which their rebellion is to be ended.

And when the revolt can be subdued without risking the life or limb of a single man who remains loyal to his sovereign the govt would be derelict to its duty if it undertook measures of force to accomplish a result that can be effected more completely with loss to none but the rebels themselves.

It is of course true that the collapse of Belfast and other Cities of Ulster would have pernicious consequences every-where. But the results to the rest of Ireland and of civilization would be comparatively remote while the blighting devas-tation of Ulster would be complete – awful – perhaps unremediable.

All this however does not alter the fact that discontent in any part of the Country is a fruitful source of evil to every part of it. However fanciful the fears or apprehensions which have produced this movement the fact remains that the men & concern who share it are not naturally vicious, idle or ill-disposed to law and order.

To compose their doubts and reconcile them to the political system of which they are a part and a very important one is the highest duty to which statesmanship can address itself.

But so far the power of Ulster to maintain a separate existence is concerned it may be dismissed as belonging to the domain of comic opera rather than of actual political problems.

I send you these hastily jotted down notes in the hope that they may be of some use and that they may reach you in time to be available.

Anne & I are just off by motor for Southampton where we take the boat for Havre and a week's tour of the Chateau Country – we will be back on the 12th. If you be in town before the 15th perhaps we may have a chance to meet. Meanwhile wishing you all sorts of success next week and after, I am.

Very sincerely yours
Bourke[22]

While Cockran professed he had 'no reason to doubt the perfect sincerity of Sir Edward Carson or those who follow him', Churchill certainly did. Cockran was correct that, in the long run, Carson's declaration of a Provisional government would ultimately fail, but Churchill believed the resulting civil strife and bloodshed might prove politically intolerable as violence often does in democracies.

Churchill's best friend, the conservative MP and barrister F.E. Smith, wrote to him in a similar vein as Cockran a day later and urged him to 'play up' and seek a compromise.[23] Whether Carson was 'perfectly sincere' or not, he was in fact proposing a violent insurrection in response to a democratic decision that provided for the protection of individual rights by the Imperial Parliament. By contrast, Churchill endeavoured, up until the outbreak of World War I, to effect a compromise solution in Ireland which would satisfy both Ulster and the Irish Nationalists and avoid an insurrection. Unfortunately, and aided by a near mutiny of British forces in Northern Ireland in early 1914, Churchill was unsuccessful and was much criticized as First Lord of the Admiralty, for his actions in positioning the fleet in the waters surrounding Northern Ireland.

Responding to attacks in the House of Commons, Churchill said:

> [W]hen attempts are made to paralyse the Executive in dealing with rebellion by fomenting stimulating suggestions of mutiny in the Army and Fleet, when that has been actually reached in our sober, humdrum, prosaic British politics, it is about time for serious, responsible people in all parts of the House, and all parties, to see if they cannot do something to make the situation a little better.[24]

A month later, Carson's treason against the Crown culminated in the landing into Northern Ireland of 35,000 rifles and 3 million rounds of ammunition from German sources with no opposition or subsequent prosecution by the British government.[25] The long, lamentable history of Ireland and England since April 1914 has many twists and turns, and while both sides wish to take the conflict back to its origins hundreds of years earlier, the Anglo-Irish War which led to the creation of the Irish Free State under Winston Churchill's guidance in 1922 as well as the subsequent 'troubles' in Northern Ireland in the late twentieth century have their origins in the April 1914 Ulster conspiracy with England's avowed enemy, Imperial Germany. While John Redmond's Irish Nationalists were 'playing up' according to English rules of good sportsmanship, Carson's Loyalists were playing at treason with the Germans. These lessons were not lost on Michael Collins and other physical force nationalists in the south of Ireland.

The remainder of the lives of Churchill and Cockran are beyond the scope of this book. Given the close-knit nature of the extended family of the Jerome sisters, Churchill and Cockran probably saw each other more frequently than most relatives who lived a continent apart. Except for the years during the Great War between 1914 and 1918, Cockran and his wife annually journeyed to Europe to visit Shane and Marjorie and other friends and relatives.

The Great War took its toll on the Jerome family. Winston's cousin Norman, Leonie's second child, was killed in combat in October 1914. His cousin Clare's husband, Wilfred, was killed in France in September shortly after the birth of their son. After the death of his brother Norman, Shane enlisted in the army and, ironically, suffered a nervous breakdown in the Dardanelles, an operation conceived by his cousin Winston and which led to Churchill's departure from the Cabinet in 1915.

A letter from Shane to Jennie on 8 April 1917 upon Churchill's return to the Cabinet illustrates the close-knit nature of the Jerome sisters' families.

My dear Aunt Jane

We are equally glad and surprised at Winston's return to office . . .

The reappointment to office has pleased Americans who look on Winston as 7/8 Yankee and 1/8 Blenheim! It is a pledge that senility has not the last say in everything . . .

Bourke in his great speech last week welcoming the Belgian mission to Boston worked out the President's meaning with care. I enclose a copy of his speech which will interest Winston and I should like to be able to pass on Winston's comment. There is nobody in this whole country now, except the mute and inglorious Bryan, who can rouse the American crowd to a frenzy of tears and emotion like Bourke. He is the only orator in America who can pick up a mob of 10,000 people in the open air and sway them to and fro.[26]

Jennie passed Cockran's speech on to Churchill, who expressed his complete agreement with Cockran. Churchill's comments were relayed back to Shane, who in turn wrote to Cockran telling him of Churchill's agreement with his speech. Shane had not specified, however, which Cockran speech Winston had read. Knowing that his recent speeches had been on Ireland as well as the Belgians, Cockran wrote back to Shane that:

I am delighted to know that Winston and I are on the same side. But what speech of mine is it that he read with such approval?[27]

In 1920, Cockran's long estrangement from Murphy and Tammany Hall abruptly ended. He was selected to nominate New York Governor Alfred Smith for president at the Democrat convention in 1920 and was re-elected to Congress for his sixth term that fall where, along with the Republicans, he opposed approval of the Treaty of Versailles and US involvement in the League of Nations. Woodrow Wilson's opposition to self-determination for Ireland had persuaded Cockran of the hypocrisy behind both the Treaty of Versailles and the League of Nations. It was a mug's game, and he opposed those initiatives just as he later opposed the chimera of disarmament advanced by Secretary of State Charles Evans Hughes in the Harding administration. Cockran believed, as did Churchill, that disarmament did not lead to peace, and Cockran's 1922 speech to Congress on how rearmament could lead to world peace foreshadowed how the Cold War concluded at the end of the twentieth century.

Meanwhile, Churchill was turned out of the Admiralty in 1915, ostensibly as a result of the British military defeat in the Dardanelles and Gallipoli Peninsula, but in reality it was simply revenge by the Conservative Party, which had never forgiven Churchill for leaving them in 1904. Churchill returned to government in 1917 as Minister of Munitions; became Secretary of State for War and Air in 1919; and in 1921 became Secretary of State for the Colonies, in which post he was present at and instrumental in the creation of the Irish Free State.

In the summer of 1921, Cockran and his wife Anne once more travelled to England as her sister Marjorie was having a complicated pregnancy and Anne wanted to be at her side. Leonie was with her husband at Castle Leslie in Ireland so the Cockrans stayed in Leonie's

London home. During this time, Jennie was convalescing nearby at her home on Westbourne Street, where she was attended by an incompetent physician who could not see what her niece Marjorie clearly could: 'Jennie's leg has turned green and black – I am sure it's gangrene – why can't the doctor see?'[28] Eventually, her leg was removed.

It was a trying time when the Cockrans arrived to find Jennie recovering from her lost leg and Marjorie awaiting a Caesarean operation. Anita Leslie, Marjorie and Shane's daughter, was seven years old at the time and wrote of Cockran's arrival in her biography of Jennie:

> And through this impenetrable jungle of unhappy grown-ups, one kind person stands out – Bourke Cockran! He had come to London with his pretty third wife, Anne, who was my mother's sister. While awaiting the Caesarean operation deemed necessary, they had taken Leonie's house, and then as Jennie's condition began to cause anxiety, they had to send for her to return from Ireland. Even Uncle Bourke looked distracted, and did not show his usual interest in us, which we resented.[29]

Marjorie's Caesarean operation was scheduled for 29 June 1921, the day Jennie died. Anita Leslie described the events of that sad morning and the role Cockran played after Jennie unexpectedly went into a coma before her two sons had arrived:

> Leonie had to be notified in the hospital waiting room where she had just learnt of my brother Desmond's birth. My father and Bourke Cockran and his wife, our Aunt Anne, were there with her – all distraught. It was Bourke who drove Leonie to 8 Westbourne Street, where her sister was still breathing. Jennie had not expected to die and Leonie felt she was still there wanting to know about the next generation.[30]

The Cockrans had arrived in London earlier in June, and no record remains of whether Cockran and Churchill met and talked during the days prior to Jennie's death. Both being in London, it would be unusual if they had not. And they would have talked of Ireland. As Colonial Secretary, Churchill was exceptionally busy with problems in the Middle East – Palestine and Mesopotamia – as well as Ireland, where the Anglo-Irish war still raged. Five days before Jennie's death, the Cabinet

approved an approach to the Irish leader. Eamon de Valera about a truce
in Ireland which subsequently came into effect on 11 July 1921.

Having once solicited Cockran's thoughts on Ireland in 1913, it is not
difficult to imagine Churchill doing so in 1921 nor Cockran volunteering
them unbidden as the two old friends discussed public affairs. Cockran
knew all the players in the Irish tragedy which unfolded in the teens
and early 1920s. John Redmond and T.P. O'Connor of the Irish
Nationalists, Eamon de Valera and Erskine Childers of Sinn Fein and John
Devoy of Clan na Gael, the American branch of the Irish Republican
Brotherhood. Ireland fills an entire chapter in James McGurrin's biography
of Cockran. Like most Irish Americans, Cockran had condemned the
British for their summary execution, without trial, of the leaders of the
Easter Week Rebellion. On 30 August 1919, he testified before the Senate
Committee on Foreign Relations regarding self-determination in Ireland, a
speech described by Henry Cabot Lodge, the ranking Republican member
of the Committee, as 'one of the greatest speeches ever delivered inside the
walls of Congress'.[31]

The Cockrans returned to England the following summer, and it was
the venue for the last letter in the Churchill–Cockran correspondence.
Written on 17 August 1922, Cockran's letter came in the midst of the
Irish Civil War, five days after the death of the Irish Free State leader
Arthur Griffith and five days before the Irish Republican Army's (IRA)
assassination of Michael Collins, Commander and Chief of the Irish Free
State's army.

August 17th 22   Turville Park,
                                                    Henley on Thames.

My dear Winston

The enclosed copy of the New York Annalist issued May 14th 1917
contains a letter addressed by me to the then Chairman of the Ways
and Means Committee of the House of Representatives which may
[be] of interest to you at this moment.

Pray treat it as confidential communication (for the present)
between you and me. The reason why I make this request will be
explained if we should meet while I remain on this side of the Atlantic.

We will be here till the 30th (a week from Wednesday) when we go
to Paris – crossing London – but not stopping there – en route.

I shall like very much to see you before sailing for home from Cherbourg Sept 9th. Should you find yourself at leisure for a chat I will gladly go anywhere that you may fix in England between now and the end of this month – or in France between the first and eighth of next month.

Yours very Sincerely,
W. Bourke Cockran

P.S. After you shall have finished with my letter to Kitchin will you be good enough to mail it to 100 Broadway New York – as it may be difficult to obtain another copy.[32]

Whether the two old friends were able to meet as Cockran requested is unknown.

The enclosure Cockran refers to was a letter he had written as a private citizen in 1917 to the Chairman of the House Ways and Means Committee upon American entry into World War I. He and Churchill had apparently discussed the subject of German war reparations and American loans to the Allied Powers because Cockran's 1917 letter was a brief in favour of a seemingly innocent suggestion: convert all American loans to the Allies into 'gifts'. Had the United States adopted this policy either at the time in 1917 or at almost any time during the 1920s, especially when Churchill was Chancellor of the Exchequer, the entire history of the twentieth century might have been changed. By 1922, the harm being done to Germany by the oppressive reparations unilaterally imposed at Versailles was obvious. Churchill favoured then and later easing the burden on Germany, but the key lay with the United States. Great Britain and France could not ease the burden on Germany unless the United States eased the burden on its loans to Great Britain and France.

As Cockran wrote in his 1917 letter:

An attempt to establish a relationship of debtors and creditors between two sovereignties must inevitably prove to be a fruitful source of dispute, probably of difficulties, possibly of war. It would be a sad ending of this glorious struggle for international right, if it left us in a position where our rights as creditor could be maintained only by invading the sovereignty of one or more among the countries which are now in alliance with us for the very purpose of guarding, defending, rendering unassailable the sovereignty of every nation, great and small.[33]

Cockran, like many statesmen, gave serious thought to disarmament after the war. Having opposed the Treaty of Versailles and US membership in the League of Nations, Cockran did not dispute a common belief at the time that disarmament among the major nations was a good thing. Indeed, Cockran thought it absolutely essentially, not merely for the restoration of prosperity but to the survival of human life. Cockran did not agree, however, that disarmament could be effected by treaties among nations. Speaking on the floor of the House in 1921, he said:

> I think the suggested agreements between nations to limit armaments are equally absurd. If you are going to fight a man, just think of agreeing with him how hard each of you would strike the other. This is practically what these agreements would seek to effect. The mere statement of it, I think, shows its absurdity.[34]

When Cockran gave his disarmament speech to Congress, all the great nations of Europe were exhausted from the unrelenting struggle of the Great War. Not so the latecomer America, so that Cockran could say without fear of contradiction that 'we are today preeminently the strongest nation in the world'. Cockran's prescription for disarmament was for the United States to out-arm the rest of the world. By doing so, Cockran said:

> . . . the President will be in a position to say to all the nations of the earth, "We seek no domination; we only seek equality, but it must be an equality of disarmament. Put away your armament and we will gladly accompany you in that act of renunciation. The experience of the world shows that while any nation retains armaments, no other great nation can disarm; and, therefore, if you do not disarm, if you persist in maintaining armaments, we will outarm any or all of you."[35]

There is no evidence that Churchill and Cockran ever discussed their views on disarmament after the Great War, but given the wide range of topics they had discussed over the years it would be surprising if they did

not. It took a Second World War before the United States established
a military policy in the last half of the twentieth century similar to what
Cockran had proposed in 1921. America indeed out-armed the rest of
the world after World War II and the Cold War eventually ended as a
consequence. It was never politically in the cards to do so in the 1920s,
but it is intriguing to speculate how the history of Europe between the
wars would have played out if a militarily-strong, if not dominating,
United States had forgiven its war loans to the Allies and conditioned
doing so on the Allies showing similar magnanimity to Germany,
something Churchill attempted unsuccessfully to effect during his five
years as Chancellor of the Exchequer in the 1920s.

Six months after his last letter to Churchill and possibly their last
time together, Cockran died on 28 February 1923. It was his birthday.
He was sixty-nine years old. He delivered his last speech that afternoon
on the floor of the House of Representatives opposing a farm credit bill
providing for a $600 million government loan to farmers. He spoke
for forty-five minutes and once more educated his colleagues on the
history of banking in England for the last two centuries, complete with
quotations from Macaulay. Anyone who ever read his 1903 speech to the
Liberal Club in London would have recognized the familiar theme of
Cockran's conclusion:

> ... When the day dawns that any number of citizens are taught to
> believe that there is a more rapid road to prosperity, to wealth, to
> the possession of capital, than the employment of industry and the
> exercise of self-denial, and that this more rapid way is through the
> Treasury, by the complaisance or the connivance of politicians, then
> the knell of this country's prosperity is sounded.[36]

His wife Anne gave a dinner party in his honour that night, which included
Nicholas and Alice Longworth, Mary Roberts Rinehart, Alice Robertson
(one of the few female members of the House of Representatives), the
writer Salisbury Field and his wife Belle, Robert Louis Stevenson's
stepdaughter and one of Anne's closest friends.[37]

After the dinner party, a gifted and generous man died peacefully in his
sleep from a massive cerebral haemorrhage. His motto had been 'Live
intensely, die suddenly'. In 1903 when he accepted nomination to
Congress, he had said 'When I quit the field of political contention,
I hope it will be on the shoulders of my pall-bearers'. Cockran had his

wish and today, sadly, he is recalled by few of his countrymen. But memory of him lived on in the hearts and minds of his friends and his family and, as it turned out, one indispensable man.

Time magazine, then in its first year of publication, wrote of Cockran in his obituary:

> Fearless, magnificent, king of orators, his public career lasted for 40 stormy years . . . He quarreled numberless times with Tammany leaders, over whom he towered majestically.[38]

Seventeen years later, people would be using the same words to describe Cockran's protégé Winston Churchill: Fearless. Magnificent. King of orators.

Adult developmental studies show that mentoring relationships for men are the exception, not the rule. Successful mentoring relationships are rarer still. Good mentors represent skill, knowledge, virtue and accomplishment, qualities for a young man to emulate. Good mentors offer a young man love, admiration and encouragement in his struggles. Good mentors combine the qualities of a good father and a good friend.[39] Cockran offered all this to Churchill and more, and at an early age, Churchill absorbed and internalized what he learned at Cockran's feet.

By any measure, Bourke Cockran was a good mentor to the young subaltern he met in 1895. Winston Churchill knew that. Moreover, throughout his own sixty stormy years in public life, he never forgot the man who 'instantly gained [his] confidence' so long ago.

How much did Cockran actually influence the young Churchill in forming his political thought, his approach to politics and his speaking style? Taking Churchill at his word, Cockran's influence in all three areas was substantial. To understand why requires an appreciation of the kind of man Bourke Cockran was, the times he lived in and the issues he faced. This we have tried to do in these pages: Cockran was a man who could light up a room just by entering it; a widely read intellectual and student of economics and politics; a close adviser to two presidents; a man fluent in many languages; a politician with good friends in both parties; an orator who towered over others in the golden age of oratory; a man who could draw Senators and Supreme Court Justices alike to hear him speak in the House of Representatives; and, above all, a nationally known public figure who placed principle above politics and who walked away from power more than once rather than betray his beliefs. All in all, not a bad role model.

Mentors typically have direct influence on young men for only few years. Cockran's influence extended over a longer period in two distinct phases. His influence over Churchill arguably reached its peak in 1896 when the young Churchill had begun his intensive course of self-education based on 'first principles'. It was during this time that his correspondence and meetings with Cockran were most frequent. Shortly thereafter, Churchill declared himself to his mother as 'a Liberal in all but name. My views excite the pious horror of the Mess.' But for Ireland – one of the few issues where he and his mentor initially disagreed – he told her he would enter Parliament as a Liberal.

Reading can only take someone so far in forming political and economic views, however, and Cockran was the only adult in Churchill's life so actively and intensely involved in reinforcing and encouraging him as he did so. As a consequence of his self-study, Churchill came to Parliament in 1900 with well-formed political principles destined in time to estrange him from the Conservative Party under whose banner he was elected. By this time, Cockran's relationship with Churchill had evolved from mentor to close friend. At the same time, Cockran had also become a close friend of Churchill relatives as well, including his mother, brother Jack, Uncle Moreton, Aunt Leonie and her oldest son Shane. Long before Shane married Marjorie in 1912, Cockran had become an honorary member of the Jerome sisters' extended family.

During this same period, Cockran also served as a role model for the young Churchill's development as an orator from his first political speech in 1897 onwards. We know this mostly because Churchill has said so and also by comparing their speeches on similar subjects. Their correspondence does not touch upon oratory per se as that came in their many conversations because Cockran had definite views on oratory and freely expressed them in many newspaper interviews. He would have done the same for his protégé. It would be wrong, however, to separate the subject of oratory from the two men's political and economic thought because that would miss the point of their relationship, i.e. that they shared common views on so many important issues of the day.

Indeed, political events in England in 1902 and 1903 over the issue of free trade served to bring about the second phase of the mentor aspect of their relationship. Free trade was the cornerstone of the two men's political and economic beliefs, and the defining event of Churchill's young political life was to turn on that issue. While his mentor had opposed his own party in 1896 over the issue of sound money, he had also declined a cabinet seat in the McKinley Administration as a reward because he was a free trader and the Republicans were not. For Cockran, principle always trumped power.

With free trade in peril and Cockran visiting England and Europe several months every year after his protégé's election to Parliament in 1900, Churchill literally had at his side the most eloquent advocate of free trade in England or America, a man whose own oratory and political courage on that issue would be emulated by Churchill in 1904 when he defied the leaders of his father's Conservative Party and joined the Liberals. It was the most significant act of political courage in the young politician's life.

It would not be the last. He was to do so many times over the next fifty years. But when he once more placed principle over power in the decade leading up to May 1940, again defying the leaders of the Conservative Party, the stakes were ever so much higher. His courage on that occasion saved his country. And the world.

List of Illustrations

Epilogue

Jennie and Bourke began as lovers in 1895 and ended as friends, their families forever entwined by marriage. Along the way, he mentored and forged a lifelong friendship with her son Winston, something Churchill would write and talk about for the rest of his life. In his Introduction to James McGurrin's 1948 biography, *Bourke Cockran: A Free Lance in American Politics,* Jennie's nephew and Churchill's first cousin Sir Shane Leslie wrote a tribute to his aunt's old lover, his own brother-in-law and the man his daughter Anita fondly called 'Uncle Bourke'.

> Bourke Cockran! The magical name, the silver tongue and the golden heart!

* * *

> Where do his memories begin and how soon will they die away? The speed with which America recompenses the shortness of her history accounts for the forgetfulness with which she buries decades as quickly as other countries submerge centuries. History in America is the life of the living, not the memory of the dead. Nevertheless, who shall knit the scenes of Bourke Cockran's dramatic life and drop the curtain with the same perfect and resplendent precision with which his last day was rounded upon earth?[1]

We have tried to knit those scenes in this book because we believe Lady Randolph Churchill and her remarkable son Winston are the answers to the rhetorical question posed by Jennie's nephew. No better curtain can be dropped upon Bourke Cockran's dramatic life with the 'same perfect and resplendent precision' than the words of Churchill's youngest daughter, Mary Soames, in a note she passed to her ninety-year-old father in his last days and with which Martin Gilbert closes his one-volume biography, *Churchill: A Life*: 'In addition to all the feelings a daughter has for a loving, generous father,' she wrote, 'I owe you what every Englishman, woman & child does — Liberty itself.'

America's greatest orator could not have said it better. Liberty itself. Cockran was a modest man and he would have deprecated his role in shaping the young Churchill's principles, political courage and oratorical style. Winston Churchill never did.

It began with a love story, but the curtain never dropped on the lives of Bourke Cockran and Jennie Churchill until the young man they both so lovingly nurtured had saved Western Civilization in its darkest hour and preserved all that Bourke and Jennie could ever have hoped. Liberty itself.

Authors' Note

The Churchill – Cockran correspondence reproduced in this book was transcribed by Curt Zoller and contains the full text of all available Churchill – Cockran correspondence. While the correspondence was more extensive, only twenty-three letters survive, fourteen from Churchill and nine from Cockran. Of the Churchill letters, four have not been previously published and the other ten appear in the Companion Volumes which accompany the first two volumes of Churchill's official biography by Randolph S. Churchill. Six of the nine Cockran letters have not been previously published. The full text of two Cockran letters and an extract from a third appear in the Companion Volumes. Many of the letters are holographic, and as a consequence, the versions here represent Mr. Zoller's transcription, which may occasionally differ from the versions reproduced in the Companion Volumes. Where possible, spelling and grammatical errors have been corrected to avoid the distracting use of '[sic]' in the narrative. As a consequence, any remaining spelling or grammatical errors may be those of the correspondents, proofreading errors by the authors or both.

The fictional narratives which begin each chapter were written by Michael McMenamin. They are based on known facts or inferences drawn from those facts. So that readers may determine themselves how reasonable these inferences are, Mr. McMenamin has placed at the beginning of the notes for each chapter the inferences he has made and the occasional literary license he has taken in dramatizing the thoughts of Churchill (seven chapters), Cockran (six chapters) and Lady Randolph Churchill (one chapter).

Acknowledgements

A large number of people have helped in many ways to bring this book about, and we gratefully acknowledge their assistance.

Celia Sandys, author and Winston's granddaughter, for her kind and generous foreword. Winston S. Churchill, Winston's grandson, for his equally generous permission to use four previously unpublished letters from his grandfather. Richard Langworth, editor of *Finest Hour*, the quarterly journal of the Churchill Centre in Washington, D.C., for bringing the two authors together over their common interest in Bourke Cockran. Sir Martin Gilbert for his many kindnesses and assistance to both authors extending back fifteen years. James W. Muller, Chairman of the Board of Academic Advisers, of the Churchill Centre for commissioning the 2004 American Political Science Association paper by Michael McMenamin 'Becoming Winston Churchill: How the Political Thought and Orator of Winston Churchill Was Shaped by His Irish-American Mentor Bourke Cockran' which directly led to this book. Simon Mason, Senior Acquisitions Editor, Greenwood World Publishing, whose early vision of what this book could be inspired the authors to make it more than they had intended. Alice Lutyens and Gordon Wise of Curtis Brown Ltd. for permission to quote from Winston Churchill and Randolph Churchill material. Tarka King, the son of Anita Leslie and grandson of Shane Leslie, for permission to quote from material by Anita and Shane. Gert Zoller for her help in deciphering Winston's handwriting. Carol Breckenridge, art therapist, for her insight into Winston's attention deficit disorder and his early adult development. Wayne Furman, Office of Special Collections, New York Public Library, for permission to use material from the William Bourke Cockran collection. Mary McDermott and Alexis Dragony, personal assistants to Mr. McMenamin. Matthew Rarey, our Research Assistant for the Shane Leslie papers at Georgetown University. Matthew Chayes, our Research Assistant for the William Bourke Cockran papers at the New York Public Library. Leon Stevens, Law Librarian, Walter & Haverfield LLP. Katie McMenamin, novelist. Les Roberts, novelist. Paul H. Courtney, Senior Editor, *Finest Hour*. Daniel N. Myers, Executive Director, Churchill Centre. Allen Packwood, Director Churchill Archives Centre, Cambridge. Andrew Riley, Churchill Archives Centre. Natalie Adams and Sue Foster, Archivists, Churchill Archives Centre. Nicholas Scheetz, Manuscript Librarian, Georgetown University Library. Thomas Venning,

Associate Director, Manuscripts, Christies. Elizabeth Bugbee, Christie's Client Service, New York. Sarah Martin, Research Assistant, Imperial War Museum. Katrina MacDonald, Library of Congress Prints and Photograph Division. Kelly McAnnancy, Kristin Paulus and Nicole Wells, New York Historical Society. Thea Blair, Gayle Meldau and Jeff Price of Mission Viejo, California Library. Edward Hochman and Frank Scaturro, Presidents of Grant Monument Association. Chicago History Museum and Chicago Historical Society. Anne Sebba, author, journalist and former foreign correspondent. Mrs. Elizabeth Churchill Snell, author. Mrs. Yvonne Spencer-Churchill. John and Celia Lee, authors. Marcelle Adamson, Illustrated London News. William Burke, New York Public Library, William Bourke Cockran Collection.

Notes

CV refers to the series of *Companion Volumes* to the Official Biography, *Winston S. Churchill*, by Randolph Churchill and Martin Gilbert.

OB refers to the Official Biography by Randolph Churchill and Martin Gilbert.

Churchill Speeches refers to the *Complete Speeches of Winston Churchill*, Robert Rhodes James, editor.

Cockran Papers refers to the William Bourke Cockran Papers; Manuscripts and Archives Division, The New York Public Library; Astor, Lenox and Tilden Foundations.

Chapter 1: 'He Was My Model'
The fictional narrative which begins Chapter 1 attempts to recreate Churchill's state of mind while writing the speech accepting the honorary degree from the State University of New York. All of Churchill's reflections are based on fact with one exception, the Adlai Stevenson story. The story is explicitly Anita Leslie's and is based on her conversation with Stevenson. We draw the inference that Churchill realized at the time that Stevenson did not know who Bourke Cockran was.

1. Churchill Speeches, vol. VIII, page 8560.
2. Ibid.
3. James McGurrin, *Bourke Cockran/A Free Lance in American Politics* (New York: Charles Scribner's Sons, 1948), page 93.
4. Mark Essig, *Edison & The Electric Chair: A Story of Light and Death* (New York: Walker & Company, 2004), page 168.
5. Shane Leslie Papers, Georgetown University.
6. Randolph S. Churchill, OB, I, pages 272–273.
7. McGurrin, *Bourke Cockran*, page 52.
8. W. Bourke Cockran, Memorial Addresses Delivered in Congress, page 14.
9. McGurrin, *Bourke Cockran*, page 76.
10. Anita Leslie, *Lady Randolph Churchill: The Story of Jennie Jerome* (New York: Charles Scribner's Sons, 1969), page 215.
11. OB, I, page 271.
12. Daniel Levinson, *The Seasons of a Man's Life* (New York: Ballantine Books, 1978), page 99.
13. CV, I, page 596.
14. Churchill Archive Centre.
15. Cockran Papers.
16. Churchill Archive Centre.
17. William Bourke Cockran, *In the Name of Liberty*, ed. Robert McElroy (New York: Ballantine Books, 1925), page 200.
18. Winston S. Churchill, *For Free Trade* (London: Arthur L. Humphreys, 1906), page 32.
19. CV, II, page 894.
20. Winston S. Churchill, *Thoughts and Adventures* (London: Odhams Press Ltd., 1947 1932), page 33.
21. Florence T. Bloom, 'The Political Career of William Bourke Cockran' (PhD thesis, City University of New York, 1970), pages 354–355.
22. Paul Addison, *Churchill on the Home Front 1900–1955* (London: Jonathan Cape, 1993), pages 440–441.
23. Martin Gilbert, *Churchill's Political Philosophy* (New York: Oxford University Press, 1981), page 110.

24. Robert McElroy, ed. *In the Name of Liberty*, page ix.
25. Churchill, *For Free Trade*, page 78.
26. Cockran Papers.
27. Ibid.
28. Chartwell Trust.
29. Shane Leslie Papers.
30. CV, II, pages 893–894.
31. Churchill, *Thoughts and Adventures*, page 30.
32. Ibid., page 32.
33. Ibid., pages 32–33.
34. Ibid., page 33.
35. CV, V, page 34.
36. Churchill Speeches, vol. VII, page 7288.
37. Ibid., page 8560.

Chapter 2: 'One of the President's Most Trusted Advisers'

There is no evidence that Cockran met Sir Edgar Vincent or that Sir Edgar would have spoken to other men about Jennie in the same way as he later wrote. He is reputed to have been one of Jennie's lovers. Further, there is no evidence that Frewen told Cockran the story about Jennie's campaigning. Her question to the constituent comes from the film *Young Winston*.

1. Winston S. Churchill, *My Early Life: 1874–1904* (New York: Charles Scribner's Sons, 1987), page 4.
2. Carl Foreman, script for film *Young Winston*, 1979.
3. James McGurrin, *Bourke Cockran/A Free Lance in American Politics* (New York: Charles Scribner's Sons, 1948), page 42.
4. Ibid., page 39.
5. Cockran Papers.
6. Cockran Papers; McGurrin, *Bourke Cockran*, pages 60–62.
7. Ibid.
8. Cockran Papers; McGurrin, *Bourke Cockran*, page 62.
9. McGurrin, *Bourke Cockran*, pages 66–67.
10. Paxton Hibben, *The Peerless Leader: William Jennings Bryan* (New York: Farrar & Rinehart, 1929); McGurrin, *Bourke Cockran*, pages 80–81.
11. McGurrin, *Bourke Cockran*, page 91; Florence T. Bloom, 'The Political Career of William Bourke Cockran' (PhD thesis, City University of New York, 1970), page 29.
12. Cockran Papers.
13. Ibid.
14. McGurrin, *Bourke Cockran*, page 110.
15. Ibid.
16. Ibid., page 106.
17. Ibid., page 111; Bloom, 'Political Career', page 36.
18. Mark Essig, *Edison & The Electric Chair: A Story of Light and Death* (New York: Walker & Company, 2004), page 187.
19. Ibid., page 253.
20. *Dawson v. State*, 274 GA 327 at 335 (2001).
21. McGurrin, *Bourke Cockran*, pages 127–128.
22. Cockran Papers.
23. Ibid.
24. Ibid.
25. Ibid.
26. Ibid.

27. Ibid.

28. Ibid.

29. Ibid.

30. Ibid.

31. Ibid.

32. Ibid.; McGurrin, *Bourke Cockran*, page 143.

33. Ibid.; Bloom, 'Political Career', page 90.

34. Ibid.

35. McGurrin, *Bourke Cockran*, page 115.

36. Ibid.

37. Cockran Papers.

38. Ibid.

39. Matthew P. Breen, *Thirty Years of New York Politics Up-To-Date* (New York: Arno Press, 1974); McGurrin, *Bourke Cockran*, page 170.

40. McGurrin, *Bourke Cockran*, page 175.

41. Cockran Papers.

Chapter 3: 'I Have Been Paid Out For All My Own Iniquities'

Lady Randolph Churchill's many affairs are taken for granted by Churchill's biographers as well as Jennie's. But they are largely undocumented and appear to be based more on her contemporary reputation and gossip rather than love letters, diaries and the like. Her affairs with Count Kinsky and Bourke Cockran, by contrast, are well sourced. Not so her alleged affair with the Prince of Wales. They were certainly good friends, and unlike other lovers Jennie may or may not have had, she saved all of the Prince's letters. They frequently dined together, alone, and he lavished her with gifts. The inference certainly can be drawn that they had an off-and-on affair over the years, but based on the same evidence, Anita Leslie reasonably draws a different conclusion in her biography of her great-aunt. We believe that the Prince's desire for revenge against Lord Randolph's earlier blackmail combined with Jennie's extraordinary beauty argues in favour of an affair between the two. But it is not well sourced, and Anita Leslie could be correct.

1. Anita Leslie, *Lady Randolph Churchill: The Story of Jennie Jerome* (New York: Scribner, 1969), page 112.

2. Ibid., page 113.

3. Peregrine Churchill and Julian Mitchell, *Jennie, Lady Randolph Churchill: A Portrait with Letters* (New York: St. Martins Press, 1974), page 153.

4. Ibid., page 154.

5. Ibid., page 156.

6. Ibid., page 157.

7. OB, I, page 226.

8. Anita Leslie, *Lady Randolph Churchill*, page 199.

9. Elisabeth Kehoe, *Fortune's Daughters: The Extravagant Lives of the Jerome Sisters – Jennie Churchill, Clara Frewen and Leonie Leslie* (London, Atlantic Books, 2004), page 174.

10. Peregrine Churchill and Julian Mitchell, *Jennie, Lady Randolph Churchill*, page 168.

11. Anita Leslie, *Lady Randolph Churchill*, pages 210–211, 213–215.

Chapter 4: 'A Startling Letter'

Only the scene is imagined. All the facts are well sourced.

1. CV, I, page 589.

2. Winston S. Churchill, *My Early Life: 1874–1904* (New York: Charles Scribner's Sons, 1987), page 13.

3. Celia Sandys, *The Young Churchill* (New York: Dutton, 1995), page 55.

4. Churchill, *My Early Life*, page 13.

5. CV, I, page 123.

6. Ibid., page 125.

7. Peregrine Churchill and Julian Mitchell, *Jennie, Lady Randolph Churchill: A Portrait with Letters* (London: Arnold, 1974), page 160.

8. Carol Breckenridge, 'Art as Therapy: How Churchill Coped', *Finest Hour*, Autumn (2003), 20.

9. CV, I, pages 168–169.

10. Ibid.

11. Ibid., page 204.

12. OB, I, page 170.

13. Ibid., page 174.

14. Ibid., pages 182–183.

15. CV, I, pages 388–389.

16. Ibid., pages 390–391.

17. Ibid., page 206.

18. Churchill, *My Early Life*, pages 45–46.

19. CV, I, pages 459–460.

20. Ibid., page 461.

21. Daniel Levinson, *The Seasons of a Man's Life* (New York: Ballantine Books, 1978), pages 72–78. Levinson's study was based on forty men born in the 1920s representing four widely different groups of men: hourly workers in industry, business executives, university biologists and novelists. Those unfamiliar with Levinson might be sceptical that such diverse groups could have much in common but they would be surprised. The results are as relevant today for those born in the 1940s as they are for children born in the 1970s or, indeed, for those born in the 1870s.

22. Ibid., pages 78–84.

23. Ibid., pages 84–89.

24. Ibid., page 90.

25. Ibid.

26. Churchill, *My Early Life*, page 62.

27. CV, I, page 579.

28. Ibid., page 587.

29. Ibid., page 590.

Chapter 5: 'I Have Great Discussions with Mr. Cockran'

The suggestion in this narrative that Cockran read Lord Randolph's speeches before meeting Churchill in November 1895 is an inference. Cockran was well versed in Irish politics and would have heard of, if not read, the speech in Ulster. It is doubtful that he had read any others. He did read Lord Randolph's speeches eventually because Churchill sent him two volumes of his father's speeches in 1896. Cockran's opinion of Lord Randolph's lack of principle on Ireland is also an inference, but no Irish Nationalist like Cockran would have had a different opinion.

1. CV, I, page 583.

2. Ibid., page 585.

3. Ibid.

4. Mother Mary Margaret Crowley, O.S.U., Bourke Cockran Orator (PhD thesis, University of Wisconsin, n.d.), pages 243–244.

5. CV, I, pages 596–597.

6. Ibid., pages 597–598.

7. Ibid.

8. Ibid., pages 599–600.

9. Ibid., page 601.

10. Cockran Papers.
11. OB, I, page 266.
12. CV, I, page 620.

Chapter 6: 'A Very High Opinion of Your Future Career'
Everything in the narrative is well sourced.
1. CV, I, page 623.
2. Cockran Papers.
3. Ibid.
4. Daniel Levinson, *The Seasons of a Man's Life* (New York: Ballantine Books, 1978), page 99.
5. Churchill Archive Centre.
6. Levinson, *The Seasons of a Man's Life*, page 100.

Chapter 7: 'You Have Won a Glorious Victory'
Cockran's opinion of William Jennings Bryan expressed in the narrative to Chapter 7 is an inference in the sense that Cockran was never recorded as saying that Bryan 'wasn't very bright'. Anyone who reads Cockran's 1896 Madison Square Garden address, however, will recognize that this is a reasonable inference to draw. The phrase 'I'm standing up tonight, not sitting, and that will remain my posture until the campaign is over' is an imaginary quote but in keeping with Cockran's character as is his comment to the *New York Times* reporter 'your paper should do the same for the likes of Mr. Hearst surely will not', which is also imaginary. The rest of the narrative is well sourced.
1. Cockran Papers; James McGurrin, *Bourke Cockran/A Free Lance in American Politics* (New York: Charles Scribner's Sons, 1948), page 149.
2. Cockran Papers; McGurrin, *Bourke Cockran*, page 150.
3. Cockran Papers; McGurrin, *Bourke Cockran*, page 150.
4. Cockran Papers; *In the Name of Liberty*, page 17; McGurrin, *Bourke Cockran*, page 155.
5. CV, I, page 676.
6. McGurrin, *Bourke Cockran*, pages 149–150.
7. Cockran Papers; McGurrin, *Bourke Cockran*, page 158.
8. Cockran Papers; Ambrose Kennedy, *American Orator, Bourke Cockran His Life and Politics* (Boston, MA: Bruce Humphries, 1948), page 71.
9. Cockran Papers
10. Cockran Papers; McGurrin, *Bourke Cockran*, page 161.
11. Cockran Papers; McGurrin, *Bourke Cockran*, page 162.
12. McGurrin, *Bourke Cockran*, page 164.
13. CV, I. page 695.
14. Ibid., I, page 696.
15. Cockran Papers.
16. Daniel Levinson, *The Seasons of a Man's Life* (New York: Ballantine Books, 1978), page 98.
17. Ibid.
18. McGurrin, *Bourke Cockran*, page 164.
19. CV, I, page 697.
20. Christie's Catalogue, 2 December 2003, page 48.
21. OB, II, page 109.

Chapter 8: 'Ambition Was The Motive Force'
The narrative is well sourced.
1. Winston S. Churchill, *Savrola: A Tale of the Revolution in Laurania* (New York: Random House, 1956), page 27.

2. Ibid., pages 31–32.

3. Ibid., page 64.

4. CV, I, pages 740–741.

5. Ibid., pages 753–754.

6. OB, I, page 307.

7. CV, I, page 746.

8. Ibid.

9. Ibid., page 751.

10. Lady Randolph Churchill's Papers.

11. Cockran Papers; Florence T. Bloom, 'The Political Career of William Bourke Cockran' (PhD thesis, City University of New York, 1970), page 112.

12. Cockran Papers.

13. Churchill, *Savrola*, pages 64–65.

14. Churchill Speeches, pages 26–27.

15. OB, I, page 333.

16. Ibid.

17. Winston S. Churchill, *My Early Life: 1874–1904* (New York: Charles Scribner's Sons, 1987), page 122.

18. CV, I, page 779.

19. Ibid.

20. Ibid., page 781.

21. Ibid., pages 784–785.

22. Ibid., page 792.

23. Ibid., page 797.

24. Ibid., page 794.

25. Ibid., page 809.

26. Ibid., pages 811–812.

27. Ibid., page 815.

28. Ibid., page 839.

29. Ibid., page 863.

30. Ibid., pages 863–864.

Chapter 9: 'How Little Time Remains'
The telephone conversation between Cockran and Secretary of State John Hay is imagined. The inference that Cockran called him directly is reasonable, however, because Cockran knew Hay socially and entertained Hay's close friends Henry Cabot Lodge and Henry Adams at his home between 1891 and 1894. It is a reasonable inference that a nineteenth-century gentleman like Hay would have reacted as portrayed here, especially given Hay's Anglophilia and Cockran would not have hesitated to use all his considerable influence to learn of Churchill's fate.

1. Mother Mary Margaret Crowley, O.S.U., Bourke Cockran Orator (PhD thesis, University of Wisconsin, n.d.), page 102.

2. Cockran Papers; James H. Andrews, 'Winston Churchill's Tammany Hall Mentor', *New York History*, April (1990), 151.

3. Ibid.

4. Cockran Papers.

5. CV, I, page 893.

6. Ibid., page 912.

7. Ibid., page 913.

8. Ibid.

9. Ibid., page 922.

10. Christie's Catalogue, 2 December 2003, page 30.

11. CV, I, page 950.

12. Winston S. Churchill, *My Early Life: 1874–1904* (New York: Charles Scribner's Sons, 1987), page 164.

13. CV, I, page 969.

14. Ibid., pages 973–974.

15. Cockran Papers; James McGurrin, *Bourke Cockran/A Free Lance in American Politics* (New York: Charles Scribner's Sons, 1948), page 191.

16. Cockran Papers.

17. McGurrin, *Bourke Cockran*, page 180.

18. Cockran Papers.

19. Cockran Papers; McGurrin, *Bourke Cockran*, page 182.

20. McGurrin, *Bourke Cockran*, page 187.

21. Cockran Papers.

22. Ibid.

23. Shane Leslie Papers.

24. CV, I, page 989.

25. Ibid., page 994.

26. Ibid.

27. Ibid., page 1007.

28. Christie's Catalogue, page 31.

29. Correspondence, Winston S. Churchill to Christine Lewis Conover, 1899–1943, The Churchill Centre, page 23.

30. Ibid., pages 23–24.

31. CV, I, page 1015.

32. Churchill, *My Early Life*, pages 223–224.

33. CV, I, page 1036.

34. OB, I, page 434.

35. Ibid., page 435.

36. CV, I, page 1055.

37. OB, I, page 450.

38. Churchill, *My Early Life*, page 252.

39. OB, I, page 469.

40. Cockran Papers.

41. Ibid.

42. Ibid.

Chapter 10: 'The Perfect Man'

Churchill's thoughts about Pamela and why they didn't marry are inferences. Winston destroyed all of Pamela's letters as he had promised to do early in their correspondence. Thankfully, she did not do the same. Unfortunately, all of the Churchill-to-Pamela correspondence was sold individually at a Christie's auction in 2003 and all are in the hands of private collectors. The only complete letters that remain are contained in the Companion Volumes to the Official Biography. The available letters do not offer sufficient insight into why two people so very much in love did not marry. Excerpts from each of Churchill's letters were contained in the Christie's catalogue of 2 December 2003, and we have used those letters to piece together our tentative view of why they did not wed. We believe it was parental pressure, based upon Winston's finances. An additional inference in the narrative is not well sourced because Pamela's letters do not survive and that is Pamela's belief that she would always come second in Winston's life because he did not return home to her – as she asked – after his escape from prison in South Africa. Churchill was a correspondent, no longer in the army, and did not need to accept the commission which General Buller gave him. He claimed in a letter to Pamela it was a matter of honour but that was Churchill putting a good face on it. Churchill already had a hard-earned reputation for personal bravery, which would not have been diminished by staying on as a correspondent, not a soldier. Without Pamela's letters, no one will ever know the real reason why Pamela did not marry him. And that may be just as Winston wished.

Cockran's introduction of Mark Twain to Churchill is also an inference without a direct source. It is a reasonable inference because Cockran was the most prominent pro-Boer spokesman in the country and he and Twain knew each other and served together on pro-Boer organizations. Cockran was understandably eager to assist Churchill in his tour, and it is reasonable to believe that Cockran persuaded Twain to give the introduction at the inaugural speech of the tour of his young friend whose name, by now, was well known in America because of his escape from a Boer prison.

1. OB, I, pages 224–225.
2. Winston S. Churchill, *My Early Life: 1874–1904* (New York: Charles Scribner's Sons, 1987), page 272.
3. CV, I, page 1093.
4. Ibid., page 1146.
5. Ibid., page 1147.
6. Christie's Catalogue, 2 December 2003, page 36.
7. Ibid., page 7.
8. CV, I, page 1159.
9. Ibid., pages 1177–1178.
10. OB, I, page 513.
11. CV, I, page 1178.
12. Ibid., page 1189.
13. Cockran Papers.
14. Ibid.; James McGurrin, *Bourke Cockran/A Free Lance in American Politics* (New York: Charles Scribner's Sons, 1948), pages 199–200.
15. Cockran Papers; McGurrin, *Bourke Cockran*, page 202.
16. Cockran Papers.
17. CV, I, pages 1172–1173.
18. Ibid., page 1158.
19. Cockran Papers.
20. CV, I, page 1222.
21. Cockran Papers.
22. Todd Ronnei, 'Churchill in Minnesota', *Minnesota History*, 57 (Fall 2001).
23. CV, I, page 1223.
24. Roy Jenkins, *Churchill: A Biography* (New York: Farrar, Straus and Giroux, 2001), page 70.
25. CV, I, pages 1224–1225.
26. 'Churchill's Love Letters Fetch Half a Million Dollars', *Agence France Presse*, 3 December 2003.
27. Christie's Catalogue, page 31.
28. CV, I, page 1225.
29. Christie's Catalogue, page 38.
30. Ibid., page 40.
31. Ibid., page 41.
32. Ibid., page 42.

Chapter 11: 'One More Sacrifice'
The conversation between Cockran and Sir Henry Campbell-Bannerman is imaginary, but Cockran being asked to stand for Parliament by Redmond, Campbell-Bannerman and others is not. Cockran's conversation with Jennie about her returning to live in America is also an inference.

1. James McGurrin, *Bourke Cockran/A Free Lance in American Politics* (New York: Charles Scribner's Sons, 1948), page 226.
2. CV, II, page 2; Churchill Speeches, vol. I, page 66.
3. CV, II, page 8; Churchill Speeches, vol. I, page 70.
4. CV, I, page 746.
5. Ibid., page 751.
6. Churchill Speeches, vol. I, page 72.
7. Ibid.
8. OB, II, page 15.
9. Ibid., page 20.
10. CV, II, pages 62–63; Churchill Speeches, vol. I, page 82.
11. CV, II, page 104.
12. Churchill Speeches, vol. I, page 131.
13. Ibid., page 149.
14. Winston S. Churchill, *My Early Life: 1874–1904* (New York: Charles Scribner's Sons, 1987), page 372.
15. Ibid.
16. CV, II, page 152.
17. Ibid., page 164.
18. Cockran Papers.
19. Ibid.
20. CV, II, page 174.
21. Churchill Speeches, vol. I, page 192.
22. CV, II, pages 182–183.
23. Ibid., page 184; OB, II, page 58.
24. Shane Leslie Papers; Florence T. Bloom, 'The Political Career of William Bourke Cockran' (PhD thesis, City University of New York, 1970), page 167.
25. McGurrin, *Bourke Cockran*, page 226.
26. Ibid., page 227.
27. *London Times*, 16 July 1903; Richard Lee Stovall, 'The Rhetoric of Bourke Cockran: A Contextual Analysis' (PhD thesis, Ohio State University, 1975), page 147.
28. *New York Tribune*, 27 July 1903; Mother Mary Margaret Crowley, O.S.U., 'Bourke Cockran Orator' (PhD thesis, University of Wisconsin, 1941), page 118.
29. Cockran, *In the Name of Liberty*, page 186.
30. Ibid., page 187.
31. Ibid., page 201.
32. Ibid., page 190.
33. Winston S. Churchill, *For Free Trade* (London: Arthur L. Humphreys, 1906), page 34.
34. Ibid., pages 31–32.
35. Cockran, *In the Name of Liberty*, page 211.
36. Churchill, *For Free Trade*, page 30.
37. CV, II, page 243.
38. Churchill Archives Centre.
39. Cockran Papers.
40. Shane Leslie, *American Wonderland: Memories of Four Tours in the United States of America (1911–1935)* (London: M. Joseph Ltd, 1936), page 43.

Chapter 12: 'An English Liberal'
There is no source for Leonie hinting to Churchill that Cockran and his mother had an affair. It is likewise an inference that Churchill intentionally chose the day he switched parties to write to Cockran.

1. James McGurrin, *Bourke Cockran/A Free Lance in American Politics* (New York: Charles Scribner's Sons, 1948), page 256.

2. Winston S. Churchill, *For Free Trade* (London: Arthur L. Humphreys, 1906), page 68.
3. Cockran Papers.
4. Ibid.
5. Florence T. Bloom, 'The Political Career of William Bourke Cockran' (PhD thesis, City University of New York, 1970), page 200.
6. McGurrin, *Bourke Cockran*, pages 249–250.
7. Ibid., page 251.
8. Cockran Papers; McGurrin, *Bourke Cockran*, page 264.
9. McGurrin, *Bourke Cockran*, page 265.
10. Cockran Papers.
11. Ibid.
12. OB, vol. II, page 98.
13. Roy Jenkins, *Churchill: A Biography* (New York: Farrar, Straus and Giroux, 2001), page 96.
14. Churchill, *For Free Trade*, page 89.
15. Cockran Papers.
16. Churchill Archives Centre.
17. Cockran Papers.
18. Churchill Speeches, vol. I, page 370.
19. Ibid., page 382.
20. Ibid., page 392.
21. Cockran Papers.

Chapter 13: 'Confound the Hostile and Surprise the Indifferent'
All the details regarding Cockran's travelling companion, The Java Girl, are imaginary.
1. Churchill Speeches, vol. I, page 397.
2. Ibid., page 401.
3. Ibid., page 406.
4. Ibid., page 413.
5. Ibid., page 419.
6. Ibid., page 436.
7. Cockran Papers.
8. Cockran Papers; Florence T. Bloom, 'The Political Career of William Bourke Cockran' (PhD thesis, City University of New York, 1970), page 142.
9. Bloom, page 141.
10. Churchill Archives Centre.
11. Chartwell Trust.
12. Ibid.
13. Bloom, page 78.
14. James McGurrin, *Bourke Cockran/A Free Lance in American Politics* (New York: Charles Scribner's Sons, 1948), page 272.
15. Ibid.
16. Ibid.
17. Seymour Leslie, *The Jerome Connexion* (London: John Murray, 1964), page 70.
18. McGurrin, *Bourke Cockran*, page 277.
19. Roy Jenkins, *Churchill: A Biography* (New York: Farrar, Straus and Giroux, 2001), page 104.
20. Cockran Papers; Churchill Archives Centre.
21. Cockran Papers.
22. Bloom, page 178.

23. CV, II, pages 587–588.
24. Chartwell Trust.

Chapter 14: 'Sins of the Father'

Churchill's thoughts about his father, Ireland and Ulster in 1913 are inferences only and are contrary to what he wrote of his father in his two volume biography published in 1906. Churchill's attitude towards Ulster Loyalists and their threat of force are accurately portrayed. Churchill's regret that Cockran did not stand for Parliament in 1903 when invited is an inference as is Churchill's reaction to Cockran's suggestion to cut off Ulster from the outside world.

1. James McGurrin, *Bourke Cockran/A Free Lance in American Politics* (New York: Charles Scribner's Sons, 1948), page 279.
2. Cockran Papers; Florence T. Bloom, 'The Political Career of William Bourke Cockran' (PhD thesis, City University of New York, 1970), page 231.
3. McGurrin, *Bourke Cockran*, page 284.
4. Ibid., page 281.
5. Ibid.
6. Cockran Papers; McGurrin, *Bourke Cockran*, page 283.
7. OB, II, page 234.
8. Ibid., page 241.
9. Ibid., page 243.
10. Ibid., page 260.
11. Ibid., pages 261–262.
12. Christie's Catalogue, 2 December 2003, page 43.
13. Ibid.
14. Ibid., page 45.
15. Ibid.
16. Ibid., page 48.
17. CV, II, pages 893–894.
18. Elisabeth Kehoe, *Fortune's Daughters: The Extravagant Lives of the Jerome Sisters – Jennie Churchill, Clara Frewen and Leonie Leslie* (London, Atlantic Books, 2004), page 235.
19. Ibid., page 282.
20. OB, II, page 432.
21. Ibid., page 456.
22. Chartwell Trust.
23. OB, II, page 461.
24. Ibid., page 483.
25. Ibid., page 485.
26. Shane Leslie Papers.
27. Ibid.
28. Anita Leslie, *Lady Randolph Churchill: The Story of Jennie Jerome* (New York: Scribner, 1969), page 393.
29. Ibid.
30. Ibid., page 394.
31. McGurrin, *Bourke Cockran*, page 238.
32. Chartwell Trust.
33. Cockran Papers.
34. Cockran Papers; Ambrose Kennedy, *American Orator, Bourke Cockran His Life and Politics* (Boston, MA: Bruce Humphries, 1948), pages 186–187.
35. Cockran Papers; Kennedy, page 187.

36. Cockran Papers; Kennedy, page 211.
37. McGurrin, *Bourke Cockran*, page 330.
38. *Time* magazine, 10 March 1923.
39. Daniel Levinson, *The Seasons of a Man's Life* (New York: Ballantine Books, 1978), pages 333–334.

Epilogue
1. James McGurrin, *Bourke Cockran/A Free Lance in American Politics* (New York: Charles Scribner's Sons, 1948), pages xiii–xiv.

Index